In *I*
Bakl
inve
sem
Mik
bey
pre
cult
cisn
assu
suc
Hit
inel

TO
Uni
liter
the
Pre

Literature, Culture, Theory

General editors

ANTHONY CASCARDI, *University of California, Berkeley*
RICHARD MACKSEY, *The Johns Hopkins University*

Ideology and Inscription

"Cultural Studies" after Benjamin, de Man, and Bakhtin

TOM COHEN

CAMBRIDGE
UNIVERSITY PRESS

PUBLISHED BY THE PRESS SYNDICATE OF THE UNIVERSITY OF CAMBRIDGE
The Pitt Building, Trumpington Street, Cambridge CB2 1RP, United Kingdom

CAMBRIDGE UNIVERSITY PRESS
The Edinburgh Building, Cambridge CB2 2RU, United Kingdom
40 West 20th Street, New York, NY 10011-4211, USA
10 Stamford Road, Oakleigh, Melbourne 3166, Australia

First published 1998

Printed in the United Kingdom at the University Press, Cambridge

Typeset in Palatino 10/12.5 pt. [VN]

A catalogue record for this book is available from the British Library

Library of Congress cataloguing in publication data applied for

ISBN 0 521 59048 5 hardback
ISBN 0 521 59967 9 paperback

For Michael Sprinker

The theory of ideology depends in many of its features . . . on this theory of the ghost.

Derrida, *Specters of Marx*

Contents

Acknowledgements

This volume owes overt debts to a few and oblique ones to many. Of the first, I want to thank Chris Diffee and Jason Smith for lending me perspectives of critical readers to come at a formative stage of the manuscript. I am grateful to Neil Hertz for his earlier-stage shrewd readings of the text together with the provocations and insights his legendary critical eye provided. Additional appreciations go to Barbara Hernnstein Smith for her discursive prods and generosity as a reader, to Cary Wolfe for his knowing solicitation and feedback, to Ray Ryan for his patience and editorial guidance and to Barbara L. Cohen for her timely and moral suport. Perhaps most crucially, I am indebted to Michael Sprinker, to whom the book is dedicated, for his general encouragement and more than allegorical example.

Parts of several chapters have appeared in earlier, subsequently revised versions: chapter 1 in *the minnesota review*, chapter 2 in *Cultural Critique*, chapter 4 in *American Literary History*, and chapter 8 in *Electronic Book Review*. I gratefully acknowledge in each case permission to reprint.

❖❖

Introduction
Webwork, or "That spot is bewitched"

❖❖

[S]uch "spectators" dispose me against the "spectacle" more than the spectacle itself (the spectacle of history, you understand); I fall unaware into an Anacreontic mood. Nature, which gave the bull his horns and the lion his *chasm' odonton*, why did nature give me my foot?

Nietzsche, *Toward a Genealogy of Morals*

This volume explores several openings for what might be called a return to "theory" within the contemporary critical scene – or, more specifically, to material technologies of reading irreducible to any *representational* schema. The argument of these essays is that, rather than being surpassed by the intervening "returns" to history, mimesis, humanism, and identity politics, the materiality of language lingers as a repressed trauma. Instead of being a pragmatic political turn, the supposed supersession of what is labeled "high theory" might prove to be a detour, or even regressive fold, within a broader transformation of signifying orders. Such a transformation may persist as an epoch-defining project upon which diverse *virtual* futures continue to depend. Despite such a perspective, this book will not primarily be "theoretical" as such. Rather, it can be said to explore three ideological clusters in which the need to rethink "materiality" in linguistic terms – that is, at a site of inscription out of which the aesthetico-political or epistemo-critical takes place – emerges with transvaluative claims. These will be: first, in what might be called the ghost genealogy of the critical "present," the way in which key

1

figures or ciphers, Bakhtin and de Man, have been effaced (the one through embrace, the other through abjection), creating a crypt within the efflorescence of contemporary historicist styles that remains to be interrogated; second, the ocular-centric tradition by which cinema has been installed as a mimetic operation (the counter-cipher here will be "Hitchcock"); and third, the way that a transformative mode of reading I will not quite call *allographics* operates today as a form of (perhaps post post-Marxist) ideology critique, applicable to the general domain of cultural mapping. Is the call to create new networks of cultural and mnemonic trace-chains, today, merely the compulsive attempt to compensate for an increasingly inescapable fault in the referential functions of language in an *information* age – that is, a recuperative gesture? Or is it the labor by which a translation is being prepared into a different epistemological model, and with that, conception of agency?

1.

In a famous letter to Benjamin after reading *The Paris of the Second Empire in Baudelaire*, Adorno complains of a perceived paralysis in the former's writing project. While Adorno misreads Benjamin's allegorical style as a merely descriptive one ("at the crossroads of magic and positivism"), he presciently reflects on a malaise or arrestation present more broadly today in the "age of cultural studies." Adorno finds Benjamin's work merely, it seems, descriptive or wishful, trusting to mimesis:

> The "mediation" which I miss, and find obscured by *materialistic-historio-graphic* invocation, is nothing other than the theory which your study omits . . . If one wished to put it drastically, one could say that your study is located at the crossroads of magic and positivism. *That spot is bewitched.* Only theory could break the spell . . . (my italics)[1]

If we take this bewitched place as at least as double – in Adorno's reading (it may refer to himself), in or beyond Benjamin's practice – the aporetic "spell" of this spot expands, reduplicates erratically. To be effective, to break its specular spell, to get away from the mimetic blind of a pretense to the sociological as such, to

---

[1] Adorno's letter appears in *Aesthetics and Politics*, 131.

become political (again) requires a (re)turn to what had, ostensibly, been effaced. What is called for has itself a loaded name: theory. The first logic of this accusation is that the will to empirical or pragmatic critique has become transfixed in a specular ideality, while the theory effaced and here unread in Benjamin harbors the key to historical, transformative, in fact political work. Why this inversion, and what wider application does it have today?

As a parable of the critical "present" rather than of Benjamin's work, of being stuck in a descriptive and historicizing model that pretends to a political practice sometimes the opposite of what it accomplishes, the idea of this bewitched spot has some resonance. To open this productive misreading would involve questioning, of course, just where Adorno seems to misapprehend the performative import, in Benjamin, of particular words – among them materiality, or what he calls above "materialistic-historiographic invocation." Such an "invocation" returns decisively in his *Theses on the Philosophy of History*, where Benjamin explicitly questions how an alternate practice of writing-reading to current epistemo-critical models – largely mimetico-historicist – is required to rupture the fixed and inherited narratives of a foreclosed notion of "history." That is, is required to open the possibility of alternative futures to what, for him, was the apparent triumph of Euro-fascism, and this by conjuring alternate pasts to those produced by a received model of reference and archiving, that same historicism that still rules knowledge formation. For Benjamin, however, contrary to the mimetic implications of Adorno's complaint, such a writing practice involves a kind of séancing of the past and future. At this séance a figure of *materiality* associated with the non-human aspect of language ("materialistic-historiographic") – that is, one superseding anthropomorphism and historicism – stands in attendance.

Benjamin will give this projected *practice* different names across his text: allegory for a prolonged moment (in the *Trauerspiel*, but then it recedes), but elsewhere translation, at times the machinery of cinema (a kind of disruptive re-inscription of the sensorium), or in the *Theses*, as Adorno anticipates, "*materialistic* historiography." No doubt, the last figure seems almost impossible to read without rewriting not only its own components (material, history, graphematics) but the once benign term "allegory" itself. We will remark, for now, only that seemingly pivotal terms which thread

3

Benjamin's work – allegory and "translation," but again cinema, as well as "materialistic historiography" – all invoke parallel logics. These non-words undergo a translation of their own whose implications are not always clear: they begin as traditional and extremely mimetic categories (translation reproduces supposed originals, cinema the real, "historiography" facts) then are reflexively altered as apparatuses that engulf and actively reconfigure the mimetic as such, mnemonic policing, anteriority. Each adopts an interventionist logic that, as it unfolds, all but consumes its representational pretext. For Benjamin, mnemonic or inscriptive interventions are the most politically necessary to explore, since they alone stand to alter the archival basis by which "experience" is programmed, decisions taken. Each parallel logic or itinerary in the terms mentioned addresses the invisible manner in which representational habits like "historicism" operate to protect and enforce cognitive regimes that may be called "ideological" and destructive. (For Benjamin, these are directly linked to what is called "fascism.")

Somehow, what Adorno will call "theory" leads back through issues of mnemotechnics, inscription, translation, "pure language," and allegory that perhaps we – like Adorno – have lost track of. What is meant, here, by a recommended return to "theory" to break a certain appalling spell if not a return from the mesmerizing pretense that description (or context) has a socio-ontological import of its own ("magic and positivism"), *to* a site of anteriority, of programming, of installed and blinding epistemo-political models, of the "materialistic-historiographic"? *Inscription*, in this sense, pretends to name not only "being inscribed" in another's textual field or narrative skeins, in invisible relations of programming and networks, but the virtual facticity of a prefigural mark or cut that cannot be preceded by a metaphoric discourse or value-formation structured "from" (or against) it. For Benjamin, "materialistic historiography" would expose the trace-chains that manage anteriority as *virtual*, together with their semantic capital and canonical accounts – and this, *en route* to a projected re-decision of sorts. Since the facticity of inscription itself is to be conceived of not as a private crypt of memory but essentially external, material in its manifestation, we will refer to this virtual act of intervention, later in these essays, as a moment of (dis)inscription and exscription.

The "spot" in question may thus be likened to a familiar critical moment today. This moment, what I call for convenience the protocols of certain currents in "cultural studies," situates itself within an imposed history or histories. According to this map – which remains popular to the degree that diverse versions of the "present" locate themselves by its legend – the advent of what is referred to as "high" or post-structuralist *theory* was associated with a philosophically inflected amalgam of programs interfacing linguistic concerns with the redefinition of "history" (or, for that matter, human agency, meaning, impositions of power, and so on). It displayed a certain auto-reflexivity associated with its linguistic preoccupations – one that, in turn, would be eventually stigmatized variably as "modernist," as aestheticist, and so on. Against this moment, we witnessed a turn away from the fetishization of language or the text – what would have only led back, as it seemed, to close reading's tricks or new criticism, an imminently institutional form of depoliticized labor – toward political criticism. Away, that is, from "high" theory – or simply "theory" – back to real practices one could, finally, recognize as politically engaged, "secular" (in Said's sense), pragmatic. This shift, hailed as a "return to history," and hence seemingly affiliated with a cultural left or Marxian itinerary, traversed new historicism, neo-pragmatism, and a stunning array of identity political agendas. Turning away from the sterile formalism of linguistic analysis, one could not dissociate a return to the political from a return to a re-asserted agency of the subject (this time, socially constructed). To a degree such reclaimed "subjectivities" and their associated motifs (return to the everyday, to socio-figural context, the "body," to lived "life") involved a return to familiar names and mimetic epistemological models. For if, *according to this story*, a linear march of progress would be represented by the super-session of mere "theory" toward the pragmatics of history, con-text, the everyday, identity politics, and so on, on behalf of a generally leftist trajectory, one is struck by one odd *fact*: that throughout the period associated with this march – perhaps, most decisively, the last decade and a half – there has been a steady return to more conservative politics both within the university and in the national and global polis. What we are reminded, here, is that today more than ever the epistemological is the "political." Thus there is a little-noted counter-genealogy to this "official"

5

one – a narrative, but one which is non-linear, a narrative of folds and counter-folds, or regressions. According to this, "cultural studies" – with its return to *mimetic-humanism* and historicist methods – would appear a detour, a regressive parenthesis or counter-move to what remains a central epistemo-historial re-orientation or shift, upon the outcome of which diverse virtual futures continue to depend. One might address this unofficial "history" that hovers over and re-writes the above at the very moment it seems to have achieved its end – that is, with a sort of installed academic hegemony of "cultural studies." The moment is interesting because it revives the possibility that linguistic pre-occupations need not appear fetishized sites fixated on material signifiers' auto-referential behavior, but operate as mnemonic technologies servicing a "transvaluation" more interrupted than gone beyond, more abjected as trauma than displaced by the intervening and inevitably mimetic programs of today's critical "present." From this perspective, the current shift to tele-techno-logical networks is not an abrupt break with the traditionalist archive, so much as the acceleration and phenomenalization of what had all along been a more or less institutionalized manage-ment of cultural mnemonics, textual switchboards, canonical pro-cessings of anteriority – that is, at the very site in which humanist discourse is serviced, an overwhelmingly formalist bureaucratiz-ation.

One might recall that as part of the return to the pragmatic, there was asserted a total break between the realm of the political and something called epistemology – with which "philosophic" and linguistic trajectories of *reading* were associated. The political was designated as the realm of the mimetic. If arguments emerged that challenged that very definition of the political, they could be bracketed, since the epistemological – which is above all a certain model of how reference is to be generated, or anteriority managed – had already been declared not political, not to do with the (increasingly "global") polis. This programming by familiar models of mimesis or historicism, what themselves stood to be transformed by movements of and within "theory," would ap-pear to narcoleptically re-instate what had become an intricately threatened regime of signification.

Whatever Adorno meant by "theory," it occupies a position in this narrative of origin and anti-origin – what Benjamin might have termed *Ursprung*, not as site of origination but where diverse pre- and post-histories converge and stand to be redecided.[2] I will argue that this scapegoating of "theory," by which we mean the more general occlusion of a *materiality of language*, can be examined in privileged ciphers and counternarratives that continue to harass this site. In the following essays, this will occur as an attempt to re-examine the prehistory of the critical "present" itself under the signatures, at first, of "Bakhtin" and "de Man" – and, finally, Benjamin himself, as though a less explored triangulation can be drawn between these three. What we call "cultural studies" today may seem like an alluvial plain absorbing remnants from the above-mentioned sequence of post-theoretical preoccupations (new historicism, identity politics) while naming as pragmatic or political a return to representational modes – what appears, in practice, by manifesting the corresponding contradiction in the process, a "bewitched" spot. While I will further distinguish a *counter-genealogy* to this place in a moment, we cannot but be impressed with how the above narrative presents itself to us with a certain legitimizing aura. "Cultural studies" arrives as if at the "end of (critical) history" – an occurrence affiliated with a hypothetical globalization of formal democracy, with the installation of new transnational or hyper-media, the end of the Cold War. Yet there remains an unsettling subtext – and politics – that ghosts this narrative, essentially *rewriting* its political claims.

2.

As a means of conjuring this alternative site, I defer proposing merely to modify the term *allegory* – a self-cancelling, or depleted term, as we will see, all but unusable today – with a simplification like *allography*. Theory, it seems, never quite meant "theory" to begin with, but a different sort of praxis; one that, for the moment, we may call anti-mimetic, epistemo-political. Keeping something in play of what Benjamin terms "materialistic historiography,"

---

[2] The problematic of *Ursprung* in Benjamin's *Trauerspiel* study, presented as the virtual or cross-site conjured by the intersection of pre- and post-historical vectors (*Vor- und Nachgeschichte*), is examined by Samuel Weber in "Genealogy of Modernity: History, Myth and Allegory in Benjamin's Origin of the German Mourning Play." *Ursprung*, as an *ur*-leap rather than "origin," opens a site in which historial inscriptions themselves can be altered or (dis)installed.

7

allography suggests the shifting mechanics of a certain *technology* of inscription implied. With this word I would gesture at a conception of (dis)inscription and mnemotechnics which, however banal, might lay claim to a spectral "materiality." Such a *task* might be preceded by identifying where, if at all, the term "allegory" in Benjamin was recirculated, that is, *not* as a modified trope of literary aesthetics, but as a *techne* of historial intervention as such.[3] For to ask where allegory in its prehistory (which is all that it has had, in a sense) prefigures an *allographic* practice to come, is also to note where the latter suggests not only that mnemonic otherness evinced by the facticity of prefigural inscription but the *altering* impact of material signs on (and against) anterior traces, altering or engineering the teletechnological routing and force of trace-chains, the recasting of anteriority and the production of reference.[4]

In Adorno's letter, much depends on how one reads Benjamin's use of the term materiality or "materialistic."[5] Adorno himself is torn on this, but overcomes a certain resistance, recognizing first that it does not echo the Marxian use that he, Adorno, more or less deploys:

> The impression which your entire study conveys – and not only on me and my arcades orthodoxy – is that you have done violence to yourself. Your solidarity with the Institute, which pleases no one more than myself, has induced you to pay tributes to Marxism which are not really suited either to Marxism or to yourself. They are not suited to Marxism because the mediation through the total social process is missing, and you superstitiously attribute to material enumeration a power of illumination which is never kept for a pragmatic reference but only for theoretical construction. (130)

Let us note, first, that the "violence" or violation Adorno perceives will involve the word "materiality" – yet it is a peculiar

---

3 The only other use of the neologism "allography" that I am aware of occurs in Nicholas Royle, *Telepathy and Literature: Essays on the Reading Mind* (Cambridge: Basil Blackwell, 1991), where it is nonetheless used of an alterity effect within the work of cryptonomy: "One might venture to call it an allography –a writing on behalf of another – but only if this 'other' is acknowledged as being non-human, unrepresentable and irremediably cryptic" (33)
4 This excursus may be heard as a "theoretical" supplement to essays I previously presented under the title of *Anti-Mimesis from Plato to Hitchcock* (1994).
5 We might think of Benjamin's use of "materialistic" as a cross between what de Man calls inscription and what Althusser implies by the materiality and semiotic rituals of "ideology" in which one is interpellated (or inscribed).

violence ("to yourself") in that it is really a violation of a Marxian orthodox use, a catachretic deployment Adorno takes for a kind of pandering, a position he modifies momentarily as the term becomes distinct, shadowed against familiar reference. Indeed, "materiality" evokes what Benjamin in his letter of reply will term a *monad*: "In the monad everything that used to lie in mythical rigidity as a textual reference comes alive" (137) – that is, the site where an entire model of "reference" may be altered by virtue of an intervention in a meaning system, the "mythical rigidity" of inherited interpretation, a coming "alive" of the dead that leads to a virtual site of (dis)inscription. Above, Adorno remarks that Benjamin's unreferenced "materiality" seems self-cancelling in its effects ("violence to yourself"): first, it devolves to a kind of "material enumeration" that liquefies the conceptual or dialectical term and with it reference ("never kept for a pragmatic reference"), and second, it emerges as a kind of censorship at the level of parody, a precensorship: "you have denied yourself your boldest and most fruitful ideas in a kind of precensorship according to materialist categories (which by no means coincide with Marxist categories)" (130). Having begun by distancing Benjamin's prefigural trope of materiality – rejecting it, suspecting it of aping and dismantling his own ("Marxist categories") – Adorno shifts to Benjamin's side, encouraging the development of another, this time a-referential site:

God knows, there is only one truth, and if your intelligence lays hold of this one truth in categories which on the basis of your idea of materialism may seem apocryphal to you, you will capture more of this one truth than if you use intellectual tools whose movements your hand resists at every turn. After all, there is more about this truth in Nietzsche's *Genealogy of Morals* than in Bukharin's *ABC of Communism*.   (131)

Leaving aside Adorno's safeguards ("God knows . . ."), what is this "materialism" that apes while dismissing "Marxist categories," voids routine concepts of reference, links something like "enumeration" to "illumination," yet insists on miming – or preceding – the categorial or verbal-monadic site from which Adorno's more conventional usage derives (and feels itself dislocated from)? Why, moreover, does Adorno turn to Nietzsche here – in the context of what "materiality"?

What is this *materiality* which, "invoked" (Adorno's word) like a kind of counter-magic linked to "enumeration," is the opposite of any claim to material reference in the tradition of the Greek *hyle*, or "matter," or the body? Why, moreover, when it is encountered in the *Theses* as "materialistic historiography"[6] – the format to which Adorno alludes – will it be associated with a virtual technique of historial intervention intended not only to counter the spell of historicism ("where historical materialism cuts through historicism" (255)), of received narratives of linear time as an empty "continuum" ("telling the sequence of events like the beads of a rosary" (263)), but as what stands to alter the past ("the dead") by way of a certain caesura-effect, or "standstill," in which pasts and futures offer themselves as *virtual*? Perhaps the texts of the *Theses* are sufficiently well-circulated that we may point to one or two problems without a full exegesis. What is involved is not this or that liberatory desire but a prospective warping of inscribed modalities of the sensorium, of hermeneutics, of an already formalized pretense of succession. To have accepted the history of mimetic historicism is to have acceded to one or another of inevitable future determinations that such predict or imply. For Benjamin this impasse provokes a different model of writing or inscription (what "defines the present in which (the historical materialist) himself is writing history" (262)), linked with a semio-mnemonic configuration called "shock": "Where thinking suddenly stops in a configuration pregnant with tensions, it gives that configuration a shock, by which it crystallizes into a monad." For today's reader, who might think too quickly that Benjamin intends, here, only to re-accent once marginalized markers on a familiar historical map, as "new historicism" or identity politics attempts, what remains puzzling is that something termed a "monad" represents an agency of transformation – that is, something like a node, or verbal relay-network about which hermeneutic encrustations accrue. Yet this monad can be converted, in a cross-historical switchboard or cultural mnemonics, to produce new possible configurations or futures. It is a term, as we noted, allied to an alteration in systems of reference as such. The time of this occasion like the non-present of the so-called *Jetztzeit*, a "state of emergency" or *emergence*, implies a momentary voiding of received contents – as if by the sheer assertion of *formal* or

---

6 Walter Benjamin, "Theses on the Philosophy of History," in *Illuminations*, 262; *Illuminationen*, 278.

material elements. Such a materiality, drawing on the always exterior domain of prefigural inscription, does not achieve some new meaning or determination by virtue of a messianic revelation (such could, at best, only repeat a past historicist narrative). It passes, or seems to *pass*, through an *aesthetic* formalization of this materiality itself, optioning in a virtual mode that caesura-effect associated in "The Task of the Translator" with something called "pure language," *reine Sprache*. The very possibility of an intervention in the historial, it would seem, depends inversely on the invocation of something like a sheer exteriority – in the absence of any determined other, and hence of its own topographical position. (Rather than being viewed as a domain of play set aside at the margins of philosophy, the "aesthetic" – referenced to the Greek *aisthanumai*, evoking perception – is linked to a programming of the senses by mnemo-inscriptive grids, from which already interpretive "perceptions" appear generated: in this conceptual remapping, notoriously present in the *Birth of Tragedy* (but also from before the "dawn" of the West, as is apparent in counter-canonical readings of texts going back to and preceding Plato),[7] the aesthetic appears rewritten as one "materialistic" conduit and cipher for a more general, pre- and post-historial graphematics out of which "experience" is shaped and produced.)

The linkage between a logic intrinsic to Benjamin's linguistic meditation on *translation* and Nietzschean "transvaluation" implies an overlooked itinerary. It returns us, moreover, to the elusive logics of allegory itself. Nietzsche's "transvaluation of all values" is hyperbolically proffered to mark the passage not (only) *as if* from one putative "epoch" to another but *from* one system of manufacturing history and meaning (passive, reactive, mimetic, "humanist," that of *ressentiment*) to a putative *other* – at war with the first, yet inhabiting it, even preceding it, a pro-active mimesis without model and copy. What, after all, can an over-arching conceit such as Nietzsche's have to do with "materialistic historiography"? Anyone who wished to retrace the so-called modernist itinerary of "allegory" may be led to a site disarticulated at its own point of departure. "Allegory," a largely vacant term today, emerges as an anamorphic and pro-active *techne* on behalf of mnemonic intervention – within what, to begin with, are and

---

[7] See, for instance, my own "P.s.: Plato's scene of reading in the Protagoras," chapter 2 of *Anti-Mimesis*.

were received and constructed pasts. Since what is presented as history would always also be the more or less legitimated product of installed networks of notational systems and genres, "allegory" would suspend naturalized genres on behalf of a pragmatic cut – opening alternative itineraries to those of fixed inherited narratives legislated by mnemonic and historicist regimes. It proposed to do so by altering the very model out of which reference (or "experience") is generated, anteriority managed. If what has been called a formal *reflexivity* is not (as some have assumed) the mark of an aesthetic or modernist suspension of the referential, but the predicate for rewiring epistemo-critical or mimetic historicist regimes designed to manage and legislate memory, time, the past, and hence the production of "futures," then what we will still not quite call *allographies* suggests where a turn as if toward the prefigural domain of material inscription re-emerges as one predicate of a mnemotechnics or "materialistic historiography." It emerges under the sign of what might be termed a *séance-effect* and as a putative counter-stroke to a "bewitched" mimetic politics, and it raises – as for Benjamin – the prospect of intervention. At the invocation of "the dead," come to table in a virtualized present, there occurs a *knocking* as if under the table – a prefigural *semiosis*, an irreducible material sequence preceding all phenomenalization or mimetic imagery, *as if* coming from a certain outside. It is this prefigural occasion that can be heard, today, in what Benjamin calls *reine Sprache*, in Hitchcock's bar-series signature, in de Man's "materiality," in Bakhtin's differential evisceration of received "concepts," in the formalization of Apollonian "music" in early Nietzsche or, even, the concept of measure itself (*metron*) stretching back before Protagoras . . .

3.

But why yoke this very worn term, *ideology*, to a more strategic word, *inscription*, which is resistant to all formats of representational logic? Does ideology not almost always operate by replacing a logic of inscription with one of representation, expression, "subjective" or "objective" correspondence, *description*? Why speak of virtualities, or virtual inscriptions? If we hear in *ideology* the epistemo-political effect that an already reactive and preinterpretive programming of the senses entails, then we may be closer to further explicating why the term *materiality* arises here. That is, in a way entirely other to how it is referentially evoked in the discursive webs of "cultural studies." A contrast is useful here. In place of the manner in which a contemporary analyst, the Lacanian Žižek, treats the figure of ideology as an *inverting* and "symbolic" reaction to the mock-epiphany of the "Thing" in its various banal incarnations – that is, to the prepersonified irruption of a Lacanian *metaphorics* of the Real (Žižek's phallophany) – we must insert a *graphematic* facticity or mnemonic network that is itself prefigural. What eludes Žižek in his appropriation of Lacan appears at the very site which he returns to in a covert rhetoric of transparency, to a beyond of "language" (the latter too hastily identified as the Symbolic *tout court*), a Cartesian scene of post-anthropomorphic identification. Instead of the "Thing," of any site of the Thing identifiable *as such*, we get or always depart from something like the facticity of a mark or inscription – caught already in a drift of pre- and post-historical forces. The prefigural powers of this materiality are those *against* which ideological or interpretive languages of identification, "meaning" (the correlative of property), or interiorist metaphors are staged. It is important to explore the political consequences of such distributions of reference and anterior force, together with the occlusion of inscription itself, this deferral of the "material," and of the powers of intervention – of disinscription and reinscription – that attend this anamorphic site. Such are anticipated in Benjamin's hypothesis of constellations or networks in which sites of *monadic* intervention arise: monads, that is to say, the always entirely singular *node* in the mnemonic switchboard from which diverse "presents" stand routinely to be programmed or projected.

It is in Benjamin's essay on "The Task of the Translator" that he invokes the topos of *reine Sprache* ("pure language"). This metaphysical sounding figure appears not as a trope of full language or theological ideality of meaning, as one still finds remarked, but very clearly as both the material and perhaps formal – at all events, sheerly exterior – networking of prefigural linguistic differences, including agencies of sound, letteration, grapheme. "Pure" is to be heard as the purely material order of effects shared by the work of the trace in all tongues, all languages. What aims to be true to an original for purposes of translation, and thus seems to return or fold back to such, must pass through this site common to the intersections of all linguistic entities or mutations. Yet this passage, this recollection that is not an anamnesis and which is always virtual, not only empties "meaning" (as Benjamin tells us), rewriting the ideological topoi of experience or content in terms of fully exterior, void, and networked signifiers (should we use this anachronism), but itself serves a translational, transitional, transvaluative role. Curiously, everything that usually blocks off "modernism" as an aestheticizing, linguistifying episode would be contained, neutralized, at just this point, for here the possibility of intervention, or re-inscription, depends as though first on a radical exteriorization of such pure linguistic agencies, themselves non-human, "materialistic" potentially. Here too lies another inversion that haunts Benjamin's ceaseless recurrence to literature: that rather than being auto-referential, in some self-absorbed and cut off way, this reflexive moment becomes instead the predicate for accessing a radical otherness present in mnemonic and representational networks out of which managing and blinding images of history issue. By contrast, it is the humanist and historicist project which appears from this perspective auto-referential, insisting upon a phantom at the center of all reference systems. The "task [*Aufgabe*]" of the translator appears metaphorically related, again, to the "task" of a historial transvaluator. All language systems, or cultural memories stand to be disarticulated and rearticulated by this external, material, virtual, formal – and historial – *crossing*. It is not without interest that this is the Benjamin text that de Man presents his sole and extended commentary on:

Pure language is perhaps more present in the translation than in the original, but in the mode of trope. Benjamin, who is talking about the inability of trope to be adequate to meaning, constantly uses the very tropes which seem to postulate the adequation between meaning and trope; but he prevents them in a way, displaces them in such a way as to put the original in motion, to de-canonize the original, giving it a movement which is a movement of disintegration, of fragmentation.[8]

There are traces of Benjamin throughout the late essays of de Man, as though the latter were acutely aware in this phase of his project of the "material" moment Benjamin isolates. To "de-canonize the

---

[8] Paul de Man, "The Task of the Translator," in *The Resistance to Theory*, 92. The notion of "pure language" is interestingly clarified by Jonathan Sheehan in "The Remains of History", *Qui Parle*, 8, 1 (Fall/Winter, 1994) as when "language comes to exist as such, pure materiality without the burden of signification" (66).

original" implies a dislocating transformation on the way to another site ("giving it movement"). As we often see in Benjamin's text (or for that matter, Bakhtin's), such an invisible but eviscerating transposition occurs without being marked openly, when the "same" terms have been desemanticized and provided new formal itineraries. For de Man, this *movement* involves a voiding of metaphor or figuration, which is to say the linguistic technologies by which interiority is produced:

> Benjamin insists that the model of their derivation is not that of resemblance or of imitation. It is not a natural process: the translation does not resemble the original the way the child resembles the parent, nor is it an imitation, a copy, or a paraphrase of the original. In that sense, since they are not resemblances, since they are not imitations, one would be tempted to say they are not metaphors. The translation is not the metaphor of the original; nevertheless, the German word for translation, *übersetzen*, means metaphor. *Übersetzen* translates exactly the Greek *metaphorein*, to move over, *übersetzen*, to put across. *Übersetzen*, I should say, *translates* metaphor – which, asserts Benjamin, is not at all the same. They are not metaphors, yet the word means metaphor. The metaphor is not a metaphor, Benjamin is saying. No wonder their translators have difficulty. It is a curious assumption to say *übersetzen* is not metaphorical, *übersetzen* is not based on resemblance, there is no resemblance between the translation and the original. Amazingly paradoxical statement, metaphor is not metaphor. (83)

De Man's insistence on the movement beyond metaphor or mimesis ("of resemblance or of imitation") raises the issue of what Adorno called a "materiality" irrecuperable to an overtly referential (or Marxian) model, to a dialectical or mimetic politics. A certain "invocation" of the non-human, the "material" as a ghosted site suggests a séancing effect that traverses bio-logics and organically policed boundaries of living and dead. Such materiality would not be a "natural process," yet it may – as Benjamin suggests, first in the *Trauerspiel* – accord with a different, translational conceit of "natural *history*" in excess of the auto-referentiality of the human. This other non-natural nature, which harbors and is refracted through non-human time(s), ruptures mimetic and historicizing models on behalf of a material semiosis irrecoverable to anthropomorphisms – preceding what de Man in exploiting the trope of prosopopeia names face as a site (or "state") of (virtual) emergence.

Benjamin's essay suggests under the rubric of "translation" a movement in which received language (the original) is relieved of its coded referential status and, momentarily remarking itself ("to turn the symbolizing into the symbolized" (*Illuminations*, 80)), closes out the discourse of interiority or expression; here, the figure of "pure language," of course, the non-human perspective from which discourse is transposed, is not a structuralist notion of linguistic differences. It is, above all, a principle of passage and selection that renders the mechanics of "translation" parallel to that of allegory or its surrogates: like allegory or cinema, translation begins with mimetic or representational claims (to fidelity) that Benjamin inverts and dissolves ("a theory that looks for other things in a translation than reproduction of meaning" (78)). Benjamin summons the non-human or material aspect during the séance-work of translation as "pure language fully formed in the linguistic flux" (80) – corresponding to where a constellation of terms including allegory, materiality, and translation itself appears similarly voided of their received conceptual content. *Pure* language, "which no longer means or expresses anything" (80), rather than epitomizing self-referential formalism as conceived from the position of mimetic humanism, brings with it the assertion of a reflexive materiality that actively disfigures the entire reserve of a received epochal order or mimetic model of reference – a hypothetical moment of *disinscription* we witness, implicitly, at least performatively, in Bakhtin's writing as well.

4.

Have we simply evaded explaining the monstrous linkage of the two non-words of the title – ideology *and* inscription – a pretense eroded by a hinted *al*literation which penetrates the mimetic history of the first term with the prephenomenal idiomatic (one might say idiocy) of the latter? What to make of the mock-connective "and," buttressed *as if* in some fictive sequence or pairing? In what ways must they be heard *otherwise*? In what way does the connective "and" link, decouple, or imply a logophagic relation – in which the second term, say, absorbs the first, or the first is conceived as an anamorphic defense against the second? If "ideology" is today an emptied term, moreover, "inscription" drops like a stone in a pond – as if without resonance beyond evoking a certain facticity, the trace of anteriority, or for that matter a kind of black-hole effect. "Inscription" seems, on the surface, the less problematic of the two words because the less familiar or familial today – pointing, in ways still discernible, toward the idea of a *matrixal* or prefigural graphematics out of which interpretive and perceptual programs stand to be generated. When one of the former term's contemporary champions, again Slavoj Žižek, "categorically asserts the existence of ideology qua generative matrix that regulates the relationship between visible and non-visible, between imaginable and unimaginable,"[9] it is the trope of the "matrixal" that seems inescapable. "Matrix" can, of course, be heard still as an anthropomorphic figure: as the maternalization or naturalization of a non-human order – what may be echoed, among else, as and against what Derrida explores as *Khora* (or what he differently names, assuming a paternal metaphorics, "archive"). While in the strictest sense non-existent, such would be also always double: at once a sheer order of differential semaphores – such as are invoked as the prefigural domain of "pure language" – *and* the multiply networked historical mutations of force and representation by which we tend to narrate perception and experience, reference and temporal plotting. What we call "inscription," given its irreducibly exterior occurrence at the site of phenomenality, might be simultaneously heard as *ex*scription. It implies a radical publicness, hence the social, as well as being interfaced with the programming of any "sensorium." Does the non-site of such inscription connect diverse planes of historial "experience" to mnemonic relays which are themselves managed by reactive hermeneutic formations, institutionalized names or knowledge-routes? On the one hand, inscription in this premimetic sense seems encountered as a kind of facticity, as the crypt of some reigning or deterritorialized law, once posited and installed. On the other hand, it is precisely in the non-site of inscription that the possibility of historial intervention and the virtual arise. It is only when an instituted and hermeneutic trace-chain is disrupted, suspended (as with Benjaminian "shock"), that alternatives to programmed historicist models can appear accessed. The perspective of such a critique derives from a non-anthropomorphic trace, rather than a foundation from which

---

[9] Slavoj Žižek, "The Spectre of Ideology," introduction to *Mapping Ideology*, 1.

"false consciousness" can be named. Here the term "ideology" returns, albeit this time in its afterlife.

Ernesto Laclau addresses something like this dilemma within the term "ideology" in "The Death and Resurrection of the Theory of Ideology," where he assesses the term's contemporary evisceration "as a result of its own imperialistic success."[10] He defines this crisis by noting the spread of "discourse analysis" to include every supposed "extra-ideological ground" that had anchored the term in the past, or given it import. Without a norm from which *variation* or perversion can be tracked and labeled "ideological," fissures such as "distortion" or "false consciousness" appear relativized and void: at this point, essentially, "there is no extra-discursive ground from which a critique of ideology could proceed" (299). Yet rather than an honorable retirement of this term, it appears to undergo a *mutation*, a translation of sorts. This occurs through a process involving the self-(re)marking of the material agency of signification. It appears to take on another, implicitly guiding role at the very point that it loses its "ground" (Derrida will, in a way, call the effect of such a *movement* "justice"). Instead of an extra-discursive referential anchor, (a)*materiality* appears refracted through a movement of trace. From this movement a critique of hermeneutically or "ideologically" invested positions is not only derivable but seems impossible to arrest.

Laclau projects beyond the death of "ideology" a ghostly revivification, "resurrecting" the term in the absence of the notion of a distortion *from* a norm or ground (one that is non-ideological, extra-discursive). Yet while proposing the notion of a *"constitutive* distortion" (*"a contradictio in adjecto"*), it is perpetually marked by a metaphysical compensation. Ideology confers teleological import, subjective import, transparency: "to project into something which is essentially divided the illusion of a fullness and self-transparency that it lacks" (301). Or again: "what an ideological distortion projects . . . is the impossible fullness of the community" (303) – as in social or communitarian rhetoric. Rhetorically, the structures of investment are similar. Differently put, the so-called distortion-without-norm of such projections occur like variations of Voloshinov's alternately critiqued semantic models, "subjective expressionism" (the idea of the subject's interior con-

---

[10] Ernesto Laclau, "The Death and Resurrection of the Theory of Ideology," 298.

tent) or "abstract objectivism" (the idea of full meaning adhering to a formal construct). They can be recognized as anthropomorphic or structurally objectifying projections onto a reflexive (a)materiality that in itself voids tropes of interiorization, appropriation, meaning. This ghostly trajectory of "ideology" involves several consequences. For one, the gesture of disengaging such "constitutive distortions" happens from within these sites (there being no outside), yet this occurs in the name of a prefigural and non-anthropomorphic agency – a materiality of the trace that may change or alter with it the very terms or concepts of temporality, representation, the "event," the human itself. This excess operation beyond a self-canceled use of "ideology" as "false consciousness" is no longer presented as a mimetic category but as a transformational, translational, or transvaluative station – if ideology was all along language ("practical consciousness," says the Marx of *The German Ideology*), the former would be increasingly cast as an effect from the perspective of the latter's material or formally reflected status, conceived now as an agency for the reterritorialization of historial relation. Ideology appears simultaneously marked and ghosted by a process of exteriorization, of *ex*posure (without inside or out as such). Here would ensue the precondition for a virtual deterritorialization and recoding of the virtual. The movement of such a portmanteau *"ideology critique" without ground* stands to not so discretely alter the status of the historial, the political – much as exceeding any tautologic of the term itself mimes a (Nietzschean) supersession of the structurally circular logic of recurrence.[11] Differently put, these projections involve phantasms of interiority – arabesques of subjective and objectivist codings, institutions of knowledge and identity production – voided and redistributed before the sheer exteriority and agencies of this active *re*marking. Among the traces that the non-word "ideology" bears is that of displacing, as in citation marks, the logic out of which ideation, idealization, and concep-

---

[11] Clearly, one could connect the juncture ideology–inscription to a graphematics of the "fetish," proceeding to theorize the prosthetic import both of the fetish-investment and the dissolution of the status of fetish-logic before a general conception of the technological supplement's role in all such ideographical inversions, clusters or historical eddies. To speak of an ideallographics, here, would not be superfluous, since the unbinding of an ideological protrusion into an allographic *movement* – directed, inversely, by the de-anthropomorphized trace – indicates where the project of a post-ideological "ideology critique" (which will have other names) partakes in a translational problematic.

19

tualization itself tends to be antithetically generated over against differential mnemonic grids – incisions, faults, events in mutating archival logics. Rather than addressing "false consciousness," one shifts ineluctably into a speculation on the currency of conceptualization, telecommunication networking, and ideational marketing or commerce that traverses semio-political and zoographic systems. The momentary pairing of "ideology" in its afterlife with "inscription" delivers us to a logic of translation or crossing – as though from one signifying order into another that has absorbed and marked its "materialistic" and exteriorizing premises. It implies that what would have been called an ideology-effect within the inherited ideology of ideology may be tracked, as if today, at sites where a discursive logic or institution occludes the problematic of (material) language in order compulsively to confer interiorist phantasms. Such could appear in the parodied guise of a critical technique.

One further twist adheres to any *use* of "ideology" persisting beyond the evisceration of this paleonym's history – a history that has always shadowed teleological narration. There has been an ideology *of* ideology that, as Žižek and Laclau note, is difficult to relinquish. It will have been associated with something encrypted, an inverse inscription of the real, a counter-truth (the metaphoric *camera obscura*), and hence unveiling of sorts, a crypto-antiapocalyptics. Yet since this figure today carries with it not only post-Marxian but post-Nietzschean resonance, a shift to "discourse analysis" without ground becomes the predicate not for wanton aestheticism (indeed, the "aesthetic" must here be defined anew in relation to the phenomenalization of inscriptions), nor linguistic play, but for a transmutation of the epistemo-political management of reference, temporality, and the archive itself. Here "intervention" can only occur with an abrupt break within programmed chains – what Benjamin might call "shock," or caesura. This seems choreographed before a reflexive, even formalized alertness to a "materiality" void of interiority, allohuman. The site, in short, where "aura" heard as anthropomorphism and personification has been (all along) relinquished. If the self-dividing facticity of the trace tends to be encountered as prefigural inscription, "ideology" in its turn is usually expressed through a *mimetic* logic that invests a self-policing model of reference as a guarantor of the real (that is, the same model for produc-

ing reference, knowledge, catalogs, ledgers). The ideological gesture effaces a reactive, inverting or expelling force while faking a
retroprojective source. It fields a mimetic counter-translation to a
putative archival or mnemotechnic "event," one which restitutes
an anthropomorphic logic of the proper and a policed code of
reference. The same texts held to legitimize and produce representational regimes and canons of interpretations (Plato, say, or
Kant, but everyone virtually) can be read otherwise as perform-
atives: for instance, that Plato from whom a routine "platonism"
is derived can be seen to have spawned the figure of the eidos
through a textual management of the repetition of an experience
of the mark, or letters – what casts that epistemological *ur*-plug,
ideas, in a wholly other, material light, dissolving and transforming the historicized edifice it was supposed to uphold or lend
legitimacy to. In such considerations a re-distribution of nodes on
the cultural and mnemonic switchboards is posited – from which
interpretive rules and perceptual protocols, temporal charts and
"experimental" norms are, always virtually, generated. Any
transformation of the archival involves, as Derrida suggests,
"transforming the entire public and private space of humanity,
and first of all the limit between the private, the secret (private or
public), and the public or the phenomenal," itself to be "accompanied by juridical and thus political transformations."[12] Any
mock resuscitation here of "ideology" (Laclau's "resurrection" is
perhaps too theological) caroms as the term shifts from a mimetic
notion of politics to a transformative logic shorn of coded, referential, phenomenal, "subjective" or "objective" assurances. The
afterlife of ideology suggests, among other things, the *passage* or
translation from one historial system of reference management
(frayed, become counter-efficient, dangerous) into an *other*, nominally "materialistic" and materialistically nominal. It moves
from an epistemo-aesthetic regime that had defined the "human"
toward an altered and altering of the terrestrial itself. It forecasts a

---

[12] Jacques Derrida, *Archive Fever*, 17. Such a project gambles on an alteration in and
of the archive itself, recalling Derrida's notation: "The archivization produces as
much as it records the event." (17) Such an archival network, Derrida further
suggests, is always a place of exteriority, "an external place which assures the
possibility of memorization, of repetition, of reproduction, or of reimpression"
(11) – that is, the material as we encounter it: "*No archive without outside.*"
Correspondingly, the institution of a certain mnemonics represents, materially
speaking, "a *prosthesis of the inside*" (19).

21

politics of "earth" in which that set of systems in which word-name we hear both *eat* and *ear* is not accorded status as ground *as such*. It is such an other "earth," not unconnected for man to traversing systems and competing laws of inscription, which Nietzsche commends as the *ethical* focus projected beyond the auto-referentialism of a globally destructive humanism.

That it has never been adequate to name any "preceding" epoch metaphysics, or to proclaim that to be closed (in a way, since Plato) seems clearer today than ever. If there never quite was a "metaphysics" to be closed, that may be because what was so termed in mock-historical fashion depended all along not on an "epoch" as such but institutions of representation, forced coding, programmings of the "sensorium," a hermeneutic management of mutating histories of virtual "events" that stand to redistribute or defer, channel or occlude, the force and laws of anteriority. Contrary to appearing "theoretical" issues, these are structures or psychotropes – invariably embedded in and shaped by linguistic and mnemonic habitats – that occur, are performed, or re-inscribed in minutiae of daily rituals. They program the "every-day." Since the dismantling of mimetic ideologies – subjective and objective, humanist and historicist – accompanies any passage toward such virtual politics, all political resonances return to "ideology" the instant they must seem erased. A trembling within the term ideology reappears the instant its old political force is lost, lost as ideological. As such, this afterlife of the term necessarily appears at the point of its own abandon – passing over the horizon at the moment that, as a familiar term, it loses all force of currency.

The preposition "after" in my sub-title – " '*after*' Benjamin, de Man, and Bakhtin" – suggests, like the connective "and," a number of turns. What may be most at issue is the manner in which these figures insist on linking a *materialist* address of language with the technical power to shape and intervene in epistemo-political orders or historical systems. The term "after" must, then, be heard multiply. It can imply a chase or pursuit, as of what lies before one still. It can imply a merely allusive regard. "After," in that case, can suggest a transformative participation which attempts to *pre*cede received familiar codifications by which problematic energies tend to be contained. In Benjamin's relinquishing of the aura of anthropomorphism, in de Man's prosopopeia preceding "face," in Bakhtin's "alien" or "dead word" a radical otherness is potentially encountered as the sheer anteriority of received mnemo-telematic systems. Here, at the pragmatic site or non-site associated in Adorno's letter with "theory," the "bewitched" spot migrates from representing impasse(s) merely of our current critical culture to naming a broader problematic which pertains, perhaps, to coming impasses in the human relation to terrestrial "life" itself – Aporia which will require more than nineteenth-century models of history, economy, the event, agency or time. Such impasses perhaps solicit perspectives more in line with what Benjamin called a sort of semaphoric "natural history" that is neither natural nor historicist, a radical otherness not primary human or humanist yet linked to the materiality and technicity of the trace. If a primary resonance of the "after" in my sub-title is to be heard in the more immediate sense of being *in the wake of*, it projects the possibility of a cultural criticism to come which – instead of situating itself in the general reaction to the epistemological traumas associated with an abjected "theory" and a return to historicist grammars – proceeds to the responsibilities of a post-humanist turn which the fetishes and timidity of current critical culture already languish behind (obvious in the corporate transfigurations looming over a relatively stunned University culture today). The question I would raise pertains to whether *other* practices of critical intervention, or "cultural studies," must not today be mobilized over against familiar humanist, historicizing, and mimetic codes whose imbrication in "older" archival protocols and machines of knowledge production we may no longer have the personal or collective luxury to simply repeat with variations. It is certainly interesting, when we contemplate the *likely* accelerations and dominations of techno-science unfolding before us, and the economic and ecologic impasses that may or may not be negotiable *en route* – in many cases, a question of redefining a metaphorics of the house and homelessness (*eco*), identity, animality, the material – that rather than posturing about post-modern and post-historical inertias in a sort of *faux* ennui, critical culture does not apprehend everything to date as merely preparatory, as a prehistory.

5.

The three clusters of essays loosely accord with three central variations in Benjamin's project: a reconfiguration of literary and historical programming under the rubric of *allegory*, a shift into a machinal simulation of the projection of the sensorium in *cinema*, and the more overtly named "materialistic historiography."

"Ciphers – or counter-genealogies for a critical 'present.'" This section explores three scenes that can be read, today, as ciphers within the "inner history" of critical theory. Through examining how de Man and Bakhtin have been constructed and situated, and how Benjaminian "allegory" conflicts with cultural studies today, we hunt for clues both to our own critical evasions (why have they been constructed with such and such variations?), but for where each suggests alternatives to the impasses of historicist models that seem to have been re-installed. The enigma would be: why is linguistic materiality the underlying target of a certain suppression of the "theoretical" itself? Why does this immaterial materiality re-emerge, today, as a question before us?[13]

"Expropriating cinema – or, Hitchcock's mimetic wars." How is it that "cinema," which should have been installed (at least, according to Benjamin) as a cultural and aesthetic apparatus destined to void humanist culture and the metaphorics of identification invariably associated with the "eye" and mimetic regimes of interpretation How has this inversion been legislated? What testimony of or resistance to this can be appealed to today? Benjamin sketches out an analysis in which *cinema* would repeat and vary the interventionist logics of what he calls allegory and "materialistic historiography." Such would entail a cinema associated with the loss of the "aura," and the logic of mnemonic and historical "shock." For Benjamin, the collective apparatus called cinema accords with a kind of techno-simulacrum of projected memory or "consciousness," a prosthetic site for the reconfigura-

---

[13] Elaborating an intersection of "biological" and "informational" models in the virtualization of the real embedded in a future epistemo-semiotic mapping found on tele-technicity, Mark C. Taylor speaks of where "the material becomes immaterial and the immaterial materializes" (*Hiding*, 15). Like Benjamin's constellations, Taylor's proposed "webs" are "not preprogrammed but are in a state of constant emergency" (63), patrolled by linguistic agencies or relays that interface zones imprinted as "living" and "dead," such as "allelomorphs": "allelomorphs mark the site of intersection between the biological and the informational" (66).

tion of the latter's constitutive trace-chains and mnemonic imprinting, as well as a writing model which openly (de)programs
the "sensorium." Yet "cinema" has been culturally installed as
the opposite: a technology guarding mimesis, as though invoking
a regressively literal interpretation of "technical reproduction"
(accenting the latter rather than prior term), guarding the metaphorics of the eye (hence classic economies of knowledge and
"light"), reinvested with logics of identification almost to surplus.
A counter-signature to this appropriation will be Hitchcock. We
will be interested in a "Hitchcock" engaged at the site
Benjamin can be said to theorize, one rethinking the materiality of
inscription as the premise for reconfiguring history, the aesthetic,
the human itself.

"Tourings – the monadic switchboard." This last cluster of
essays fans out, slightly, in parodic search of the Benjaminian
trope of the monad - that site, at once textual and situated within
the mnemonic network from which representation can tend to be
programmed, in which the teasing out or putting into play of a
(linguistic) materialist logic can function, virtually, as a proleptic
intervention of sorts. The present examples are no more, perhaps,
than occasions or case studies – yet each carries forward, in a
different micro-milieu or ideological site, traces of an agenda that
I had begun to earlier articulate: *a mnemotechnics of cultural inscription.* In these preliminary probes, the rhetoric of science in cultural
studies, the politics and linguistic logic of drugs (in the example of
Benjamin), and the protocols of writing "travel" are engaged.

Each of the essays diagnoses a suppressed crypt within contemporary critical practice. Each of these essays, moreover, asks
where the figure of aporia or impasse – openly associated with de
Man – had all along been evinced not as the epistemological
dead-end of some caricatured or programmatic "skepticism"
(skeptical, exactly, of *what?*) but as a *techne* underway toward a
more general translation, transformation, or indeed passage.

The concerns here extend terrain I began to address in a previous volume, *Anti-Mimesis*, which focused on the politics of "materialistic" reading. That is, how questioning operative models of
reference by drawing on where the prefigural domain of language
suggests alternative systems of agency contests traditional programs of difference and memory management. That volume explored how installed or canonical interpretations controlled the

25

roles played by *key* texts in diversely related traditions ("from Plato to Hitchcock"). Repeatedly, that work found that the most "material" or banal of markers – sound, letters, signatures – provide public entry into alternative histories of reading and force which each cluster of text-events more or less resided over and was (re)produced within. Here, the iconologies of key names were found to channel and transmute, contain and program the informatrix of cultural and historial forces – Plato as "platonist," Whitman as avuncular "democrat," Hitchcock as a mimetic auteur. Such forays suggested alternative *technologies of reading* – in each case tied to and tracking one or another trace of *materiality* (what I call the "legs of sense"). *Anti-Mimesis* accordingly projects an inescapable role for *interventionist* techniques of (close) reading in a more general politics of cultural memory – which is also to say, modes of transmission and "knowledge" production. By contrast, the present volume mobilizes the same problematic in relation less to a textual imaginary than to ideological and culturalist encounters. It moves centrally into what might be called politics of the archive. A recent review of *Anti-Mimesis* articulates this "materiality":

Once we realize that cultural identity depends on more than merely the representational strata of social forms, we can ask ourselves the more important question: what other technologies might be available in cultural production and how can these be transformed? . . . By understanding how cultural systems rely upon predetermined models of semantic determination and referential policing, [*Anti-Mimesis*] can offer a model of transformation that aims not merely at pluralizing the notion of identity or elaborating a descriptive genealogy of its construction, but in effecting the very installation of cultural signifying systems. By returning to specific moments in the late de Man associated with the materiality of inscription, [the author] attempts to understand how a pivotal linguistic materiality is not opposed to culture or identity but forms the necessary ideological matrix through which social semiosis inexorably proceeds. Such an emphasis on materiality clearly divorces his understanding of ideology from simple false consciousness and instead locates it in those signifying practices recalling what Bourdieu dubs the social *habitus*. At such archival sites of interpretive habit, historical signifying chains form a conjuncture of virtual pasts and futures that generate as effects identifiable political formations.[14]

14 Christopher Diffee, "Cohen's Furies" (forthcoming in *the minnesota review*).

The current book argues the need to reclaim some traumatic lines of force associated with problems of materiality and memory in "theory" – something we must respond to before moving on. It also suggests that there is good reason today to consider following through on epistemo-political conversions that, at one point begun, have generally been stampeded back from, spellbound. It may be that before opening the possibility of a post-humanist era, we will need to redefine the non-human, the animal, the dead with greater porousness – much as the aporetic markers tripped upon almost everywhere today in the "older" mimetic and binary logics must, when encountered, be acknowledged less as stop signs triggering anxieties of paralysis and disappearance than cheerful points of translation and departure for the cultivation of chronographic networks and nervous systems without models. Concealed within the word allegory is the supposition of a non-human site associated with a disinheriting premise of language as such. Concealed within the modernist use of allegory is the presupposition of a movement, or *passage*, as though from one representational-temporal technology and economics of the real ("history") to a multiplicity of others without a unifying code. In Benjamin this work is called a "task," as though a pro-active ethical call marked this trajectory. This "task," of translation or transvaluation, is anything but academic even where academic writing partakes of it – actively positioned as the latter is within assignments and technologies of transmission, in the politics of the archive and memory *tout court*. For those with an eye for such movement, this translation from a mimetic archive into "materialist" terms and agencies from which there is no return – or interiors to return to – is apparent today across very diverse individual gestures, projects, disciplines, communities, walks of life, experiments in human relations and technology. Without ground, it is heard in those intriguingly aware of a historical and perhaps survivalist bottleneck stalking the logics of reference our culture seems, still, sinisterly watched over and reproduced by.

PART I

Ciphers – or, counter-genealogies for a critical "present"

1

❖❖

Reflections on post
"post-mortem de Man"

❖❖

1. The trouble with Paul

We are known by our labels. So when, having studied at Yale, I am asked to do a piece on "Post-Mortem de Man" (what, after all, *is* the role of rhetorical reading today?), it is assumed I have an agenda; even I assume this – de Man and close reading today, "after" you-know-what (allow me to allude to the "scandal" as a kind of obscenity, including the double inflection that may have).[1] It would almost seem a closed book, for now, but some corpses, like Harry in Hitchcock's *The Trouble with Harry*, never stay where you put them. More: I always prided myself on a sort of psychotic ethic (even though it has never worked) – never mourn, just incorporate – so I had not quite written "on" de Man as such. Nor have I ever relinquished a focus on the materiality of language, which has kept me alert in the epoch of cultural studies to where a de Manian problematic might be said, recurrently, to emerge (even under other names). We cannot, after all, get rid of *reading*, and a certain "problematic of language," though beaten up by the right and the left at a necessary juncture as merely textualist (insufficiently exterior, worldly, political), has never seemed entirely possible to escape. The once violent foreclosure of the public space associated with de Man's name seemed, if anything, to have created a repressed wound, itself never worked through, a wound

---

[1] This phrase and topic, proposed by the editor of *the minnesota review*, Jeffrey Williams, may be glossed by the particular nadir in de Man's fortunes registered in Lindsay Waters, "Professah de Man – he dead," in *American Literary History* 7, 2 (Summer 1995), 284–303.

that invariably would have to be reopened sometime to take another look. Indeed, in trying to address the place of ((fore)close(d)) reading today – its relevance to what we call pedagogy, its role in the critical market-place – or even its association with the name "de Man" in the sense of a "post-mortem" (the editor's suggested phrase) or a post post-mortem (my own), one would need to retake the pulse of contemporary positions, particularly as the present state of post-theory is, if you will excuse the term, so unreadable. I needed to locate again – or look for – the *corpus*.

In reviewing this scene, however, something has struck me repeatedly which I will try to pursue here: that the cultural left has made a central error in assuming that "politics" must be defined in mimetic or representational terms alone (a supposition that has led to the impasse of identity politics), and that what has been suppressed, for which the site of "de Man" is one particularly troubled *cipher*, is the increasingly felt lack of a premimetic or anti-mimetic politics. I will return to this later. It is reasonable to expect that if a certain corpse of de Man functioned as the founding sacrifice (or erasure) of the edifice of new historicist and cultural studies (as, in the Andes, they use llama fetuses under new building sites), a certain process remains, here, to be read.

I realized I was not interested in the *Signs of the Times* sort of debate at all (I had always wondered, maliciously, if de Man himself set a time-bomb to disperse his own monumentalization), and found myself posing a little asked question: even given the abjection of "deconstruction" in the return to History in the 80s, what would a post-deconstructive and post-Marxist de Man look like? Moreover, what were the broader ideological uses to which the public abjection of "de Man" were put? Are we still, for instance, in the tired "link de Manian reading to new criticism" phase, targeting the text as a scene of mere *internal* play, of in-difference cut off from the real, the political, and so on? How would de Man (have) be(en) read, "today," without *you-know-what*? How, on the other hand, do "we" currently use or deploy the trope of fascism, regardless of its referential status, when brushed upon de Man or, less problematically but still within an ideological agenda, Heidegger? Even when negatively packaged – as "nihilist," bigamist, carpet soiler – had the icon of "de Man" always *also* been circulated as a screen, a decoy, for other social and cultural energies to stage themselves against? And what is not surprising, now, is that if we review the outline of this official history, certain impasses and disturbances seem increasingly visible. If "de Man" has been tainted publicly, that certainly seems in excess of someone who focused merely on newer refinements of close reading, on the impasses of an unpolitical model of undecidable meaning structures in the text. Indeed, they are more in line with someone who posed a very political problem. That is, one cannot quite dissociate the *public* abjection of de Man – a convulsion which perhaps only seems now, for equally historical reasons, somewhat subsided – from the history of "theory" or its course in the intervening years. What seems to me buried with the name "de Man" during this time, though, may be the obverse of that public history or narrative, and it raises important questions for whatever might be called pedagogy today. It goes something like this:

The official history of criticism since de Man's death (to choose a convenient if arbitrary mark) involved the abjection of "post-structuralist" theory (an exclusionary focus on the supra-agency of language or power), and a *pragmatic* return to history and the social, from the allegorical to the concrete and political: indeed, this took the progressive form of what seemed a movement from inside to out – one through, say, new historicism, the multicultural left, cultural criticism and its return to context, and identity politics. While this story ends in an upbeat sort of way – say, in the functional problems of formal democracy – it also has several problems, and has not been quite as linear as the official history suggests. Indeed, in "identity politics" alone, the abjection of theory (well before the biographic degradations of de Man, or Althusser and Foucault) has taken its toll, as though the return to the foundational subject and lived experience involved less the celebratory restitution of the subject after its prematurely announced "death," than precisely a phenomenon that confirms that death – the staging of numerous ghosted or simulacrum subjects for which appearance that death was a condition. In short, the self-forgetful return of the dead, we might say, as the living. Moreover, the trajectories of the left led not only to the "crisis of the left" and post-Marxism, but another enigma yet to be analyzed: why, given the politicization of critical interests in the 80s, did we enter the mid-90s in so much *more* of a neoconservative and nationalist atmosphere? And with that, how much of

33

the stylistic turn toward personal or autobiographical writing has devolved now to the repetitious, low-energy, and factious atmosphere that floods the echo chambers of a ceremonial and autoarchaeological institution like the Modern Language Association convention (the ebb of autobiodiarists, post- and retro-identity politicians, revanchist pseudo-pragmatists, theory nostalgists and Marxian nostalgists, neo-Habermasians of the right-right and left-right)? Was "high theory," however abjected – the token of which is surely visible in the icon of de Man as the apolitical textualist – also suppressed for *other reasons*? May we even ask whether, rather than having gone too far, the focus on language's materiality *had not yet been taken far enough* in undoing the pan-mimeticism that led, first, back to a historicism whose "political" effect, despite its intentions, actually played into the right? Is it accidental that today, to be properly historical, new historicism appears more and more visible as a Reaganite phenomenon for all its politically "subversive" concerns, or that the return to the foundational subject on the left accorded with a right agenda that, at least institutionally, seems to have prevailed? Was a *certain* "high theory" (let us leave the possibility of further distinctions open) all along more politically problematic – and dangerous – than the pan-mimeticism of the late 1980s or mid 1990s would assume? Did it, rather than tarry in the Hamlet-like portico of undecidability, serve to force some matters all too prematurely to a decision?

As I ask these questions, I am left with the stain of a suspicion: that together with a set of genuine and intricate historical problems, de Man had been dealt with so ferociously not because close reading was apolitically fetishized or nihilistic (a curious, clearly perspectival term), but for another reason. An obvious candidate would be because his exposure of the technological and materialist model of language put those adhering to the ideology of mimesis, on which so many institutions intricately depend, in an increasingly uncomfortable position. This has little to do with his value, moreover, as a critical interpreter of texts. Finally, it is not because de Man pedaled a "literary" version of deconstruction, but because the public image of "deconstruction" had become increasingly irrelevant to his trajectory. In order at least to question this suspicion – which leads into a brief consideration of de Man's late work – I will look at how he is dealt with "now," in the marketplace, in an attempt to generate a narrative.

As a critical style associated with allegory as a mode of intervention re-emerges as an antidote to the groaning pan-mimeticism of identity politics and its impasses – a figure whose roots are, still, in Benjamin – some of the arguments recently used to abject "de Man" sound to the ear increasingly misdirected and mechanical. Thus when Jeffrey T. Nealon discusses the death of deconstruction in a recent issue of *PMLA* and uses a certain de Man to genealogize its double death ("attributed either to suicide – to its falling back into the dead-end formalism it was supposed to remedy – or to murder at the hands of the new historicists" (1,266)), we see an attempted ideological cleansing at work. What might have passed for a routine dismissal five years back, even a "fact," now appears so codified that its fractured familiarity tends to dissolve the narrative's authority. According to this story, "deconstruction" was misappropriated from Derrida's philosophic texts by the Yale School (de Man, Miller) as a technique of mere literary reading, which it was then reduced to ("For them, the impossibility of reading is the telos of deconstruction – it is what deconstruction readings seek to reveal" (1,272)). Following Gasché in *The Tain of the Mirror*, Nealon presumes that Derrida all along had really been doing "philosophy," to which purer confines he should be returned, a move which then allows us to rehabilitate a certain cleansed Derrida and even see "deconstruction" as acceptably traditional in its rigors. Thus purged of the name "de Man" (of course, argues Nealon, "in no way am I calling for Derrida to denounce deconstructive criticism – to issue a sort of papal bull on a doctrinal matter" (1,276)), Derrida can be restituted from the "death" of deconstruction, saving "the specificity at the heart of Derrida's itinerary" from the creation of anything like a discipline of reading literature.[2] Of course, while the sacrifice of "de Man" in this way is designed to save Derrida (a gesture of questionable good faith not limited to hostile critics), Derrida himself is by this means put back on the reservation – kept, moreover, in "philosophy" and out of literature departments. Nealon, of course, is

---

[2] For Nealon, once de Man is exposed by his real roots in new criticism and the "scandal," and the "siege mentality" subsides that excuses Derrida's public defense of de Man, Derrida can be readmitted to the fold even after the "death" of deconstruction that Nealon (as the other condition of this generous gesture?) affirms. De Man should, however, be the sacrifice as the price for that readmittance.

assuming an avuncular and helpful posture to "deconstruction,"
retrieving it surgically from a precipitous death if only it will
behave. Everything that is packed into the black hole of "unreadability" is, in a common sense fashion, cleansed, with "de
Man" as *pharmakon*. Nealon's rhetorical bid to discipline deconstruction is complete with de Man sent to the woodshed: as a
traditionalist, "deconstruction" is cut off from literary institutions; and, as a "friend" of deconstruction, Nealon restores Derrida from impure associations. (We will ignore how such *friendly*
purification of Derrida, in turn, operates as attempted contain-
ment and occlusion – like Bakhtin in the hands of American
slavicists.)

A somewhat mannerist variant of classic deconstruction-bash-
ing is argued by Mas'ud Zavarzadeh in "Pun(k)deconstruction
and the Postmodern Political Imaginary."[3] Zavarzadeh's pitch is
similarly linked to Gasché's philosophic reregulation ("a rigorous, serious, philosophical reading of Derrida (e.g. Gasché)" (7)),
yet he in general sees *all* post-structuralism as a means of extending a parenthesis of speculation that narcoleptically *defers* true
revolutionary action. For Zavarzadeh, post-structuralism merely
reinscribes an ideology of humanism, which works to still the
grand old referential, labor.[4] What might have seemed a mainline
dismissal of deconstruction ten years ago now encompasses
Foucault. In a post-Marxist milieu, this sounds shrill, miring "intervention" in a vague totalizing trope of revolutionary action – a
return to a truth of the referent muddied by the diversion of
intervening "post" theories. More interestingly, the writer performs here a specular occlusion, since what the return to the truth
of class struggle remains itself inscribed in is the *mimetic ideology*
of "traditional humanism." ("Mimetic ideology," in a de Manian

---

[3] The term "pun(k)deconstruction" is Zavarzadeh's coinage. It is used to indicate
a late phase of deconstructive praxis extending to other aesthetic domains, such
as visual arts (Joseph Beuys). In this phase, the supposed patterning of material
signifiers (anagrams, signatures, glyphs) prior to conceptualization is pursued,
one intending to produce an altered form of mimesis itself.
[4] Thus Zavarzadeh: "humanism is the traditional mode of producing an acquiesc-
ing labor force through reading texts of culture as embodiments of transcendental moral and ethical values and as the site of sophisticated aesthetic pleasures"
(8); however, "(post)structuralism has 'reinscribed' the ideological effects of
humanism in the post-modern moment" (9). Or again, less originally: "in the
ethics of (post)structuralist textuality there are no grounds upon which to found
a decidable 'resistance' or a radical 'intervention'" (19).

frame, might be considered a tautology – since the effects of "ideology" are always contracted with the generation of a descriptive, interiorist or structuralist, mimeticism as a deforming response to the implications of an inscribed event.) Here we see the uncanny affinity that some on the left bear to the right and, moreover, why: what they share is a referential theology, the need for a signified to speak on behalf of, compared to which compulsion the ultimate signified supplied for that system may be secondary (and we know, by the mid 90s, which of the two prevails). As Zavarzadeh – a kind of Pat Buchanan of the left – argues against the drift into pun(k)deconstruction, something else emerges:

At the same time, it is a celebration of a new empiricism, the empiricism of trace and difference, and a new mimesis, the indeterminate mimesis, of high-tech civilization. The politics of this double move – the deconstruction of 'natural' and thus determinate (mimetological) experience and its reinscription as 'aleatory' and therefore indeterminate (mimetic) experience – is to reject and jettison those elements of the dominant ideology of experience that have lost their historical usefulness in late capitalism. The double move of deconstruction . . . is in fact a means for this renewal of the ruling ideology.   (34)

At issue is the typical plaint of a drift into a pure, and therefore auto-reflexive universe of language, yet what is missed is that such a language can be rendered, in its active capacity to void a received set of conceptual habits, as a material site required to exceed or transpose the yet more auto-reflexive closure of a programmatic mimesis or humanism – themselves conventions. The pun(k)deconstructive shift into an altered practice of the "signifier" seems, at first, a *pragmatic* or materialist "intervention" within the domain of mnemonics, a domain precedent to *mimesis*. Zavarzadeh's move is to invert the terms in advance, so that this form of post-structuralist "theory" is viewed as a practice that returns to the ideology of "experience" unwittingly, while the Marxian pragmatic stays true to the effaced realm of the "concept" that is unmoved by this latter day evasion of action. In the end, the decibel level of this Lefter-Than-Thou rhetorical posture may not suffice to obscure a certain melancholy, particularly where the nostalgia is for a "Marx" that may not quite have been the case to begin with. It is melancholy, not because the staunch loyalty to a memorialized rhetoric cannot fail to effect the opposite of its stated intent, but because the force of argumentation contains other economic motives. It needs enemies and expends itself in the sound and fury of excoriating demon-others (post-structuralism, "deconstruction") at a time when the best political energies are metamorphosed by absorbing, simply, these as technologies of thought in a changing and accelerating historical signscape. I will later ask from the perspective of a certain "historical materialism" where de Man's contribution may appear privileged in this regard.

The traditional attack against deconstruction, or "de Man," relies on an inside/outside binary by which "language" is presented as interior, cut off from the world of reference and history. Yet for de Man or Derrida, as for Lacan or Bakhtin or Peirce, language is already the outside at all points – the site that precludes any return of interiority, and whose suppression, inversely, tends to reestablish a new (old) interiority of the subject, of the theologized or immaterial self. It is not accidental, say, that Judith Butler, thinking "gender" as sheer performance without recourse to causal forms of identity, must rigorously foreclose the "illusion of interiority" ("the question of agency is not to be answered through recourse to an 'I' that preexists signification" (143)). She does this, moreover, by an appeal to the public role of "inscription," cultural or mnemonic.[5] I mention this because it seems, more and more, that the problem with "deconstruction" and what to do with it – the need to abject it, the inability to do so definitively – turns on the fact that "language" was never quite what it was converted into by this post post-structuralist revision. It was never an *interiorizing* topos, but quite obviously the opposite. Moreover, the machine-like transposition of a material and external topos into its opposite only served what were, either on the right or the left, continuing interiorizing interests. In readdressing this inside/outside binary, those who purportedly champion the concrete, like neopragmatism or modes of identity politics, end by reinventing a privileged interiority or "self" (which is itself abstract). What is overlooked is that politics within signifying practices is always (also) a politics of memory, of "inscriptions" and how they are managed, guarded, purged,

---

[5] Butler's model will always appear to be Foucault, but a "Foucault" who becomes a cipher for diverse associations the term has.

restored, projected – the very function, say, of the academy. As case studies in contemporary revanchism, Nealon and Zavarzadeh are above all guardians of mimeticism. But the "political" battle lines today seem less left and right than between the transvaluations posed by the thinking of exteriority and those reasserting the destructive privilege of interiorizing models of meaning. It is here that the word ideology returns, and if it is clearly and thankfully a ghost of its former self (not, that is, "false consciousness"), it is a *revenant* with a mission.

For Althusser, one word for this radical exteriority of language is *ideology* or its ritual repetition in the "state apparatus" by which the subject is interpellated and enacted. While Zavarzadeh invokes the acceptably "Marxist" Althusser against his specular image of pun(k)deconstruction ("experience is not a given but is in fact a construct of the dominant ideology" (38)), we must recall that any opposition between Althusser and de Man on the question of the radical exteriority of language or its ritualized status as ideology may be shortsighted indeed, much as the return in the 80s to the *opposition* of history and language may turn out to have been, potentially, *a historical regression* – one that we need to retrace again. Thus Althusser: "what thus seems to take place outside ideology (to be precise, in the street), in reality takes place in ideology . . . Which amounts to saying that ideology *has no outside* (for itself), but at the same time *that it is nothing but outside* (for science and reality)" (175). From this perspective, what de Man represents is neither a formalist extension of "new criticism" nor a reduction of deconstruction to "literary" models but an attempt to use the model of reading to situate epistemology as the site of the political. This, since representation at all times involves the ritualized *backloop of memory*, of the prerecorded *in*scription, of the ritual apparatus of "ideologies" chiasmically dissimulating the incursion they represent. De Man sketches and prefigures the topos of reading as a post-human(ist) technology not for historicism but for intervention – a future politics of inscription, which is also to say disinscription, reinscription, and *ex*scription. For de Man, that is, the sheer exteriority of signification and its public space are guaranteed by the scriptive, material facticity of "the machine of mechanical memory," as he notes of Hegel: "In order to have memory one has to be able to forget remembrance and reach the machine-like exteriority, the outward turn, which is retained in the German word for learning by heart, *aus-wendig lernen.*"[6]

It is not irrelevant that Nealon locates one of the many "deaths" of deconstruction in the dubious hands of the new historicism – a by now fairly suspect suspect. If we recall the terms of a text like Benjamin's *Theses on the Philosophy of History*, it would seem that what "historicism" actually opposes, and distracts us from by merely generating new *causal* chains, is the transvaluative import of what Benjamin calls "historical materialism," that interventionist historiography which is always also that of the *Jetztzeit*, and which depends on blasting an image from the delusive mimetic continuum into an allegorical moment of crisis. It suggests a radical textualization of historicality before which "historicism" presents an evasion of history. It is not accidental that this is the domain that de Man's late essays seem to define. As recent work by Michael Taussig has tried to perform in its valorously eclectic manner (in *The Nervous System* or *Mimesis and Alterity*), Benjaminian allegory situates the praxis for such historical intervention within the facticity of a *style* that confutes continuity or narrativization, and does so by assaulting the institutions or histories of mimesis.[7] This notion of "allegory" most consistently and proactively developed by de Man occurs not, that is, as an evasion of the historical, but as the evasion of historicism's evasion of history, as a *"historical materialism"* in Benjamin's catachretic terms. We are further from the icon of the internal play of ironized signifiers, of the rootless play of hypertextualism, if we understand that for de Man the topos of *reading* is used to stage such "interventions" within the ideological rituals of language, or memory out of which the world is constructed – that is, within conceptual and hermeneutic formations, the prerecorded modes out of which "politics" or identities are generated.

It would seem that among the public histories of de Man's abjection lies the following logic *as well*: that what required *de*legitimation in de Man was less a tainted apoliticism consolidated and overwhelmed in the blizzard-like signifiers of "scandal," than something else – a deliberate approach to politics, to "changing the world." To point this out, moreover, does not constitute a defense

[6] "Sign and Symbol in Hegel's Aesthetics," in *Aesthetic Ideology*, 103.
[7] For an elaboration of this thesis in a literary format, see the introduction, "The Legs of Sense," to my *Anti-Mimesis*.

of "de Man," who is thankfully desacralized at the very least, but utilizes him, now, to return to a still inescapable problem. We can now call this by other names than "new criticism," nihilistic unreadability, the literary misappropriation of deconstruction, or even a return to "humanism." De Man assumes an Archimedian point where the staging of mimetic identity can be preceded (a site he probes with the term *prosopopeia*). Here the facticity of "inscription" precedent to phenomenality and performance can be evoked. And not only addressed aesthetically, as in intertextual interpretation, say, but in pragmatic terms that make *dis*inscription, transcription or reinscription – the altering of the prerecordings themselves – thinkable; that expose the possibility of new pasts, which is also to say, the condition for exploring alternative futures to those which one or another inherited narrative defines or predicts for us. What de Man labored toward can be called, from a certain perspective that requires such terminology, a pragmatics of hope – a phrase it does not take that much irony to arrive at, but which one would not choose to retain. One may gloss it on the most technical of grounds: the "direction" that de Man takes, we might say, hardly stops at some logical aporia, since it clearly anticipates a notion of the material, or prefigural, against which a different sort of memory grid might be installed, a mode in which inherited narratives (historicisms) stand to be rewired in the manner which Benjamin, it seems, envisioned interventions in historical *monads* as operating – key nodes on a transhistorial switchboard capable of reshuffling the agency of historical events, generating different pasts. The bizarre labors of de Manian reading (who, let us not forget, mobilizes all tropological names, allegorized players, only to question such systems of "transformation" entirely) work, then, with the gamble of a future thinking of the "event." From such a perspective, "undecidability" is not the paralysis of interpretation and action, but a *tool* for neutralizing a mechanical, learned, or inherited mode of arriving at a routine "choice" or designation that could not be questioned or halted – a place where decision becomes, for the first time, possible. For the late twentieth century, this raises important issues. At the same time, de Man may have been abjected most for disturbing the regime of a mimetic ideology.[8] And this may indicate the very point of his interest today

---

[8] In "Hypogram and Inscription" we read: "Description, it appears, was a device to conceal inscription" (51).

following the dead-end of identity politics, the moralist drift of various pragmatisms, that is, the array of new historicisms. The figure of "aesthetic ideology" seems to have been the unread remainder of de Man's work – the post-deconstructive and post-Marxist agenda that stands most philosophically remote from yet practically close to current concerns.

2. Tales from the crypt

Yet perhaps the narrative I have just outlined is already erased, supplanted by another. The question may now be whether, if we are entering a post "post-mortem" phase, we will approach "de Man" primarily as an interesting story. If so, then an interventionist element to which his entire text is dedicated may remain elusive.

If there have been two main phases of de Man's post-mortem to date – initial mourning and monumentalization, interrupted by the release of the wartime writings and the polemics and defenses to follow, a first death and a second – one could project, now, a third. Such would focus less on the de Man of undecidability and unreadability as such, on the logic of tropes of cognition and persuasion, than on a post-deconstructive *and* post-Marxist figure already ghosting itself in the late texts, the de Man focused in various ways (including as *mere pretext*) on "aesthetic ideology." Aesthetic ideology as trope encompasses not *only* ideological constructions of the "aesthetic" that create it as an abjected reserve ("merely aesthetic") but all ideology, all "consciousness," in so far as that can be addressed as the dissimulative revision of material or linguistic effects. Rather than being philosophically remote from today's pragmatic concerns, this work may be the most paradoxically useful to it. Perhaps unsurprisingly, the reason these essays remain relevant in the "wake" of identity politics has to do with their attempt to engineer a critical moment that precedes the staging of identity, a moment that, nonetheless, can be called "materialist." To bring out the contours of this prospect it may be useful to contrast his text with a recent project of "post-modern" ideology critique drawing on late Lacan that has had curious impact, that of Slavoj Žižek. A parallel and opposition between late de Man and the late Lacan – or a recent use of him – has been largely overlooked, though it helps bring out a shift that has not been entirely pursued.

Žižek's differentiation between a *middle* and *late* Lacan involves a fictive parallel to de Man's last productions. Žižek's "late Lacan" stands beyond what Žižek terms post-structuralism, which, in a polemical caricature, he identifies with the symbolic and hence with language's metonymic play. Yet the turn toward the supposedly post-modern rhetoric of "the Thing" that places the late Lacan (and Žižek) within a program focused on *the real* bears a significant difference from where the late de Man moves as if beyond a rhetoric of tropes toward the unnarrativizable and premimetic. For Žižek, the turn to the real involves a pretended shift "beyond" language itself that is played out, as he sees it, by the move in a ventriloquized Lacan from metonymy to metaphor. But for de Man, the very aspect Žižek ritualizes as a "beyond" of language is only another, more ineradicable form of language – the materiality of inscription, sheer anteriority, a site buried with in and emerging from the historical shifts and erasures of *infra*-textual cross-currents. As such, it presents the pragmatic possibility for a site or *technology of inscription*, a material address of where numerous "presents" are generated from the prerecordings of the realm of inscription.

This may be why, with de Man, the category of inscription is primarily approached through a negation of figure, and also why allegorical reading involves an obvious irony: rather than using terms that can denote abstract or fixed meaning, allegory converts each term into a *techne* poised to stage historical and ideological "interventions" in the realm of *mnemotechnics* – at the site out of which representations are produced, events staged, cognitions assembled. For de Man, we might say, *ex*scription occupies the site that Žižek would call "the Thing," the radical exteriority that is at the dispossessing core of whatever would recuperate itself ideologically as interiority. Such exscriptions are not mock-epiphanies of otherness (the Thing). They are already haunted and traversed by (historical) trajectories, aleatory narratives, compulsive yet effaced destinations. The prefigural is not, like Žižek's circus-like Thing, removed from the striations of power it disrupts, able to offer its own fetishization as a delusive form of mock-pleasure, staged as a distraction for what it cannot offer (i.e. radically immediate Otherness). Beyond (and predating) "pleasure," the prefigural takes a negative format: "True 'mourning' is less de-luded. The most it can do is to allow for non-comprehension and

43

enumerate non-anthropomorphic, non-elegiac, non-celebratory, non-lyrical, non-poetic, that is to say, prosaic, or, better, *historical* modes of language power" (*Rhetoric*, 262).

There is a *double* inflection, clearly, with regard to what is called "mourning" here – that is, mourning as the attempt to retrieve and fill, to interiorize (and recuperate) loss as a mode for producing the evasions of meaning, whereas *"true* 'mourning'," nonetheless in quotes, "allows" for a relinquishment, passes into a mode of enumeration. The latter uses the occasion to reposition its own formalization (no longer that of a conventional "subject") near *"historic* modes of language power" that are non-anthropomorphic, non-interiorizing. The aporetic logic is superseded by a space that demands – if it is to be accounted for – a transformation of the very system of accounting (the speaking being, human), one in which "true 'mourning'," like language use, appears as a fulcrum accessing a non-human site where materiality and form converge as sheer exteriority. Increasingly, in so-called "late" de Man, the *systems* of trope whose displacements preoccupied him are viewed as interchangeable, totalizable, and dissimulating the presence of premimetic events. Mimesis, in general, is a *faux* premise of cultural language, with its referential codas and mantras – rather (and this remains, in ways, a penultimate refinement of Heidegger's historicization of "representation" and "Western Metaphysics"), the mimetic premise is always an ideological blind, the evasive conversion of a form of inscriptive programming. Before metaphor, the mode of inscription *cata*logs "events" that, themselves forming switchboards and signature-networks, can be addressed on the order of linguistic and textual occurrences which it remains the province of cultural hermeneutics broadly conceived to mute, invert, re-inscribe: traditional or academic hermeneutics is not "wrong" (alone) because it props up self-referential mimetic and humanist systems but because it systematically transcribes and forecloses the material nature of historical events (of language power). These appear often in collusion with the programmed, dissimulative logic of a writing project ("platonism," say, as a calculable effect of Platonic writing, anticipated, shaped, exceeded or even discarded in the text). In the case of Kant, for instance, in what is a total reconfiguration of the relation of "Enlightenment" thought and the amodernism that persists through present attempts at periodization, a subtext remains unread, that of "a materialism more radical than what can be conveyed by such terms as 'realism' or 'empiricism'" (*AI*, 121), so that "in the whole reception of Kant from then until now, nothing has happened, only regression, nothing has happened at all" (134). One can see why the institutionalization of hermeneutic surveillances functions, in de Man, as the preclusive enforcer of ideology – in ways, its locus. Yet if, like Althusser, that is a kind of imaginary, a fictional relation to the real "event" (or mnemonic eventuation of an incision or inscription one might locate in the place of the real), the latter is nonetheless politically effective for being, strictly, non-existent, a non-event itself. Canonical "meaning" is not one among other types of interpretation – it is, it comes to appear, ethically corrupt and positively destructive (like the "nihilistic" allegories of historicism) to the precise degree it contracts to sustain an obliterative and narcissistic system of consumption, deferred responsibility, and faux memorialization. A certain intervention in reading systems corresponds with what Benjamin's premise for intervention in the historial – by way of monadic clusters, evocative of the Greek notion of *kairos*, in which prefigural mnemonic systems (or inscriptions) emerge from beneath their mimetic guises – emerge as the site of sheer exteriority that they always inhabited. In doing so, they become again virtual, like the site of prosopopeia that precedes the *Nachkonstruction* of face or voice. Yet in the above sentence, still, de Man stops at the site of "enumeration," as at the site where the linguistic subject is itself altered, *less at an aporia than a place of passage into different terms.*

To continue this parenthetical gloss, we may note how the problem of the prefigural is mapped out in the lecture "Kant and Schiller,"[9] in which the two names serve as ciphers – in a sense, allegorical figures – for the problem of the "event," of the decisive shift from tropological systems into material inscription that opens alternate pasts (Kant), if one may in passing mark this incision with a label whose very logic would be entirely rewritten, and the manner in which that is, systematically, foreclosed by mimetic interpretation (Schiller). (Missing, in a sense, is a third "and . . ." which would include the Schillerized reader negotiating, from a yet third position, the problematics of historical foreclosure and intervention that the critical engagement of

[9] *Aesthetic Ideology*, 129–162.

this pair opens.) Kant will be associated with the model of such an event, then, though it will be a different "Kant" than that received traditionally by the mimeto-humanist tradition (which is already Schillerian), with the event of a disarticulation of that very tropological system Schiller would re-instate (like cultural studies in relation, say, to "theory"). This Schiller will do so in the name of a practicality, a return to practice, that in the end appears (to de Man) as a sheer "ideality" and evasion of materiality itself. This event, Kant's text, is described as "the materiality of something that actually happens, that actually occurs" (132) – that is, a shift on the level of inscription, out of which virtualization subsequent "presents" stand to be optioned (or precluded). "Inscription" stands, like a facticity that is also prospective, as if before the subsequent (ideological) evasions and tropological re-inscriptions which, often in the name of "history," work to foreclose the openings and discontinuities of such occurrences. Even when merely used as a rallying point to re-institute tropological evasions of such events themselves – or precisely so – textual occurrences of this sort become icons within narrativized histories (what Žižek might term an evil "kernel"). The notion of "history" that ensues does not have to do with the accumulation of experiences, since such would be more or less programmed (preinterpreted, not "experienced"): "History is therefore not a temporal notion, it has nothing to do with temporality, but it is the emergence of a language of power out of a language of cognition" (133). *Out of a language of cognition*: that means, bluntly, a preinscribed, prefigural apparatus that determines what Benjamin calls "the sensorium" – the site where the senses themselves, perception (the aesthetic), appears interpretively programmed. Since numerous "presents" will be generated from this locus precisely its disposition – that is, where a language of power erupts out of a language of cognition – would be politically contested to the highest degree. In this schema, the import of the "event" – its potential impact on received or interpreted "causal" chains – is ceaselessly imperilled by the narrativizations of mimeticism, humanist interpretation that contrives to efface the order of a materiality that precedes the production of referents. In de Man's mapping of Kant and Schiller (by now a kind of system), we witness "the regression from the event, from the materiality of the inscribed signifier in Kant" (134). And more specifically, this "regression" (the term is recurrent) forestalls history, imperils the human encounter with the material, and by a disfiguring mechanism. That is, "Schiller's" return to a merely tropological system of substitution (Žižek's Symbolic), his apparent privileging of the practical, his return to a sheer ideality in the name of the practical reminiscent of cultural studies – to the politically compromised mimeticism that, by the end of the essay, will itself be allied to fascism. De Man's example – one encrypted anticipation of charges to be brought against him based on use of his war-time juvenilia – is Goebbels' appropriation of Schillerian ideas. Like Benjamin's fascist "historicism," de Man's "Schillerism" works by chiasmus, we are told, to return to the machine-like predations of an epistemo-critical program, an aesthetico-political regime disguised (but then, what else is ideology?) as a pragmatic model of reference.

There remains an interesting analogy to cultural studies today: "The important thing is that this apparent realism, the apparent practicality, this concern with the practical, will result in the total loss of contact with reality, in a total idealism." (142) Today, when there seems a certain urgency in rethinking a materiality that is not mimetic or the mytheme of a dialectical narration – and this, with reconceiving the very definition of the human in relation to terrestrial "life" and logics of time, bio-systems, the management of anteriority and reserves, the disposition of legal and linguistic borders, and so on – the need to exceed the auto-referential foreclosures of mimeto-humanism appears as a rather banal if not ironic imperative (ironic, since "mimeto-humanism" never really can be said to have existed – which has not made its effects any the less real, or disastrous). Schiller, who represents such institutions, operates (de Man tells us) incessantly by chiasmus – re-inscibing the "event" of Kant's disarticulation by reversing polarities, avoiding "the performative" of materiality in his drive to transcend the materiality of the aesthetic, of the prefigural: "The transcendence of the aesthetic in Schiller differs entirely from the disruption of the aesthetic as the return to the materiality of inscription, to the letter, that we found in Kant" (146). Yet "Kant and Schiller" presents a joint system ("and") – as if the event of Kant need generate a Schiller-effect in its own name, as if "Kant" would be known through the Schillerian "regression," muting the import of the occurrence, even making "Kant" as name the echo of a non-event, a restoration of the systematic occlusion itelf, the very law of that. The way "platonism" does for Plato. From here, even the clarification of Kant is imperilling (for the event of the prefigural can be approached by a dispersal of figuration, canonical interpretation, mimeticism, ideology, "Schiller"). It appears an ethical demand on the part of a certain materiality, a certain "real(ism)" – demanding that the "human" exceed its hermeneutic and legislative closure and mutate – yet it is also a political gesture recalling Benjamin's opposition of a "materialistic historiography" to historicism. All of our habits and hermeneutic justifications (de Man notes that we are all Schillerians *in practice*), all language of (*faux*) interiorization on which our discursive culture appears propped is connected here to "Schiller," to tropological systems designed to institute the cognitive evasion of the material (or aesthetic) under the chiasmatic pretext of a return to practicality, or historicism, or the abstractions of cultural context. Here is the tell-tale windup, however, that resonates in this discussion: "And if you ever try to do something in the other direction" – that is, back from the *faux* return to the practical, toward the material, the event, history, "Kant" – "and you touch on it" – extraordinary figure of contact, not unlike the series of negations in the sentence on "true 'mourning'," well: "you'll see what will happen to you." (142)

You'll see what will happen to you. Paul de Man's "war," as Derrida has phrased it, would be irreducible to the mythemes of the second "world war," since the resistance signalled here – not to but perhaps of what underlies the moniker "theory" (which is to say, now, a certain materiality for which language must appear one non-human, mnemonic site preceding figuration or reference) – involves the deterritorialization of an emergent cognitive-political.[10] We are in position to ask anew why a certain parenthesis has been installed around the name "de Man" (or *theory*, for that matter). The answer may have less to do with the rhetorical opportunism of a shift in critical habits than, from the broadest possible perspective, unfolding decisions to be collectively taken before the emergent demands of a future terrestrial politics that presupposes entirely different definitions of meaning, reference,

---

[10] In chapters 4 and 5 of this book, I attempt to extend this metaphorics of war and espionage – in the name of the historial event – to Hitchcock's "political thrillers."

materiality, death, the "social," memory, "man," and the organic. "You'll see what will happen to you" – for one thing, *they* will want to take away your signature, erasing it as event. We might re-open a practical consideration of "de Man" by asking what use his itinerary is to us? Specifically, where an allo-human concept of materiality that accesses a differential allo-chronic conception of terrestrial history is of value, and why the abjection of de Man has always also been, in the strictest and most problematic sense, political. To open this space again, we might begin by seeing the micro-technologies of reading de Man explores as a template for a mnemotechnics operative in what Benjamin saw as the only site in which the historial can be accessed or intervened in: monads, nodes on the transhistorial switchboard empowered to alter the manner in which cross-historial referentials are (de)produced. Like any text that solicits our attention today, our serious attention anyway, it must respond to the question of not what it reshuffles or confirms, but what passage it leads to, and to where?[11]

Rather than being, as he has been caricatured, a proponent of working inside texts rather than in the outside world, the domain of mimetic actuality, de Man locates a radical exteriority at the site of memory, a mnemotechnic (or historiographics) at times referred to through the term *inscription* which, in advance of every hermeneutic system, marks the inevitable materiality and exteriority accorded the human apparatus – that is, the usual figural suspects whose conceptualization rests upon promoting interiorizing models: perception, experience, history, identity, the social. For de Man, there seem to be two distinct senses in which movement, or transformation can be cited, both of which are fairly traditional. It involves only a move toward assuming the implications of such materiality in the "human," rather than effacing it with the array of defensive, privileging, politically suspect gestures that unwittingly aestheticize this terrain – therefore, at the same time, it may also *not* involve an explicit movement as such. A first use by de Man of the word *transformation* would be bracketed, ineffectual, transformative only within a closed specular order. It is that of a "tropological system," say, which "totaliz-

[11] This last question, that of where the issue of "materiality" in the late de Man leads, is addressed by an array of critical and cultural theorists in the forthcoming volume, *Material Events*, edited by T. Cohen, J. Hillis Miller, and A. Warminski.

es itself as a series of transformations" (132) – that is, networks of tropes whose ability to accommodate substitution and reversal would appear structural. Then, following and breaking with that (but not in narrative fashion, since it has, recall, already occurred in advance of the installation of "tropological systems") is a second use, we might say, where "you *pass* from that conception of language to another conception of language in which language is no longer cognitive but in which language is performative" (132; de Man's italics). In *performative*, of course, echoes both of acting and action are intended. This *passage* or "direction" – *from* the entire model that encompasses mimetic humanism, historicism, the "magic and positivism" of "cultural *studies*" as such – is nonetheless said to be irreversible once initiated, one cannot return from it, partly because the "first" site never really existed as other than an installed cultural reaction-formation: "That process . . . is irreversible. That goes in that direction and you cannot get back from the one to the other" (133). The figure of passage is impossible to decode in progressive, temporal terms. Rather than the de Man we may associate somewhat facilely with the term *aporia*, then, we encounter one for whom the aporia is itself a kind of *techne* of passage, a(n(a))poretics. His project appears more in contact with a tele-mnemotechnics that seems already coming into place in a clearly post-humanist *popular culture*. For de Man, for whom the trope of cancer had some resonance, it is interesting that the move as though back to a tropological model of representation – phenomenological, experiential – from this other site, what is accomplished supposedly under the name "Schiller," is called a *relapse* rather than mere reversal ("the recuperation, the relapse, has to be distinguished from a reversal"). The historial seems configured with reference to "events" from which the relapse represents a regressive detour away from the domain of history – in part since its narrative, decisions, and experience will appear more or less programmed.[12] Indeed, what Schiller's

---

[12] It would be possible to think of de Man's enterprise, here, as a proactive attempt at a way of an interventionary approach to what Althusser names the non-historical domain of "ideology." See Louis Althusser, "Ideology and Ideological State Apparatuses," in *Lenin and Philosophy*, trans. B. Brewster (New York: Monthly Review, 1971), 169. De Man's use of materiality solicits the term's appearance in Althusser – as in the famous non-tautology from "Ideology and Ideological State Apparatuses': "[W]here only one subject is concerned, the existence of the ideas of his belief is material in that *his ideas are his material actions inserted into material practices governed by material rituals which are themselves*

recuperation represents operates repeatedly on the tropological model of mere "chiasmic crossing" (135) – what, precisely, deters or defers the other *crossing* from a tropological model (of language) to a prefigural one. De Man finds in the pairing of Schiller *and* Kant another mock opposition, not only that between an interiorizing and a materialist model, but that as if between the practical and theoretical divide with which our own discussion opened. Like the "return to history" or pragmatism out of which cultural studies was to issue – which involved a determined abjection of a literary, or philosophical, or epistemo-linguistic "theory" as aestheticizing operations – there occurs here a predictable inversion. A "relapse" is anything but harmless, and may be deadly, terminal even: after all, it restitutes a humanist and aesthetic model that can appear to (re)institute not a humane but (what Benjamin calls) a "fascistic" order – not by sympathy, not even obviously, but by an epistemo-political bias programmed into assumptions about reference, context, history, ethics. Cultural studies, today, bears some traces of such a "relapse." Thus we might ask where *this* cultural studies has reason to recalibrate its political premises – that is, its overt reinscription in a mimetic and historicist epistemology that has always, potentially, been an institutional form of anteriority-management and deferral. It might discover that any break with the anthropomorphism (and auto-referentiality) of a certain foreclosure of the historial itself accesses the traces of a "materiality" that opens different configurations of intervention, configuring alternative pasts that make possible alternate futures to those passively inscribed in received narratives. Like American neo-pragmatism that supposes itself to turn from "theory" to practice by restituting the trope of self and identity, we are told that Schiller's great "realism," over against Kant, involves an apparent blind, a mimetic blind: "this apparent realism, this apparent practicality, this concern with the practical, will result in a total loss of contact with reality, in a total idealism" (142). It is not accidental that the code which gave us "theory" (as idealist) versus cultural studies (as

defined by the material ideological apparatus from which derive the ideas of that subject." (emphasis Althusser's) Louis Althusser, "Ideology and Ideological State Apparatuses," in *Lenin and Philosophy*, 169. What Althusser calls interpellation might be compared to one sense of inscription. For a re-articulation of Althusserian materiality, see Warren Montag, " 'The Soul is the Prison of the Body': Althusser and Foucault, 1970–75," in *Yale French Studies*, 88 (1995), 53–77.

practical) can not only be inverted in this sense, but that this inversion is fraught with cultural and political consequences of an entirely determining order.

What may be most worth noting is the contemporary value of a material Archimedean point in the prefigural that vacates any notion of interiority. One, moreover, that vacates any predefined concept of the "human" (even if rather than dwelling on the prefigural aspect of "pure language," de Man probes, unexpectedly, a "constructive" site beyond this séancing effect through the category of inscription). The materiality of inscription tends, as a term, to radically revise whatever is or has been meant by the epithet of "nihilism." On the contrary, if there is a reduction operative in later de Man it involves, perhaps, a repeated falling off the mimetic platform of discursive protocols altogether. Such occurs not as a tick or provocation, but in response to an ethical call from the material toward the human. The dispersal of sedimented narratives no doubt sabotages the projection of future continuities. Interestingly, one can sometimes measure in the responding urge to mute this, the entrance of an irksome responsibility we had not expected. We might want to keep in mind that to approach the netherworld of inscription or hypograms implies the power of intervention – which, in turn, makes possible *alternative futures* to those received by a given present as prescribed, programmed in received chains or interpretive systems. This assumes the image of "futurity" that attends us at any time is routinely, in its blindness and presumed continuity, programmed by the fashion in which the event-nature of anterior inscriptions are serviced, inverted, managed, effaced as a means of ideologically derealizing the virtual structure of such events, most often in the two favored modes of a culture legislated by mimetic binarism: in subjectivist idealities (expression, phenomenology, pragmatism), and its parallel others (structuralist, scientism, mimeticism *tout court*). We could say that de Man's ethic is Burroughsian: to change what might be called the world – which is to say how the trope of "history" is produced as an ideologeme, phenomenality programmed, the "sensorium" legislated, reading contained – change its prerecordings, reinitialize its hard disk.

We are now closer to a reversal of the position we began from, the ideological posture in which "de Man" (or a certain de Man) represents through whatever reasoning a foreclosed space, one first of all linked to a trivialized fetish of close reading. On the contrary, we see what has been covered by that argument: the beginnings of a technology of signification, decisively post-humanist, in which a new "mnemotechnics" begins to present itself, all too pragmatic or interventionist, all too political in some of its implications, in which the very trope of the future opens as a prospective site of transformation – or transvaluation. "Ideology" here becomes less a the term of Marxist or post-Marxist orthodoxy than a strategic transposition, perhaps, of the term value as used in *The Genealogy of Morals*. We may go a step further, with the understanding that these are mere notations, and risk suggesting that the *materiality of inscription* which de Man concerned himself with, as the phrase suggests, was not an attempt to fetishize a narcissistic space of "language" but, on the contrary, the very dissolution of an epoch of the book in an attempt to again think *the earth*. One can say that the site of "materiality" that the late de Man points toward is implicated with the rupturing of the self-referential system of mimeto-humanism. A "materiality" that is neither mimetic (reference) nor dialectical (Marxian "base"), which traverses faux binaries such as organic and inorganic, human and animal, life and death indicates without promising an allo-human site that remains, today, virtual.

If any future *use* of this aspect of de Man's project remains to be implemented, we may speculate about the point at which, in Žižek's terms, a certain "de Man" had come to occupy the symbolic site of the obscene, the uncontainable "evil" Thing – for whom unreadability is not a dead end but a limit moment of otherness returning full signifying power to the "literary" thing, a power to destroy its symbolic encrustations. If a post "post-mortem de Man" seems possible to produce by the highlighting of altered and perhaps still unread terms like materiality, history, inscription and (as here used) ideology, it also entirely depends on or is called forth by the impasses of today's critical scene, returning to question its own underworld, a scene which responds to a text like Žižek's not only for the violent inversions and conservative familiarity of the Lacanian drug it offers – anything, after all, may be said with*in* psychoanalytic discourse – but because *the pan-mimeticism which was supposed to return us to History did not do so*, and was subtly and not so subtly coopted by regressive humanisms, dead-end identity politics, and the dubious authority of moralistic postures (on the left and right) to which the "nihilism" of a de Man, in a certain sense, offers a uniquely positive opening. Indeed, what de Man calls the "recuperative and nihilistic allegories of historicism" (*Rhetoric*, 122), and what Žižek calls historicism's "evasion" of the real, represent the site out of which such a need returns. If de Man is of any technological use at this juncture, it is certainly desirable that he has already been desacralized for the occasion – the irony of which may be, after all, that such a ritual precisely generates the desired reading. De Man, as engineer, provided extraordinary tools for that transition to a post-human(ist) epoch, on which successful transition a good deal (of future) arguably depends. What he reminds us is that the ultimate pragmatic and political decisions – as every propagandist for a ruling ideology knows – precede mimesis.

Whatever phase the rereading of de Man assumes, there are two directions worth considering. The first, is that it remains boring or unproductive to recuperate or recirculate "de Man," which seems inevitable, largely as an event in recent critical history. Such a tendency, particularly when sympathetic, unwittingly extends the logic of his recent abjection. This "de Man," in a sense, may be *not* interesting to the precise extent that interest fetishizes the story or profile of an unusual critical intelligence, since it comes at the expense of experimenting with or extending strangely won, still radical *technologies* of value in the installation of a decisively post-anthropomorphic signscape. I assume in this, as noted, an alliance not between de Man's attempt to think the materiality of inscription and "late Lacan," but with more diverse attempts to rethink "man's" relation (economic, linguistic, political) to materiality – and hence, the earth. Rather than explaining the notion of "undecidability" with clichés about moral paralysis and the apolitical, we might grasp the *undecidable* as a *technos* of historial intervention – a moment in a stage of transition in which habituated chains of reaction or logic formed in circumstances no longer historically applicable ("truths") are first suspended: and brought to a decision anew. Things, after all, are only "decidable" due to a long installed habit of language, thought, memory, or interest which is invisibly followed: the outcome of this chain of habituated response (economic, linguistic, political) is then called

a decision. "Undecidability" marks where a preinscribed historical value-narrative (one that seeks expression or institutionalization as "meaning") has been deprived of momentum, opened to
renegotiation. It is a technique to bring matters to a point of (new
or first time) decision. This is what is in part subsumed by the
self-cancelling and perhaps ultimately unusable word, "ideology" – (which may be called always aesthetic) in so far as it is
implemented, linguistically, at the very site in which perception
seems to emerge within an always already hermeneutic program.

(Dis)installing alternative pasts, the re-invoking of the virtuality of representations as a repositing of possibility and responsibility to the maintained opening of unprescripted futures – for *this*
is what de Man's project is ultimately about, the very opposite of
mere close reading – depends on the ability to suspend an "inevitable" or predetermined concatenation of signifying (or rhetorical) judgements. The second direction I mentioned above, however, is equally important: that the contemporary imperative of
pursuing materialist transvaluations such as de Man's work,
among others, supplies tools for, should *not* be linked to any
refetishization or, for that matter finally, necessary recirculation of
the name "de Man" as such – or any other name. The problems
posed at this spot, a "bewitched" spot we approached at first by
examining the profile and story of The Abjected de Man, remain
entirely contemporary to a cultural and critical present whose
very inhabitation and structure may be suspect.

2

The ideology of dialogue

It is very hard to believe that Bakhtin spilt so much ink just to inform us that we should listen attentively to one another, treat each other as whole persons, be prepared to be corrected and interrupted, realise that life is an endless unfinished process, that too much dogma makes you narrow-minded, that nobody has a monopoly of the truth and that life is so much richer than any of our little ideas about it. He was not, after all, George Eliot or E. M. Forster or a liberal Democrat.

Terry Eagleton

Following one of the more popular receptions of any theoretical opus into contemporary discourse – what was oddly called Bakhtin's "rediscovery," as if a quality of repetition were nonetheless sought here – there seems to have emerged an impasse in the use of his terms. Not so much a burnout as the gradual awareness, perhaps, of a gap, or flaw, in the dissemination and translation itself, a tension lost, an assumed import receded. Not only has no Bakhtinian criticism clearly emerged (not itself a negative), but highly interpretive decisions by Bakthin's editors have taken a subtle toll, particularly as their own roles shift from being translators to defensive priests of ideological turf. This scenario looms behind two very different collections, Gary Saul Morson and Caryl Emerson's *Rethinking Bakhtin: Extensions and Challenges*, which loosely represents an American Bakhtin as humanist poetician (anticipating their *Mikhail Bakhtin: the Creation of a Prosaics* (1990)), and Ken Hirschkop's *Bakhtin and Cultural Theory*, a quasi-Marxist (or British) Bakhtin whose hybrid interventions in "cultural theory" are philosophically sophisticated and diverse. Yet the once-famous battles over the Bakhtin empire (more a multi-

56

national corporation than the "industry" it has been called) show our continuing dependence on readings that avoid questioning the rhetorical strategies of these writings – too often viewed as straightforward or even "vocal" exposition.[1] If in the Hirschkop volume cultural theory is expanded through juxtapositions of Bakhtin and reading, Bakhtin and feminism, and so on, the "challenges" and "extensions" of the American school – mostly to and of Michael Holquist's christological reading in his *Mikhail Bakhtin* – yield a more conservative "Bakhtin," a neo-Kantian moralist and literary typologist suspiciously invested with a rhetoric of the "self" reminiscent of the late twentieth century American academy.[2] Yet a larger question looms as to whether the two *ways* of

[1] Caryl Emerson, in her Editor's Preface to *Problems in Dostoyevsky's Poetics*, suggests that Bakhtin's "works seem designed less to be read than to be over heard, in a sort of transcribed speech" (xxxiii), encouraging an assumption of transparency and "communication." This approach seems echoed in the ideological need to purify the voice of the author, "Bakhtin," either by returning all the "pseudonymous" texts to him, as in Katerina Clark and Michael Holquist's *Mikhail Bakhtin* (1984), or segregating them definitively, as in Morson and Emerson's *Mikhail Bakhtin: The Creation of a Prosaics* (1991), where the "Voloshinov" texts are discarded (and even the *Rabelais* side-lined). By naming an "American" Bakhtin school I am of course identifying, primarily, the group of slavicists who have presided almost exclusively over his translation, dissemination and editing (Holquist, Emerson, Morson).

[2] One example is "dialogism's" use in the Michael Holquist's, *Dialogism: Bakhtin and his World* (1990), where the term appears in every chapter heading as a kind of differential if conceptually vague theology of "self and other." While we are told "that for [Bakhtin] 'self' is dialogic, a relation," and that the "key to understanding . . . is the dialogue between self and other" (19), the "event of being a self" (21) is hypostasized as a unity ("The gate of the 'I' is located at the center not only of one's own existence, but of language as well" (23)), and Holquist's early Buberisms seem merely revamped. This is apparent, for instance, when Bakhtin's "principle of simultaneity" (*PDP*, 27) is misread as a transcendental ("self/other is a relation of simultaneity" (19)) rather than material and linguistic problem. Extending Holquist's iconography in this regard, Morson and Emerson consecrate a chapter of *Prosaics* to what they term, "Psychology: Authoring a Self" (172–230), oddly with special reference to Voloshinov. In writing on "Bakhtin's Imaginary Utopia," Lahcen Haddad critiques the American appropriation of Bakhtin, mostly for its "antihistoricist" character, yet appropriates from this site a precritical notion of "history" itself for Bakhtin that seems to replicate the American slavicists' anxious dismissal from Bakhtin of theory ("theoreticism"). By contrast, Anthony Wall and Clive Thomson's "Cleaning Up Bakhtin's Carnival Act," in *Diacritics*, Vol. 23, no. 2 (1993), 47–70, indict Morson and Emerson for their editorial mutilation of Bakhtin's canon in order to produce a neo-conservative figure (noting their work's determining "moralizing tone" (58)). The "debate" between the cultural critic "Bakhtin" of the British left and the American retro-humanists (Morson) flares again in a letter exchange in *PMLA* (January, 1994), where Ken Hirschkop and David Shepherd note that Morson's " 'prosaic' Bakhtin is a political creature in disguise" (117).

producing Bakhtin have not been locked in a certain specularity (left-right, ostensibly) that effectively diverts attention from a more material turn in Bakhtin's text. The question makes the story of Bakthin's American translation a key puzzle in the mimetic wars of contemporary critical politics, an ideological site or *spot*, too, where the problem of inscription plays a specifically disfiguring role.

The byzantine politics of Bakhtin's reception was and remains complicated by peculiar alliances. These misalliances include that between the Marxist and traditional humanist readings brought together to oppose post-structuralism in the 1980s yet – that seemingly accomplished – now at odds. Thus Graham Pechey in *Bakhtin and Cultural Theory* attacks Clark and Holquist's reading: "Bakhtin becomes in their hands a topic in the 'history of ideas'; a shamefaced theologian who adopts the opportunistic guise of a Philosopher of Freedom, yet another apostle of sociality as inter-subjectivity," arguing instead for "rescuing Bakhtin from the cold storage of intellectual history and from the politically compromised liberal academy which presides over this immobilising exposition" (39–40). Some of this is tediously familiar, though reflecting, as ever, back on the blocked or translational logics of such familial intrigue. Yet if Bakhtin's somewhat alien constellations were first rendered *familiar* through analogy to known texts (Buber, Sartre, Benjamin, or Levi-Strauss), much was also determined by who "Bakhtin" should not be read *as* – specifically, as is familiar, the hypertextualism or "deconstruction" for which he was to provide a social and historically grounded alternative.[3] The question remains what problems in Bakhtin's poetics – the duplicity of his terms, the allegorical role of signatures – were repressed as a dialogic "imagination" (never Bakhtin's word) emerged that was to legitimate a rhetoric of the self and the ideology of communication? Securing this origin was clearly one aim of Clark and Holquist's book, which united stylistically diverse works under the unitary "Bakhtin" signature and then ascribed a reassuringly christian "transcoding" to the opus. A certain pathos, moreover, was routinely invoked by the narrative of a life and work rescued from the injustice of censorship and

---

[3] For a reading of Bakhtin as promulgating the "return to history" of the early 1980s by his theoretical access to the "others of the text," see David Carroll, "The Alterity of Discourse."

returned, supposedly, to its true meaning. Aspects of today's impasse may be traced to demands made on this Bakhtin of the 1980s, among them the near total suppression of a permeating presence of Nietzsche throughout the early works (a presence precisely, necessarily, *un*marked in the writings themselves). To point this out is neither to play at "influence" studies nor to attempt another simple homogenization of Bakhtin's text – but rather, since resistance to this reading has been constitutive of those that have reigned, to rupture a certain pattern of translation that has framed Bakhtin's reception. Thus Ken Hirschkop opens by asking the question too often brushed aside: "What is this 'dialogism' that so many celebrate as liberating and democratic: what are its actual cultural forms, its social or political preconditions, its participants, methods and goals?" (*BCT*, 3).

If Bakhtin remains a *cipher* for any attempt to read certain impasses in cultural studies today, it is interesting how the right and elements of the left together constructed a "Bakhtin" who was supposed also to be the anti-dote of this "formalism." If there now appears a covert specularity between the right and certain left agendas in this appropriation, there also remains a specularity between "Bakhtin" and his textualist others that has often harassed this scene from within. We may remind ourselves, here, of an often overlooked fault or scandal of sorts that haunts the critical scene going into the late-1990s: that, *despite* the "return to history" and the pursuit of the political in the 1980s (and the marginalization of supposedly disengaged language-centered criticism), the mid-1990s appeared in a *more* neo-conservative national and academic environment than before – a fact virtually presaged to the point of parody in Morson and Emerson's "Bakhtin." Moreover, having joined with the right to arrest post-structuralism and return to a foundational subject, the left would be linked with deconstruction and turned on by the right (as in the "culture wars"). Other inversions could be traced as well. On the one hand, if the humanist "Bakhtin" was to escape formalism by highlighting an inter-subjective "dialogic imagination" of an imaginary self and other, it ended by producing a pallidly typological figure (i.e. another formalist); on the other hand, in cultural criticism "Bakhtin" became a patron of "new historicism" which, despite its well-intentioned politics, appears today a fairly Reaganite phenomenon – one hoarding as capital the presumption of referential "facts." If the name Bakhtin has provided the foil against which a *mimetic* crisis in criticism dissimulates itself, one could say that "theory" was abjected in the 1980s not because it was apolitical, or ahistorical, but because it represented a political problem that demanded other terms to be resolved.

My pretext for re-examining this complex involves a sort of *katabasis* or séance effect – a return to a curiously encrypted "past" scene, one of (non)reading between de Man and Bakhtin that suggests an alternate history to the official one outlined above. While much has occurred in and to the itineraries of both names in the intervening time, my intent is practical. I will ask not only why the *descriptive* poetics of "Bakhtin" seems to have led to an impasse in practical criticism, but what iconic role this repressed exchange has in any genealogy of the present scene. Specifically, if a tendency toward representational, historicist, or mimetic interpretation determined much in Bakhtin's construction, ignoring the rhetorical side of Bakhtin's performance has been costly. After surveying the terms of this exchange as staged by de Man, I will suggest that "dialogue" as used by what we might call the Bakhtins may be an intentionally sabotaged figure. Rather than implying hermeneutic exchange or communication, Bakhtinian "dialogue" may be read as a wildly agonistic scene of power, positioning, deception, seduction, and defacement in the structural absence of "communication" as we tend to define it – and that containing this problem motivated the Bakhtin's official guardians from the first. I suspect, accordingly, that beneath the story of Bakhtin's construction lies a political contest over how *referentiality* is to be conceived – and hence how politics, history, the "literary," formalism, and so on, are defined. If so, then any revision of the Bakhtin of the 1980s we are still stuck in involves the possibility of moving leftist cultural studies from a mimetic model that frequently repeats the mimeticism of the right toward a linguistic materialism that sees the problematic of language less as formalistic play than as the agency of cultural intervention. My initial purpose in the following, then, is both to make more apparent how a decision was made early about how Bakhtin should be installed and marketed, and to see *where this event still haunts the uses of Bakhtin*. That decision has to do not only with the way that language-oriented theory (post-structuralism) had been "otherated" to favor certain interpretations of history and the social, but how the turn toward the political may have been compromised by an implicit re turn to conservative representational models. A subsidiary consequence of reading this exchange is one to which I can give only brief attention: the question of the role today of de Man – let us even specify, "late de Man" – in the contemporary rearticulation of the political. For behind this conjuncture of signatures – that of de Man's and Bakhtin's – we read a cipher for the present state or impasse of critical culture, or certainly the "inner history" of that: both names being, after all, very differently handled and made to play different iconic roles for a return to history (or historicism) that has accompanied the return to mimetic humanism from more "theoretical" stances. But if we can, from our viewpoint today, see that turn more and more not as one from theory to practice, from language to history, but from a certain re-thinking of the future and materiality itself through language back toward a familiar archive of historicism and humanism, as a regression registered in the increasing conservatism and *faux* political codes of the academic and national scenes, then the conjunction of these two names, as suggested, opens up somewhat differently. For if what might unite these names today is the question of a certain "materiality" that critical culture has in each case worked to neutralize and bracket, it would be hard to say whether the strategy of abjecting de Man (re-cast of "new critic," apolitical textualist, tainted by "scandal") or the embrace of "Bakhtin" (as proto-historicist, humanist, or mimeticist) was more efficient.

1. Making Bakhtin prosaic (and why it wasn't that hard)

Read symptomatically, Hirschkop's collection has a range and philosophic depth not matched in the more lugubrious American approach, but the latter project is more interesting for what it tells us of the still current Bakhtins – particularly as the editors lay out the interpretive agenda followed in their subsequent *Prosaics*. There three totalizing "global concepts" – Prosaics, Unfinalizability, and Dialogue, the first the authors' *own* "neologism" to indicate Bakhtin's interest in prose and the everyday – are used to interpret and hierarchize Bakhtin's concerns. The collection is also interesting for containing (or, literally, trying to contain) the generally ignored essay by Paul de Man, "Dialogue and Dialogism," which has the unique status of speaking back, as it were, from within one specular meconnaissance that decisively defined Bakhtin in the 1980s. De Man's short piece, first given as a talk before an MLA audience on "Fiction and Its Referents" in 1981, seems an appropriately mock-dialogic choice – aside from the discomfitting doubling of the title. On its surface it dismantles the hermeneutic conception of "dialogue" or Bakhtin most celebrated by the editors – exposing it, essentially, as dependent on a false claim of immediate access to alterity. Interestingly, the collection immediately inserts a counter-piece designed exclusively to contain and negate this, Mathew Roberts' "Poetics Hermeneutics Dialogic: Bakhtin and Paul de Man." Yet rather than analyzing or debating de Man's apparent thesis – that Bakhtin promises an access to alterity he nowhere delivers – he suspends any possibility of such "dialogue," and this by arguing that the two critics could not possibly understand one another anyway (he notes their "mutual unintelligibility" (134)), since they supposedly have different concepts of the "self" ("the most fundamental differences between Bakhtin and de Man lie in their respective conceptions of the self or subject" (116)). In another inversion of names, he generally opposes what he terms de Man's "rigorous, unending effort to dis-close and distinguish an ontological self" (120) to Bakhtin's embrace of "the world in general" (134).

This critical tact raises suspicion as to what is at stake in de Man's piece – or what drew the editors, with a certain intuitive doom, to include it? Why do they stage a dialogue to show the impossibility of (that) dialogue? Whatever must be isolated in de Man's essay seems to subtly contaminate the collection by the emergence of the last essay, which, oddly yet tellingly in Nietzsche's name, turns against "dialogism" itself. While one could read "Dialogue and Dialogism" as a brief and minor discrimination in de Man's late work, his recurrent self-references in it give the piece a weirdly trenchant and uniquely autobiographical tone. A certain doubling, present in the title, seems imposed on de Man – a sort of (deflected) contract to address a "Bakhtin" set against deconstruction, found in that audience's construction – that required him to fend off the invariable other Bakthin engendered by the encounter, one too proximate or even irritatingly susceptible to a de Manian "reading." This fundamental duplicity and doubling pervades the simulacrum of "dialogue" in the essay (with Bakthin, with the audience, with a reader of Bakhtin to come).

I will examine this exchange by keeping in mind the manner in which the stakes of the outcome – who wins, who loses; who is read, who isn't; who is misread, and how – remain a cipher and crypt still influencing the contemporary critical landscape. Thus while de Man repeatedly exempts himself from the critical community then engaging and celebrating Bakhtin, his sweeping erasure of almost every available reading in the final line anticipates and deforms in advance any current impasse of Bakhtin's terms. Against the hermeneutic understandings of dialogue, then, de Man early on notes that we may translate the term as "double-talk" ("It can, first of all, simply mean double-talk, the necessary obliqueness of any persecuted speech that cannot, at the risk of survival, openly say what it means to say" (*RB*, 106)), thus raising the specter of a Bakhtin whose own text dissimulates substantially more than his fondest readers – or strategically, "de Man" himself – assumes.

We cannot ignore, moreover, that this *dialogue* as if between "dialogue" and "dialogism" (if this even *is* a binary) is fore-closed by and within the collection. In another sense, *Rethinking Bakhtin* conceals a family affair that is played out in the editors' subsequent *Prosaics* (like *Mikhail Bakhtin*, and doubling its doubleness, a jointly authored effort). *Rethinking Bakhtin's* programmatic introduction is designed to crystallize the inner logic of the American "Bakhtin" as managed by a small rotating group of brilliant and energetic slavicists (Holquist and his slightly Oedipal successors, Morson and Emerson). If it attempts to reverse and refine – "challenge" and "extend" – the ideological investment of Holquist's biography, what is worrisome is that the collection produces a Bakhtin refined into an oddly reduced neo-formalist or right-wing practical critic at odds with the Bakhtin familiar through tropes like the carnivalesque. As elsewhere, the rhetoric of self and other oversees a manageable economy of "difference" while asserting and defending an ideology of authorial intent and meaning. Thus the *Prosaics* distances the entire import of the carnivalesque, which involves the transvaluative import of the priority of the reversible ("like Janus") material sign in Bakhtin: "From an ethical perspective as well, the role of the 'public square word'" – that is, the word as sheer

63

exteriority, the very import of Bakhtin – "is somewhat inconsist-
ent with Bakhtin's other formulations . . . This separation of the
word from any grounding in the ethical speaking person is said
to be one of the privileges of the people's laughter" (447).[4] Where
Hirschkop would expand Bakhtin through diverse cultural juxtapositions, Morson and Emerson (henceforth ME, keeping in
mind the projected ideology of the self) respond by further par-
ing Bakhtin's territorial canon, stripping it first of the critical
"pseudonymous" production signed Voloshinov and Medvedev. The problem of signature in the Bakhtin Circle has habit-
ually been probed as a matter of attribution, rather than as a
complex system of marking that permeates and (perpetually)
alters the production and its reading from within, rewriting *in
particular* the signature "Bakhtin." It has never been literally a
case of historical evidence, of fact versus fiction, since the parameters of that dyad have been (indeed, systematically) erased
by the inability to restore anything outside the need to compulsively re-narrativize this (hi)story – a situation even given the
historical "Bakhtin's" apparent imprimatur by its own withdrawal, by his refusing to sign an acknowledgement of the
pseudonymous scheme late in life (indeed, the problematic of
signature places this text in a group of critical writings including
Plato, Kierkegaard, and Nietzsche). Such decisions seem designed primarily to control interpretive or ideological options. If in
Rethinking Bakhtin any American school to emerge appears both
occasional and parochial, the volume's culminating section on
"The Dangers of Dialogue" unveils its own anxieties. This is
most explicit in Michael André Bernstein's interesting and finally
open assault on dialogism as a figure of Nietzschean *ressentiment*
that stands opposed to the rhetoric of the speaker's authenticity
and pathos ("The Poetics of *Ressentiment*"). Billed as the critical
revision of a master who has evinced too much "hero-worship,"
the move in fact exudes a discrete hostility toward an unassimilable aspect of the text for this group of Bakhtinians (no wonder
that, in the *Prosaics*, ME will have to go on and excise from the

---

[4] By neo-formalist I mean a figure whose strategies of displacement have become
typologies, as evidenced in two different yet complementary pieces by Morson
and Linda Hutcheon on Bakhtin and "parody." In each case the writers fail to
ask where they use the term (at best, minor to Bakhtin) as an ideological tool of
centering and control reasserting the originary (or parodied) text – a strategy
barred within Bakhtin's broader deconstruction by ambivalent laughter.

scene, virtually, the carnivalesque and the *Rabelais* book). Here the early 1980s attempts to appropriate "dialogism" for the ideology of the self, from Todorov's Buberesque redaction to Holquist's communicationist ideology, come (almost) full circle.

Thus Bernstein's rejection of "dialogism" as a *techne* of *ressentiment* merely articulates a profounder resentment in the collection. Here that seems to be against the implications of a "crisis of citation" in dialogism that threatens the authenticity of the self or a voice that is its own – a direct, if unseen, resentment at a principle of material otherness. Bakhtin, who clearly had been enrolled as an unthreatening figure to help manage a restricted economy of difference, is here castigated for resisting: he has all along been a *time*-bomb. The inversion is familiar yet done, again, in Nietzsche's name: the rhetoric of the other's word empties the autonomy of the speaker or self and is that of the reactive slave, rather than the master, though it is the delusion of mastery whose blindness is expressed, here, as Bernstein's resentment at the supposed implications of *ressentiment*: "what Bakhtin understands by the 'dialogic imagination' is uncomfortably similar to Nietzsche's account of the slave's reactive, dependent, and fettered consciousness. Every word the Nietzschean slave utters, every value he posits, is purely reactive, impregnated by the words and values of others and formulated entirely in response to and as an anticipation of the responses he will elicit" (201). The attempt to bring Nietzsche into play remains insightful, if almost upside-down, since it focuses on the relation between the "other's word" as such and memory, repetition, or sheer anteriority.[5] For Bernstein speaks in the name of a restored immediacy ("The dialogic status of their words, ideas, and sentiments is experienced as pure entrapment, triggering only rage and *ressentiment*" (208)), echoing Morson's assumption of "Bakhtin's unquestioned valuation of the new, the original, the authentic" (60), as if unaware that the "living word" may only be a necessary trope for a particular recirculation of the "dead," the material, the *alien word*.

---

[5] It is a mark of how consistently the performative parameters of Bakhtin's text remain unread that Caryl Emerson, in her Editor's Preface to *Problems*, simply pronounces: "His entire understanding of the word, and of the specificity of the utterance, invalidates the very concept of repetition. Nothing 'recurs' [. . .] The phenomenon is perhaps better understood in the linguistic category of 'redundancy,' that is, as the surplus necessary for a certain mode, or force, of communication" (xxxv).

In Voloshinov's entirely performative or allegorical genealogy, the (perpetually) present age implicitly follows that of the "dead word" of formalism, as alternately the pseudo-authority of the "priest's word," where the "alien word" is hypostasized and then serviced (*"alien languages preserved in written monuments"*):

European linguistic thought formed and matured over concern with the cadavers of written languages; almost all its basic categories, its basic approaches and techniques were worked out in the process of reviving those cadavers.

Philologism is the inevitable distinguishing mark of the whole of European linguistics as determined by the historical vicissitudes of its birth and development. However far back we may go in tracing the history of linguistic categories and methods, we find philologists every-where.   (*Marxism and the Philosophy of Language*, 71)

Two things might be noted. First, that the facile attacks on writing and philology are essentially metaphoric. And second, while this narrative is used to situate the present of the text in a heartening opposition to the *dead* word of formalism, the latter is explicitly said to occur at all times ("we find philologists everywhere"). This last inversely puts into question the historical pretext of the "living word." What, here, might be called Bakhtin's *post*-formalism? Does it truly occur or is it simply a different strategy of formalization? Since what is hypostasized as the "dead word" already has a history as a concept in Russian formalism, it is mediated. Moreover, what is called the "alien word" (*chuzoe slovo*) is often the same term as what is routinely called the "other's word" of dialogue. The "other's word" – supposedly lateral, coming as if from another person's mouth – is always first a past word, a figure of *anteriority* in some sense either as memory, inscription or the reserve of already "inhabited" words. The alterity of the other's word, that is, passes through a loop of inscription, repetition, and rememoration, which the text's rhetoric absorbs and covers. What this may tell us is that in Bakhtin's text there is no "other's word" in the *immediate* sense, i.e. that of being co-present. There is no *immediate* "other" in Bakhtin – a problem I will return to, but which is dealt with rather explicitly in his analysis of texts in Dostoyevsky. Instead, there is a word that is always (also) anterior and caught in repetition, that is, already dead, alien, or a form of monumentalized writing in the

metaphorical sense. Then how "living" – immediate, vital, free of
formalism and philology – is Bakhtin's dialogic or "living word"?
Can we take the living word at its word, or is it only a variation of
the dead? It is not accidental that Menippea's "dialogue of the
dead" should be a model of anti-genre, since the most alive word
metaphorically is not that spoken immediately but that, as in the
polyphonic novel, suffused with the most antithetical (scriptive)
traces or "intonations." For Bernstein the antidote for Bakhtin's
"dialogism," or, one might add with all sorts of conditions and a
positive inflection I will return to, *nihilism*, turns out familiarly to
be Habermas ("a salutory correction to the abstractions of Bakhtin" (291 n)), though the "dialogism" Bernstein attacks is the
most comfortably affirmative redaction to begin with, the inter-
subjective version of Holquist or Wayne Booth, with whom his
own allegiances lie. (For Nietzsche, of course, there are two at
least antithetical *nihilisms*: the first, which is that fostered by a
kind of moralism of reference (including historicism, various
ascetic or Christo-Judaic rhetorics, humanism, the rhetoric of paternal meaning) and a second that exists in its (positive) negation
of the terms of the first.)

But Bernstein's allusion to Nietzsche could be developed differently. For one thing, the Bakhtinian word is repeatedly depicted
as anticipating in the other's word an anticipation of one's own
(anticipation), with the intent of overpowering and incorporating
the counter-reading of an always verbal other. What is infrequent-
ly noted is that the all important trope of the "other's word"
(*chuzoe slovo*) merges figuratively with other categories in
Voloshinov's mythographic history in *Marxism and the Philosophy
of Language* – that is, genealogy of what precedes the permanent
contemporaneity of the text – and specifically with the "alien
word" ("coalesce(d) in the depths of the historical consciousness
of nations with the idea of authority, the idea of power" (*MPL*,
75)), philologism ("the inevitable distinguishing mark of the
whole of linguistic thinking" (*MPL*, 71)), the "priest's word,"
descriptions of writing that recall passages from the *Genealogy of
Morals*, and with the "dead word" of formalism – pure anteriority
at the point that becomes another figure for materiality, exteriority, or trace as such. In each of these categories a variation on the
idea of the memory trace, repetition, and materiality is at work,
since any "crisis of citation" has to do more with the anteriority of

a word that itself generates "consciousness" (*"consciousness itself can arise and become a viable fact only in the material embodiment of signs"* (*MPL*, 11)). The reading of Bakthin as all along pragmatically theorizing an intervention in the real through *memory* rather than through some model of dialogic or historical immediacy – including what is called genre memory – is raised by Wall and Thomson. In a section titled *Memory* in their discussion, they by-pass the metonymic chain that leads from "other's word" and the "alien word" to the "dead word" (and "absolute past"), wherein the trope of materiality itself is inscribed: "Memory becomes a complex space where new communities and relationships can be forged through such inscription. It is entirely appropriate to recall Walter Benjamin's 'Theses on the Philosophy of History'" ("Cleaning Up," 62). Dismissing Morson's *faux* bid for immediacy and transparency through the pretense of purging "theory," they note that: "on the contrary, the everyday is, for Bakhtin, a theoretical concept of the first order" (63). They further wonder about the cold war anachronisms of ME's study: "Not only does their study seem to set up a traditionally nationalist opposition between the free enterprise, individualist Bakhtin and the evil, collectivist Bakhtin. In a further twist, Marxism is made to encompass everything dialectical, utopian, and collective" (67) – or *theoretical*. The American critics' obsession with the explanatory pretense of biographic "fact" – particularly in one who pointedly, biographically, erases just this – and talk of "authoring a self" indicates more than an anxiety about authority and origin that Bakhtin provokes. As a figure with allegorical traits, *formalism* appears less a concrete school or epoch – as it appears sketched in Medvedev's *The Formal Method* – than a problem posed by the permanent *anteriority* of cited, inhabited, incorporated, or repeated words. The entire configuration illuminates a duplicity within the trope of formalism: specifically, that "formalism" may be, figuratively, what *always has just been the case* and *what will return* as the material and aesthetic moment of language's phenomenality: that is, one ambivalent cipher for the materiality in language. Rather than being the mode by which external considerations (divorced from "content") are subject to quantifiable rules that evade history, aesthetic formalization here implies quite the opposite: a site of sheer exteriority – or even, metaphorically considered, visibility, the public, materiality, the *sign* – which itself determines the very modus of so-called "experience," much as inscription can be said to precede or engender (against itself) the tropological pretexts of content, interiorization, mimetic reference. The entire ideological encoding of what is formalist and what it entails (for there are, clearly, double "formalisms," and doubles of these doubles), requires demystification – for which the trope of "dialogue" itself, with its seeming invocation of voice and immediacy over trace and mnemonic spell, supplies one model. Despite the loud insistence of the hermeneutic reading of Bakhtinian dialogue, it is nowhere clear that Bakhtin even deploys the concept of "self" that American commentators so prize – any more than Nietzsche, as in Rorty's opinion, does self-fashioning, and so on.[6] Quite the contrary, this particular conceit seems interdicted openly and repeatedly in Voloshinov's anti-subjectivist *Marxism* (what he refutes as "subjective expressionism"), where personality is the effect of a self-differing and material word: *"a word is not an expression of inner personality; rather, inner personality is an expressed or inwardly impelled word"* (*MPL*, 153). The entire import of the Bakhtinian-Voloshinovian writing is toward an exposition, an ex-posure, that breaks all interiorist economies such as almost every hermeneutic redaction of Bakhtin has willed to restore. Where does this lead?

As the *Prosaics* makes clear, the deletion of Voloshinov's essay from the Bakhtin canon has everything to do with enforcing a conventional ideology: "Presenting a picture of Bakhtin's views of the self entails special difficulties, because so many earlier accounts – including our own – have been based on the belief that Voloshinov's book on Freud and his comments on psychology in *Marxism and the Philosophy of Language* belong to Bakhtin" (172). Yet, in fact, Bakhtin may even be said to practice a covert yet *systematic* Nietzschean reversal of received valorizations in undermining the too familiar concepts he empties and recirculates (sign, dialogue, value, ideology, genre), terms that negatively and anamorphically trope their "official" or philosophic meanings by moving "in between" and undoing the binaries that upheld the

---

[6] Some of the terms publicly attached to Bakhtin's work are the inventions of his commentators and never occur in his text, such as Holquist's "dialogic *imagination*" (a distinctly humanizing label), Todorov's "dialogic principle" (borrowed from Buber), and ME's "prosaics," their own "neologism" yet called one of his three "global concepts."

terms themselves. This "interindividual" or "interterritorial" linguistic and material signifying agency on which visibility, *publicness*, and materiality hinge is sometimes called, simply, the "social." However belated a Nietzschean Bakhtin might be, *Genealogy of Morals* and *The Birth of Tragedy* appear omnipresent, if pointedly uncited, in the work of the 1920s.[7] Returning now to the one piece in this collection that is out of place, virtually *atopos*, Paul de Man's strategy appears odder still, since in dismantling the hermeneutic appropriation of dialogue, he seems to set aside a very different interpretation that he shows no interest in developing – what allows us to address a third, allographical, or effaced "dialogue" in this scene. With this, it seems, we stumble onto a crypt both within recent critical history and the archaeology of the present.

2. Speculating with "dialogue"

If the problem of assessing cultural criticism's investment in a certain (mis)reading of Bakhtin is a practical one – and if the impasse in today's Bakhtin is traceable to such a move – the point of returning to this site must be itself practical. Since rewriting this (hi)story involves projecting, as it must, a different present as well, underlying questions must include: What *other* ways of reading "dialogue" exist? If the 1990s has succeeded in creating a retro-humanist ethos mirrored in the rights to (or exploitation of) "Bakhtin," what direction will dismantling this investment take?

"Dialogue and Dialogism" evinces a tendency toward auto-inscription rare for de Man. Among else, it covertly marks the framework of the performance, in which the sociological "Bakhtin" of de Man's audience is potentially doubled, if not overtly against the textualist de Man, at all events against "deconstruction." In asking whether "dialogue" cannot first be translated as "double-talk," de Man marks that as the performative premise for any reading of (which is and is not to say dialogue with) "Bakhtin," which he demonstrates by solemnly referring to Bakhtin's "highly competent and clear-sighted introducers," Holquist and Todorov. When the postscript later replaces the hermeneutic model of dialogue with Rousseau's model of "parrying, feinting

---

[7] One might compare this effacement of Nietzsche to the similar way he is treated by Freud and Benjamin, present through an elaborate removal of overt traces.

and setting traps in a sequence of attacks and defenses somewhat like a fencing match" (106), de Man implicitly exposes his own strategy of calculated entrapment at a point it can not be openly responded to or countered – thus tactically derealizing the potential to name that duplicity. While the performance proceeds before its MLA audience in the mock-dialogic manner of inscribing "I" and "you" repeatedly, de Man doubles dialogue itself (*already* "double-talk"), as the two words of the title suggest. If there are also two Bakhtins in the address, one who seems marked by "double-talk" and who, unread, is set aside, and the other of the hermeneutic reading of the audience, there is also a "de Man" clearly represented by the self-references, disqualifications and mock-exclusions in the analysis (as when de Man excludes himself from those having anything to use from Bakhtin). Thus de Man maneuvers not only to dismantle Bakhtin and deny the specular relation he inherits from outside, but to repeatedly block the reverse moment of that specularity from emerging – the generally unconsidered possibility of a "de Manian" Bakhtin. For in opposing the hermeneutic reading of Bakhtin to an agonistic and dissimulative (that is, truly social, material and pragmatic) notion of "dialogism," de Man seems to mark another Bakhtin "betrayed" by his readership.

De Man's critique of Bakhtin's *dialogism* involves splitting the same term first into two moments: "Bakhtin at times conveys the impression that one can accede from dialogism as a metalinguistic (i.e., formal) structure to dialogism as a recognition of exotopy . . . the passage, in other words, from dialogism to dialogue" (111), or from poetics to hermeneutics. (The "two distinct senses" of *dialogue* that ME distinguishes – that applying to "all language" ("it orients itself toward a listener, whose active response shapes the utterance") and that opposed to a figural monologism that attempts "to 'forget' the multiple dialogizing qualifications" (*RB*, 52) – have no correspondence to de Man's strategic binarization.) The argument may be read as a sequence of traps:

Very summarily put, it is possible to think of dialogism as a still formal method by which to conquer or sublate formalism itself . . . The self-reflexive, autotelic or, if you wish, narcissistic structure of form, as a definitional description enclosed within specific borderlines, is hereby replaced by an assertion of the otherness of the other, preliminary to even the possibility of a recognition of his otherness . . . Whether the passage from otherness to the recognition of the other, the passage, in other words, from dialogism to dialogue, can be said to take place in Bakhtin as more than a desire, remains a question for Bakhtin interpretation to consider in the proper critical spirit. (109–10)

De Man's intervention will momentarily focus on three moments: Bakhtin's aberrant exclusion of trope, his misleading binarization of lyric and dialogue, and his subsequent collapse into a precritical phenomenology. The argument moves through a series of tactical asides that obliquely revise the text's figural import, as when he notes that polyphony invokes less the Greek *phone* than differential musical notation ("as in a musical score" (109)). At the heart of the critique, however, de Man determines that in Bakhtin "trope" is itself deemed undialogic or unsocial, and this moment – related to Bakhtin's notorious exile of the lyric from his concerns – opens a contradiction:

as the analysis of dialogical refraction develops, Bakhtin has to reintroduce the categorical foundations of a precritical phenomenalism in which there is no room for exotopy, for otherness, in any shape or degree. When it is said, for example, that "the heteroglot voices . . . create the background necessary for [the author's] own voice" (*DI*, 278), we recognize the foreground-background model derived from Husserl's theories of perception and here uncritically assimilating the structure of language to the structure of a secure perception: from that moment on, the figure of refraction and of the light ray becomes coercive as the only possible trope for trope, and we are within a reflective system of mise en abyme that is anything but dialogical. (112)

When de Man first excuses himself from "taking part" in a critical assessment that has, he adds, "barely begun," that is given an active form: "since I ignore the Russian language, it is not an enterprise in which I can responsibly hope to take part" (107). This self-removal might be doubly read, if "the Russian" actively ignored is also an *other* or untranslated Bakhtin, one rhetorically set aside for the duration of the critique. The term "ignore" recurs in describing the novelists' supposed otherness ("they simply ignore such strongly suggestive oppositions as those between author and character" (108)). The non-relation that obtains between de Man and his characters, "de Man" and "Bakhtin," will not be easily expounded. In fact, de Man stages the address within the question of "fact and fiction" (107), shifting the borders of these two continually. If the reading of Bakhtinian dialogue as communication of self and other was a fiction, it nonetheless behaves like a fact of the critical community that reifies and uses it. After extending the preliminary definition of dialogue as "double-talk" to the Russian ("there is ample evidence . . . this meaning is entirely relevant in his case" (107)), he brackets its import. Later, in citing the text to be taken apart, a brief piece from "Discourse in the Novel" on "tropes," de Man notes another suspension: "if one is willing to suspend for a moment the poten-tial dialogic otherness of these statements, he seems, on the whole, to consider that the discourse of tropes is not dialogical" (110). If de Man puts aside a certain Bakhtin – he who speaks in effaced "double-talk," whose statements subsequently can be read in a "potential dialogic otherness," whose passages are "appropri-ate(d)" (111) – it is not clear whether de Man stages a reading (as a "battle for mastery") with the audience's Bakhtin, or whether the refusal of such an engagement is not itself strategic.

This dialogic model of fencing or entrapment further inscribes the reader in the text: "the smart reader always outwits an author who depends on him from the moment he has opened a dialogue that is never entirely gratuitous, that is always a battle for mas-tery" (113). De Man appears at times to perform a reading of "Bakhtin" that acts as the novelist does to the poet: "the novelist does not set out to take the place of his master, the epic poet, but to set him free from the restricting coercions of his single-minded, monological vision" (108), yet this is also blocked by his refusal to adopt a usurpative relation to Bakhtin. Thus de Man makes him-self the negative pivot of the "odd list" of Bakhtin's "admirers" he at first excludes himself from, only then to (pretend to) reverse: "at the moment I appropriate these passages as the ground of my own admiration. . . I have included myself in the odd list of Bakhtin admirers from which I first pretended to be excluded" (111–12). For what these *admirers* "have in common, at least nega-tively" would be the one critic who alone cannot be inscribed in Bakhtin's methodology: "a literary theoretician or critic con-cerned with tropological displacements of logic, with a rhetoric of cognition as well as of persuasion" (111) – that is, "de Man." De Man, after exempting himself from partaking of the dialogue on Bakhtin's work because he ignores (the) Russian, points to himself as what "negatively" binds Bakhtin's readers by his own exclu-sion. I, "de Man," am not a reader of Bakhtin or an admirer – the text says – though (another?) "de Man" later seems to anamorphi-cally invert this parenthesis. What must be established to follow this doubling is where dialogue is doubled into two versions (dialogue and dialogism), and whether they are fact or fiction – the topic, after all, for the original MLA panel. But if de Man recognizes his negative inscription in the "hermeneutic" Bakhtin, at least in that represented by his audience, he cannot wholly control the specular relation he so steadfastly refuses (and thus accelerates). He seems less concerned with the opposition to Bak-htin he uses to attack the hermeneutic reading than with the figure of "substitution" the latter implies. As was clear above, one of the problems of the American Bakhtin is that it always suppressed the performative dimension of the text. Like the author "Rousseau" invoked in the postscript ("it would be naive to ask who wins the match since in this model, Rousseau, as author, controls the moves of each of the antagonists") our attention is drawn to "how one fights" – dialogics, I might add, as sheer will to power, the site not of shared understanding but the fight over who will install and mnemonically control a (no doubt political, yet also) inter-pretive or aesthetic regime. So, what's at stake?

De Man's strategy is to repeatedly double back over a figure he has just critiqued, assuming its reversed position while exposing his own violation of the reader's presumed contract. Thus, after denouncing binaries ("to the extent that they allow or invite synthesis . . . the most misleading of differential structures" (103), de Man can pass unseen into producing what might be called the binary of binaries, announced in his title, by indicting "the pas-sage, in other words, from dialogism to dialogue." This passage occurs "in other words" because two forms of the same word, *dialogism*, are at stake: a passage from "dialogism as a metalingu-istic (i.e., formal) structure to dialogism as a recognition of exotopy." Since the distinction does not belong to Bakhtin, this dialogism covertly cites the expectation of the audience (an "author and a concept – dialogism – that can be made to accom-modate" various critical models). Moreover, the narrative move-ment toward the *promise of alterity* appears to almost invert the normal narrative direction in Bakhtin (one equally suspect) from monologue to dialogism. This now appears, however, as the "pas-sage" from dialogism to (hermeneutic) "dialogue," the latter be-ing, nonetheless, "not necessarily monologic." Yet the binary that

results in the doubling of dialogism appears as if already suspended in de Man's title, "Dialogue and Dialogism," where the
order is reversed in advance and the "and" declares no necessary
direction. Thus the two D's in the title and de Man's refused
doubling against this Bakhtin suggest another subtext. Rather
than "de Man" substituting for Derrida in the public opposition
of Bakhtin to deconstruction, Derrida can inhabit, momentarily,
the specular position of "Bakhtin" in relation to a certain "de
Man" within the article's staged agon – a position hilariously
criticized, by contrast, for its hermeneutic traces. The two D's of
(the) "dialogue" (or deconstruction) appear in a fractured specular model which de Man simultaneously refuses, as he does all
doubling between himself and Bakhtin. A certain specularity and
substitution opens, however, that de Man cannot master and
which, inversely, not only contracts "Bakhtin" involuntarily as a
tropological figure (ciphered, in turn, against the "official" or
hermeneutic reading of the community), but reattaches him, un-
stably, to another double or figure with whom de Man's name is
publicly linked – and, again, distanced. The text focuses not only
on fact and fiction but on otherness as such and rewrites dialogue
as who is inscribed in (or erased from) whose text – that is,
dialogue *as* usurpation and (dis)inscription.

There are moments in de Man's Bakhtin (dis)connection, so to
speak, in which the imaginary "dialogue" is, simply, cut-off,
hung up on, the switchboard dis-connected from either (ventriloquized) side. Behind this anamorphic "dialogue," however, is
another scene of reading. At the center of the critique Bakhtin is
excluded from the ranks of critics "concerned with tropological
displacements" through a bracketing of "the potential dialogical
otherness of these statements." By-passing de Man's tongue in
cheek treatment of the chosen text ("among the richest in the
canon") and his own planting there of a "conception of dialogue
as question and answer" that facilitates the polemic, two moments stand out. These include Bakhtin's segregation of lyric from
dialogic prose that "excludes tropes from literary discourse, poetic as well as prosaic," and a return to a "precritical phenomenalism" void of otherness that is indicted as "assimilating the structure of language to the structure of a secure perception: from that
moment on, the figure of refraction and of the light ray becomes
coercive as the only possible trope for trope, and we are within a

reflective system of *mise en abyme* that is anything but dialogical" (105). What is acknowledged by de Man's language is the possibility nonetheless of a *tropological* reading of Bakhtin. In fact, in playing against the Russian's own fictive binaries – that of lyric and prose, epic and novel – de Man calls him "tropological in the worst possible sense, namely as a reification." Another way to say this would be that he is *indeed* tropological, only in another or even bad "sense," or indeed, the worst, since (for de Man) Bakhtin unforgivably muddles important distinctions by his typological strategies and general imprecision. Moreover, it is in the site of a *trope for trope* that de Man fingers the collapse of "the tropological" into "a reflective system of *mise en abyme*." What is entailed, though, by a return to "precritical phenomenalism," particularly if we know that Voloshinov's dismantling of phenomenology through the primacy of the material "sign" over perception renders that regression impossible to read literally – that is, as other than a strategy?

De Man's move illuminates Bakhtin's own cultural entrapment. The closing examination of Rousseau's "Dialogue on the Novel" as a countertext presents "Rousseau" as an alternate signature of de Man. As in the case of "Rousseau," the author "controls the moves of each of the antagonists," and what appears at first as a session of question and answer (a hermeneutic exchange) comments on the preceding performance. Thus de Man rewrites the exchange between Rousseau's author and reader as that between a poetics and a hermeneutics: "The relationship between poetics and hermeneutics, like that between R the author and N the reader, is dialogical to the precise extent that one cannot be substituted for the other, despite the fact that the non-dialogical discourse of question and answer (the mode of the cited text) fully justifies the substitution" (113). The author now in question, Rousseau-de Man, guards against any slippage towards the "smart reader" ("the smart reader always outwits an author who depends on him"). De Man ends with the surprising erasure not of Bakhtin, but of those readers who imitate or apply his criticism or pretend to dialogues with him – that is, almost all *familiar* strategies of reading: "To imitate or to apply Bakhtin, to read him by engaging him in a dialogue, betrays what is most valid in his work" (114). Yet there is an equivocation in the cited Rousseau text or its commentary, where it seems that the ignored or excluded Russian – that is, the Bakhtin whose text is "betrayed" by his readership – threatens to re-enter the text as a potential reader of de Man. In the Rousseau text, de Man says, it is N (the reader) who is identified as the straight-man to the continuing irony and control of R (the author): "The character designated by R and who is the author, refuses the substitution offered to him," which is "the refusal, in terms of poetics, to grant the substitutive symmetry implied by a hermeneutics" (114). De Man supposedly refuses Bakhtin, signal broken. Yet in the text, it is in fact N the reader who *both* proposes *and* dismisses the prospect of this exchange, and not R:

N . . . I advise you, however, to switch parts. Pretend that I am the one who urges you on to publish this collection of letters and that you are the one who resists. You give yourself the objections and I'll rebut them. It will sound more humble and make a better impression. – R. Will it also be in conformity with what you find to be praiseworthy in my character? – N. No, I was setting you a trap. Leave things as they are. (114)

Why does de Man give the priority to the author, since the refusal – the controlling gesture – is not that of R, as de Man explicitly says ("R . . . refuses the substitution offered to him"), but the reader N? If the text's own dialogue is inevitably a form of double-talk – the only honest approach to poetics – what is represented as a "hermeneutics" in Bakhtin (likened to the reader N) appears marked as yet another poetics of writing and reading anyway. A new material conception of dialogue as dissimulation is opposed to the familiar icon of Bakhtinian dialogue, the hermeneutic one, only to find that this "false" reading may have been a calculated trap or moment in Bakhtin's own double-dissimulation.

The specularity which a certain de Man refuses yet differently enacts might be addressed in the use of "admire" or "admiration." The term is used to organize the intervention throughout, down through the later double reversal wherein the text feigns to "include" de Man on this list he at first exempted himself from: "What one has to admire Bakhtin for (that is, want to be in his place in having written what he wrote), as all his present readers, including myself, do, is his hope that, by starting out, as he does, in a poetics of novelistic discourse one may gain access to the power of a hermeneutics" (114). Here *admiration* exists outside the possibility of any "switching" of places, as a desire to be in the place of when writing, yet de Man's admiration is ironically effaced as the "hope" evinced is for what is never realizable, and becomes a weakness. What does it mean to admire or not to admire Bakhtin – to imitate, to (ad)*mirror*, to deface, to envy, to appropriate, to desire to substitute for? With whom is de Man conducting his battle of entrapment, the reader, the simulacrum "Bakhtin," another Bakhtin, another "de Man"? What may be rewritten as *a*(d)*mir*(ror)*ation* suspends or defaces the mock-specularity that Bakhtin seductively solicits from numerous readers. Yet the labyrinth also has no obvious exit. The obstacle presented to any subsequent reader is how to apply Rousseau's conception of "dialogue" to Bakhtin's own writing, yet in doing so to evade the appearance of merely "saving" Bakhtin from de Man (an ironic non-task). Why can we not "imitate or apply" Bakhtin – outside of a more critical reading of his text – without *betraying* (a harsh word) what may seem most valid in his project? To a certain degree, the ceaseless readjustments of de Man's attempt to undo a specular trap set for him (and engaged), registers a discrete horror of its uncontrolled dimensions – an aware-ness of all the calculable and inextricable variations in that public specularity by which both figures will come to be shaded, framed. At all events, the entire course of this history and non-encounter seems to present a fairly disruptive cipher by which the critical present tends to occlude its own precarious depositioning, having potentially regressed in its pan-mimetic habits to a site that must, once again, like the nightmare of an eternal recurrence or memory loop, work through rather than occlude this performative im-passe.

3. Transvaluating "Bakhtin"

Let us assume, for the moment, that concealed within de Man's staged agon as though with a "Bakhtin" he cannot either decon-struct nor absorb, which repeatedly opens a black hole absorbing critical force (the trap handed over by the hermeneutic commu-nity), are still other logics. In a distinct sense, de Man creates his text as a trap that cannot be gotten out of, but only *broken with* – yet it is also imbricated in the critical politics of the 1980s in a way with distinct resonance today. If anything, then, it seems one knife by which to force an exit from the enclosure of the American

Bakhtin without seeming to provide another. It is what is not in de Man's text, or the blindness and aggression that sustain its controlled vituperation and inscription in the general text of its audience that remain of interest here. I want to proceed, then, with the beginning of a reading which, decidedly not de Manian, nonetheless helps situate de Man's project of aesthetic ideology today – and a *materialistic* Bakhtin's confluence with it. Since just this reading has been (and remains?) excluded or repressed, it may be a necessary detour.

If de Man's reading of "dialogism" is the pragmatic or, indeed, materialist one – that dependent on a materialist conception of language – ME and Holquist's readings remain "subjective expressionist" in that sense dismantled by *Marxism's* evisceration of phenomenology, the text most crucial to rereading Bakhtin today. The ideology of dialogue is a prototype of ideological anamorphosis as evisioned by Žižek: the site where a piece of radical exteriority is enfolded as the dispossessing kernel for a discourse of interiority.[8] Yet de Man-Rousseau's model of dialogue as an agonistic encounter of inscription, seduction, and counter-entrapment may have all along been Bakhtin's own, blindly unread as such, as numerous textual analyses from the *Dostoyevsky* book rather explicitly testify – for example, in the penultimate analysis of Stavrogin's maneuvering with Tikhon over the inert (and unread) text of his "confession," or Zosima's interview.[9] In the prior a duplicitous battle for reverse empowerment is said to represent "the functions of the other person in dialogue, the other person as such, deprived of any social or pragmatic real-life concretization" (*PDP*, 264). In the example of Zosima and the "mysterious visitor" that *comments* on this one, the relation to the other is called "pure hatred toward 'the other' as such" (264). Bakhtinian "dialogue" here is precisely an engine of power, erasure, dislocation and representational murder, even as the figure of the "social" depends upon just that fact. While an interpretation of Bakhtin's writing as a duplicitous strategy was outlined by Holquist, it is at least interesting to ask not where Bakhtin provides us with new

---

[8] The dynamic of "ideological anamorphosis" is outlined in Slavoj Žižek's *The Sublime Object of Ideology*, 98–100.

[9] For an application of this "agonistic" reading of dialogue in multiculturalist terms, see Wlad Godzich, "Correcting Kant: Bakhtin and Intercultural Interactions."

critical terms – which has all along been uncertain, since so many of them are either very old (sign, ideology), or clunky neologisms (chronotope, heteroglossia) – but where the little remarked Nietzschean component makes the writing appear transitional, destructive (in Benjamin's sense, or ruinous in Kristeva's). Or, more specifically, *transvaluative*: en route to another site, itself non-mimetic, for which the Bakhtinian system might be understood as openly sacrificed rather than offered for canonization. (It should be recalled that the term "value" does not operate like a content or a motivating figure in *Marxism*: it is always also a retro-projection, co-extensive semantically with "ideology," "intonation," or "theme": both, moreover, are two-sided inflections *carrying* what alone matters semantically (as intonation), yet which doubleness is also reversibly put in play in carnival, menippea, ambivalent laughter, and so on.)

As noted earlier, Ernesto Laclau takes up the problem of a post-Marxist afterlife of the term "ideology" at a parallel juncture to the performative logic of Voloshinov's text. "Ideology," there, is not a key-term, but assimilated to an eviscerated series of other differential, contentless, and infratextual non-words (intonation, value, emotion). Noting "the progressive abandonment of 'ideology' as an analytic category," Laclau asks how the term survives a situation of discourse analysis where one can no longer utilize any notion of "distortion" (if there is no originary norm outside discourse) or "false consciousness" (if there is no other)?[10] This loss of any "extra-ideological ground supposed to provide the standard by means of which one can measure ideological distortion" (298) shifts the nature of the hunt.[11] What Laclau will want to term

---

[10] Ernesto Laclau, "The Death and Resurrection of the Theory of Ideology," 298.

[11] In his attempt to make Bakhtin yield a concrete "theory of ideology," Michael Gardiner comments ruefully that while everyone takes Bakhtin as addressing the social or dialogic other there is a near total absence of historical, representational, or mimetic analysis – a space without "institutional structures":

By suggesting that ideology is co-terminous with the process of signification itself (and by not developing a more precise conception of ideological processes in the negative sense), it is difficult for Bakhtin to maintain an image of ideology as a particular type of signifying practice which is intimately connected with the maintenance of class domination. As such, the "struggle over the sign" seems to be more of an expression of an abstract battle between forces of monologism and dialogism . . . In this, Bakhtin owes more to the metaphysics of Heraclitus (and to Nietzsche's duality of the Apollonian and Dionysian) than to Marx's historical materialism. What are the institutional parameters of the linguistico-ideological sphere? What are its historical configurations, its linkages to other social-cultural practices, to politics and the economy? . . . Accordingly, Bakhtin's dialogism precludes a social-historiographic analysis of the roots and dynamics of "monologism." (*The Dialogics of*

"constitutive distortion" can be recognized not by difference from
a non-distorted original but by way of the ceaseless ("constitutive") projection onto a figure or object the counter to this lack, "the
illusion of fullness and self-transparency that it lacks" (301), or
"the impossible fullness of the community" (303). Such corresponds in Voloshinov with the double critique of "subjective
expressionism" (phenomenology, "Freudianism") and "abstract
objectivism" (formalism, "Aristotelianism") out of which the theory of the self-differing and sheerly exterior "sign" evolves. It
would seem that from a *representational* notion of ideology critique
we have moved into a proactive or transformative domain, in
which a formalized trace of anteriority (inscription) supplants the
position once projected onto as "extra-discursive" real (historical
reference). Voloshinov's text implies a transformation of the signifying order it ironically inhabits: the emptying out of terms; the
auto-dismantling of every projected "fullness of the community"
(in *subjectivist* or *objectivist* codes); a shift from cognitive to performative language; the formalization of "content" (*another's
word, the dead word*); the projected deregulation of the temporal or
historicist logics by a precession of *chronotopic* "model(s) of reality" (as the polyphonic novel is called in a tacit invocation of *The
Birth of Tragedy*). That Bakhtin seems to get (theoretically) arrested
by the "modernist" moment of this trajectory – as at the point
called carnival or "novel" – tends to convert his text into the
ruined monument of a still virtual event. *Ideology* in this sense
tends always to connote mimetic ideology, the site where a logic
of inscription is countered by the chiasmic pretenses of a conven-
tionally descriptive language – one routinely inverted, anamorphic, defensively congealed.

Some directions for this reading might now be indicated. One
necessity would be reading Voloshinov's *Marxism* not only as a
performative but as an allegorical text – that is, one that reflexively

Critique: M. M. Bakhtin and the Theory of Ideology, 177–8)

Yet if Bakhtin resists translation (back) into a mimetic or referential rather than a
performative model, Voloshinov's treatise already implies a different *translation*
of "Marx's . . . materialism," one perhaps echoed in Benjamin's "materialistic
historiography," or more recently by Derrida's *Specters of Marx*. Bakhtin's
concepts of the *alien* or *other's* or *dead word* – all of which tend, eschewing
subjective (phenomenological, Freudian) and objectivist (formalist-structural-
ist, mimeto-historicist) models, to slide into one another – purvey the site of *an
anteriority that already is received as mnemonic or material inscription.*

turns up so as to alter the very signifying order from which its discourse advances. One would want to account for where in Bakhtin an anamorphic logic is frequently projected across a temporal narrative or axis, as when carnival or dialogue is said to follow in some genealogical sequence a monologic or epochal period. In such cases, the "prior" terms appear preceded or framed by categories that, like carnival, have no "before or after." It would also examine the positing of pseudo-terms or pseudo-concepts (dialogue, genre, ideology, the social) that, strategically unmarked in their difference, systematically empty the "official" meanings they cite.

What is this *other* Bakhtin, then, produced through and despite de Man's reading? The multiply inverted strategy of admiring defacement – which I have in passing termed de Man's a(d)mir(ror)ation of Bakhtin to the precession, here, of mere specularity – would not simply promote an *ironic* Bakhtin, though that would be plausible in a writer who uses "a still formal method by which to conquer or sublate formalism itself." The Bakhtin first depicted as void of tropes (who "excludes trope from literary discourse") appears now reversed and overtly tropological. It is possible, then, to read Voloshinov's *Marxism and the Philosophy of Language* not as a treatise on the "philosophy of language" but as a performative work whose title would undermine each concept it named ("Marxism," "Philosophy," "Language" as linguistics). The text properly appears as a duplex writing strategy that covertly consumes a literary subtext it means to subvert, that being none other than Hegel's *Phenomenology* – after which it is, at first, almost parodically modeled. The work presents itself as a "phenomenology" of precisely what renders any phenomenology impossible, the materiality of what is given the name sign. What comprises this "materiality" remains a central heuristic question in the contemporary use of these works, and it is illuminated by a specular excess de Man's own work here solicits. The "materiality" mentioned in Voloshinov's *Marxism* has been misleading because of the ambiguous solicitation of "Marxian" categories (like "base"), solicitations that are isolated and disjunct (that is, not even subject to the systemic desemanticization that key terms like word or dialogue are, as it were, favored with). In fact, the figure of *materiality* appears here to have a double register: on the one hand, it means precisely materiality, in the sense of sound or scriptive trace; on the other, it implies that more or less absolute trace of *anteriority* that is heard in Bakhtinian topoi like the "alien," "dead," or *other's word* – which congeals the literal implication of materiality, here, with the mnemonic force of inscription divorcing it from any facile mimeticism like a Marxian "base" or referent. "Materiality," wedded to the word (and to its differential, desemanticized properties), is simultaneously the node at which anteriority is managed, programs or converts the site of transmission or utterance. This mnemonic materiality stands behind and eviscerates any mimetic apprehension of "dialogue" as immediacy, returning us to the de-anthropomorphized import of Voloshinov's analysis of a *triadic* utterance that posits the speaker's immediately displaced and auto-personified position at the price of its (linguistic) death and virtual inscription. "Materiality" in this Voloshinovian sense can never be reduced to a referential or metaphysic site but, between mnemonic and prephenomenal trace, remains a signature of sheer *exteriority*, the public, the social nonetheless.

This prospect shifts cultural criticism from "descriptively" using Bakhtin ("imitate or apply") to exploring where his conception of the social results less in a new set of academic typologies than a technological shift in the signifying order, within the material structure of mimesis. One of the consequences of this is the closure of all models of interiority, including any theological use of the word "social" itself. *Marxism* might best be read as a (fictional or literary) text that projects across a narrative axis a movement – from sign (a covert reversal of Saussure's figure) or inner speech outward to reported speech – that is in fact simultaneous. Pivotal figures like the "dead word" of formalism or the "alien word" ("this role of the alien word led to . . . the idea of authority, the idea of power, the idea of holiness, the idea of truth" (*MPL*, 75)) similarly return as mock historical allegories for the perpetual anteriority of citational language. Moreover, its conception of an "outer word" that constitutes "inner speech" ("nowhere is there a break in the chain, nowhere does the chain plunge into inner being" (*MPL*, 11), puts into question the trope of *exteriority* that it relies on as well. It is clearly such a reading of Voloshinov that the *Prosaics'* strategic exile of it from Bakhtin's own canon is designed to preempt. If the so-called American school aims to return Bakhtin to a category of interiority or "the self," this resubjectivization seems apparent in the chapter of the *Prosaics* on "Psychology: Authoring a Self," where Voloshinov's "outer word" – what, strictly, suspends any theory of psychology as such – is familiarized, simply, as "the fundamental tenets of Voloshinov's theory of psychology" (203). Where, here, is Voloshinov's *materiality* – what now, more than ever, appears allied to the "materialistic historiography" of Benjamin, or more insightfully still, de Man's "materiality" of inscription? How must that writing associated with these signatures be read, today, not as superseding mere linguistic formalism but as, first, ruptured and submitted to the translational logic of a *purely* material, exterior, or indeed formal dimension – what Benjamin terms *reine Sprache* – before and after which there can be no return to interiorist logics, and which simulates, in often unreadable ways, the proleptic passage gestured to repeatedly in the metaphoric theatrics of *Zarathustra*?[12] Does one witness across certain of Bakhtin's signatures, or emerging from their interface, not a literary, or sociological, or representational theory – not a critical apparatus to "apply" for archival purposes – but an incipient transformation of the one set of archival logics altogether in the name of an irrepressibly material or mnemonic movement, trace, and passage?

Bakhtin's unconvincing exclusion of the lyric may be a clue here, since what it technically represses may be the apostrophic model of utterance that appears in the only detailed sketch of the dialogic utterance we have, Voloshinov's "Discourse in Life and Discourse in Art." It may be of value to resituate it – particularly with reference to de Man's concerns with apostrophe. Analyzed in the example of the utterance "Well!" made at the sight of a snowfall in May, the social scenario of dialogue turns out to be neither social nor dialogic in the received (and perpetuated) sense of each. It is not the unmediated interaction of two persons talking, but *triadic* and even narcissistic in structure. Moreover, the second person or listener (called a "reader" (105)) is not even addressed, but seems to merely *over*hear a closed address to a third participant, one that is not necessarily human ("Who is this

---

[12] For a pivotal exploration of how such a principle of *reine Sprache* may be conceived to operate within Benjamin's text, see Werner Hamacher's, "The word *Wolke* – if it is one," in *Benjamin's Ground: New Readings of Walter Benjamin*, ed. Rainer Nägele (Detroit: Wayne State University Press, 1988), 147–176.

third participant? Who is the recipient of the reproach? The snow? Nature? Fate, perhaps?" (103)). Yet this performative, triadic anti-model prefigures "the social" as such, which in Bakhtin always begins with three and not two. When the third participant is brought into speech through personification or apostrophe, the second person must be antithetically positioned or seduced – hence inscribed – as "witness and ally" (103). Finally, the first person can be said at his own canceled pre-emergence into language to be representationally murdered or disfigured by instantly becoming a third person. In this agonistic model the listener or "reader" must usurp in retort the specular position of the first person as the system itself invariably rotates. The mock-specular scenario of "dialogue" in this model appears almost self-canceling as a mobile system, erasing and supplanting as it proceeds. If Bakhtin's "dialogism" involves, as both de Man and Holquist note, dissimulation before a disfiguring power, that might as readily be called the "discourse scenario" or even (metaphysical, "official") language *as* Stalin. Finally, such double-talk extends to the most familiar and assumed words that are deployed, like the word "social" itself. Bakhtin's "social" may at times appear to close out that concept, at least as what we too quickly translate as a familiar referential of history – and in this he recalls what Baudrillard announces as the "end of the social" (at least as the metaphysical reserve it is taken for) through the acceleration of simulacra; Bakhtin's "social" forecloses what Pechey termed mere "sociality as intersubjectivity."

It is interesting that for Bakhtin dialogue is *not dialogic* – and it is interesting that this seems almost *never* noted, as if it were a scandal. *It* can only exist or be mobilized by the Listener's (or Reader's) attempted usurping of an always *imaginary* position of a first speaker, in which the latter (who, personifying his addressee, can only simulate retrospectively the first person's position) is representationally always as if *murdered* by the act of speech, becoming in turn a third person – before "utterance." Apostrophe or prosopopeia in this way is applied not to the third person (impersonal, voiceless, dead) but the "first" (impersonal, otherwise voiceless). Rather than being static or nurturingly dialogical, Voloshinov's model appears to *rotate, displace and erase as it advances* – a threshing machine in which *I*'s are harvested before the fact, recuperable as citation. It is a model that one may not like or wish on one's friends, being violent, usurpative, and without repose – yet it is Bakhtin's. Yet to read Bakhtin through de Man raises other questions. In the text cited, "Well!" appears as the general type of any utterance, yet as "a word virtually empty semantically" (102) it is also "of a kind verging on *apostrophe*" (103) – one with a "tendency toward personification." That Voloshinov locates the origin of the utterance in the pre-mimetic trope of apostrophe places Bakhtin – that is, as the signature of an entire writing project – in working contact with de Man's use of prosopopeia or hypogram.[13]

If dialogue is actually a *tri*alogue dependent on a "third" figure, it is also a highly unstable scene of multiply shifting positions that are less constituted than performatively assumed. Moreover, the "third" figure that may not even (or must not) be human can also appear like a text or *inscription*. A rupture haunts the verbal scenario that both perpetually opens a possibility of freedom or historical intervention – the suspension of causal historical chains in carnival, with the potential, preceding "face" itself, to rewrite those – and forecloses that by producing the speaker as the after-effect of a sort of self-canceling model. Aside from asserting an agonistic model of a non-communicational dialogue obeying protocols of usurpation and defacement, any Nietzschean reading of Bakhtin must ask where Voloshinov's two-faced sign without interior or identity compels a transvaluation of every term caught in the chain ("each living *ideological* sign has two faces, like Janus" (23)). Voloshinov strategically used paleonyms such as ideology, or value, or intonation, or theme, or emotion – words void of content with nearly intersubstitutible roles – as the markers of dialogic *differance*. Utterances "are joined with one another and alternate with one another not according to the laws of grammar or logic but according to the laws of *evaluative* (emotive) *correspondence, dialogic deployment, etc.*" (38), "*the psyche effaces itself, or is obliterated, in the process of becoming ideology, and ideology effaces itself in the process of becoming the psyche*" (39) – the last inserting a tautological schema to empty, and disrupt, the mnemonic circle of

13 For varying treatments of Voloshinov's text on the utterance "Well!" see Juliet Flower MacCannell's "The Temporality of Textuality: Bakhtin and Derrida," Michael Holquist's "The Surd Heard: Bakhtin and Derrida." For a treatment of how this model might effect reading, see my "Bakhtin, *Othello*, and the Death(s) of Dialogue," chapter 1 of *Anti-Mimesis*, and my "Well! Voloshinov's Double-Talk."

conceptual reinscription. While *Marxism* subscribes to a linguistic invocation of ideology, it suspends any initial identity of "value," itself reversible or two-sided, a retro-identified effect. It thus places the value of *value* momentarily – albeit, it is an interminable, carnivalesque hiatus – into active suspense, emptying its received content and returning it as a post-Marxist trope in which "ideology" functions to mark any (regressive) appropriation of this trace in logics clumsily if accurately coded as culturally subjectivist or objectivist, in effect triggering a project in which a limitless allegorical deconstruction is projected as the material means of a historical transformation. It is this way that we might read what Bakhtin called Dostoyevsky's "criterion" of evaluation: "The possibility of simultaneous coexistence, the possibility of being side by side or one against the other, is for Dostoyevsky almost a criterion for distinguishing the essential from the nonessential" (*PDP*, 29). Voloshinov and Bakhtin not only situate *aesthetics* socially, as is generally noted and banally misread, but generate the social as an aesthetic – that is, material and linguistic – event. They render the materiality of "word" – which is also to say in different incarnations the "dead word," formalism, or writing – the prototype of experience (*"expression organizes experience"* (*MPL*, 85)). De Man's proto-definition of allegory in *Rhetoric of Temporality* as the commentary of a sign on anterior signs defines "consciousness" in *Marxism*, where sign "reflects and refracts another reality" (9) that is always another material sign. Where the *materiality of the word* – or another's word, anteriority as such, or *inscription* – is the prototype of aesthetic phenomenality or perception (*aisthanumai*), as it is in Voloshinov, ideology can be rewritten as an aesthetic or linguistic effect: "Language, so viewed, is analogous to other ideological phenomena, in particular, to art – to aesthetic activity" (*MPL*, 48). For Bakhtin, the materiality of the received sign or trace produces "perception': language – that is, the trajectory of the alien, dead or other's word in transposition – constitutes its *materiality-effect* not through a referential function (that defers the import of the linguistic moment by a pretense to transparency that everything in Bakhtin abjures), but through a differential movement of received and anticipated "word" traces not dissimilar to what Benjamin implies by *translation* (without meaning or expression, sheer material trace). Such an effect – which locates the "aesthetic" in this Nietzschean sense of prefigural and material or linguistic rhythm – is experienced in part by a voiding of received sense covertly entailed by "Bakhtin's" own words: sign (now without content), ideology (shorn of false consciousness), value, dialogue, novel, and so on. Terms, that is, that not only *sabotage* their own translations (the diverse appropriations of subjectivist and humanist or objectivist and semiotic "Bakhtins" respectively), but anticipate collectively a *virtual* transformation in which the linguistic models of *expression* and representation are cross-epochally voided.

One may note, briefly, where this account leads – as de Man was no doubt aware and wished to avoid. That is, to viewing Voloshinov's proposed "science of ideologies" as a dissimulative project essentially allied to de Man's proposed analysis of aesthetic ideology (what has the secondary benefit of reading de Man as "Marxist"). Aesthetic ideology for de Man, of course, means a number of things, including the ideology of what is (or is not) dismissed by us as the aesthetic, and the manner in which the formalization of linguistic properties generates the effects we call ideology. It is entirely possible to view *Marxism*, then, as a strong and covertly Nietzschean reading of the *German Ideology*, unpacking the latter's address of language as "practical consciousness." The resistance to the numerous "Nietzschean" implications of Bakhtin's linguistic materialism has been relentless. While reducing the question to one of mere influence represents, it seems, another instance, it is the overlap between a both too present and occluded "Marx" and occluded if too obvious Nietzsche (sometimes located under another signature, like "Dostoyevsky") that looms perhaps as the most violently foreclosed site of this crypt.[14] Among other things, since it partakes of an irrecuperable translation of both – a reading of Marx, for instance, that while wholly unmarked presages that of Derrida's *Specters of Marx*. That is, a site where the prospect of historial action associated with Marx's

---

[14] For a consideration relating Voloshinov's use of sign to Nietzsche's in *The Gay Science*, see Samuel Weber (1985), and otherwise James M. Curtis "Michael Bakhtin, Nietzsche, and Russian Pre-Revolutionary Thought," in *Nietzsche in Russia*, ed. B. Rosenthal (Princeton: Princeton University Press, 1986), 331–355, and my "Reading a Blind Parataxis: Dostoyevsky (Nietzsche) Bakhtin," where the argument is made that Dostoyevsky is, in part, a signature for Nietzsche in Bakhtin's text. It should go without saying that the argument, here, has nothing to do with some study of "influence" (Nietzsche "on" Bakhtin, say).

materialism is transposed within the logics of mnemonic intervention, a "materiality" re-programmed by a monadic logic of the
séance irreducible to the mimetic or ontological reading of Marx
(what would explain, more than the problem of censorship, or a
secret right-wing agenda, the evaporation of overt Marxian alliance within Bakhtin's "own" double-signature). That such a
supposedly nihilist Bakhtin returns today as the domesticated
neo-Kantian crank or the apostle of benign communication theory
today is only one irony (albeit a particularly bitter one). While a
critical recalibration of Bakhtin may be underway, as it seems at
times in *Bakhtin and Cultural Theory*, one could excuse a call along
the lines of Baudrillard's *Oublier Foucault* to "forget Bakhtin," or
at least the more public and mock literal Bakhtin that has
saturated the critical horizon with compromised formulations. It
may be that Bakhtin's text has practiced a mode of rhetorical
entrapment against its fondest readers all along: a virus that eviscerates its predictable host languages.

A last aside on de Man's reading. If Bakhtin's metaphor of
intentionality as verbal "light-ray" can be depicted as a trope of
trope concealing "a reflective system of *mise en abyme*" anything
but dialogical, the modernist Bakhtin who is betrayed or who does
the betraying of others (or "the other") appears more problematic
still. Thus we read in "Discourse in Life" the following passage,
which links the figure of "light" not to cognition but to *value*: "They
(social evaluations) have entered the flesh and blood of all representatives of the group . . . We seem to perceive the value of a thing
together with its being as one of its qualities, we seem, for instance,
to sense, along with its warmth and light, the sun's value for us, as
well. All the phenomena that surround us are similarly merged
with value judgments" (101). The text evokes a mock-solar poetics
which precedes phenomenality, producing sense or nature as an
effect of material signs and placing "value" side by side with sense
impressions or phenomena ("along with its warmth and light").
The only possible "trope for trope" proceeds, then, as a figure in
which the "sun" has no priority, value no claim. The logic indicates
a certain nihilism in a *positive* sense obvious in carnivalesque
laughter, one which Bakhtin's interpreters back-pedal from furi-
ously – not because it is irrecoverably tragic, but because it casually
empties out the vocabulary (sign, ideology, consciousness) and
claims to *interiority* they remain mimetically dependent on. When,

pages later, Voloshinov discusses the "hero" of his triadic discourse scenario (the addressee), the "sun" appears not as a center but merely one personified object on a list of equal virtualities including "thought" itself: "How often we shake our fist at 'someone' in a fit of temper or simply scowl at empty space, and there is literally nothing we cannot smile at – the sun, trees, thoughts" (104). Rather than locating discourse in a new (old) referential sociology, Bakhtin resituates a linguistic materiality that precedes any mimetic formulation and therefore the very topos of the human. Hence, for Bakhtin, the phenomenon that is called the "social" is, rather than the metaphysical heart of human meaning, like *inscription*, an exterior and allohuman site.

We must now regard "carnival" less as a figure bursting with life and the rule of immediacy than as a formalistic or *faux* mimetic trope that, difficult to leave, in the end evades the *transvaluation* Voloshinov's text began with its radical modification of inherited terms. It pays the price of assenting, for too long, to the fictions of Bakhtin's modernist subterfuge. If so, it would be in the essay on *chronotopes* that Bakhtin attempts, and fails, to cross beyond this site – by imposing a differential typology on types of "carnival" and presenting them as a serial or narrative (literary) history leading to a "metamorphosis" as if *beyond* Bakhtin's own text.[15] As an allographical turning upon and against the mock-representational status his writing pretends to, as an interdiction of the auto-reproduction of that archive, the chronotope essay projects (beyond itself) not another *descriptive* typology for application but a reconfiguration of the cross-historial – the template of a *chronographics* to come, of inter-active inscriptive monads and conceptions of times.

The point of juxtaposing de Man and Bakhtin in this way is not to recuperate "de Manian reading," whatever that now would be (or if it ever existed), but to use the one encounter that has proven indigestible to the Bakhtin industry to help us intervene in that genealogy and impasse which haunts present cultural studies. What emerges from this juxtaposition, however, is that the apostrophic monster "de Man/Bakhtin" could appear anti-dotal for a

---

[15] An example of the remarkably flat "use" of chronotopes, as if these were descriptive models, might be Katerina Clark, "Political History and Literary Chronotope: Some Soviet Case Studies," in *Literature and History: Theoretical Problems and Russian Case Studies*, 230–247.

reigning and misleading binary that has (im)mobilized much historical and cultural criticism – the scapegoating of the problem of the materiality of language, its cold war otheration, ME's "theoreticisms," during a "return to history" that has not been unilaterally successful. It may turn out, that is, that the fall/rise of Bakhtin tells the story of an appropriation of the figure of history by a still regressive mimetic ideology. We return to the first question: what does *this* genealogy of the American Bakhtin say to cultural studies – and why does a return to the question of "materiality" (one earlier considered formalist) point to a different *pragmatics*? One, that is, different from either the humanist typologies of ME or the frequently descriptive poetics of British cultural studies – a pragmatics I would tentatively call less "Nietzschean" than that of a certain *NietzscheMarx*. I will return to the seemingly monstrous or discomfiting hybrid outlined before – "de Man/Bakhtin" – to suggest some directions for assessing what has resided beneath this whole scenario all along.

4. Dialogue as inscription; or, the mnemotechnics of cultural transformation

The prospect of a post-Marxist, post-deconstructive "Bakhtin" raises questions about where Bakhtin might be located now in cultural studies, or if the latter stands to undergo a fundamental reorientation in its project. Such a shift would be away from representational and context-centered "studies" that remain determined by a mimetic logic and toward a transvaluative or transfigural agenda that reconfigures different forms of mimesis and their dependence in relation to the materiality of language: the element most suppressed in the "Bakhtin" of the 1980s.

The question returns to why there has been a neo-conservative consolidation going into the late 1990s. The apparent error both of the retro-humanist right and certain leftist agendas in the 1980s can seem reflected in the general scapegoating of theory, or language centered analysis – the same gesture, say, that ME turns against "Marxism" in the final move on this gameboard. What certain left agendas participated in might be called a mimetic ideology: that is, a regressive desire for the immediacy or transparency of reference which, among other things, "dialogue" seemed to proffer, a desire which satisfied itself that post-structuralist discourse (by now, a code-name) represented the aes-theticizing obstacle to the more serious mission of engaging his-tory or recontracting the "subject's" political agency. Under the aegis of a certain definition of the political, such agendas could be assimilated to the right's requirement for a new foundationalism – and this alliance, irritating to the self-image of the first, no doubt, had become quite common. It could then be disciplined through official institutional organs when necessary, something made relatively easy when global Marxism was seemingly discredited. What may have been less obvious was that the sacrificial logic applied against the linguistic model (the case of deconstruction) was not only in ways self-mutilating but one that echoed, by inversion, the binary gesture of a cold war epoch – an inverting, perversely nostalgic gesture for the left. The partial result was the spectacle of leftist itineraries that depended not only on historiciz-ing logics but the covert effort to restitute interiorist economies of meaning. What the "story" of Bakhtin's production now suggests is that aspects of the politically progressive trends of the 1980s had in fact been regressive – as various identity politics and new historicisms now confirm – and must return to interrogate prob-lematics of figuration and linguistic materiality to recalibrate the tasks of cultural criticism *as historial intervention*. It may be, in this *entr'acte*, that the machinery of mimetic thought has been the most seductive and conservative force, bending the best intentioned critical ground-swells slowly back to service the very archivism that seems, today, to have programmed if not consolidated the more destructive itineraries of deferral and consumption that hostage the future. Among other things, cultural critique depend-ent upon installed habits of thinking mimesis, referentiality, or action stands to be reterritorialized if it is to exceed merely form-ing another archive within the greater field of a largely nihilistic humanism. For cultural criticism, one may anticipate a "Bakhtin" who does not lend himself to the further production of historicist narratives but to the abrupt alteration of signifying orders and systems of mimesis as such – of which, today, few activities seem more broadly political. What may be at stake is a fundamental shift from a mimetic (restorative, referential, foundationalist) to a transformative and transvaluative model – what dissolves, in the process, the model of the model. It is an intriguing aspect of the "human condition" that such cannot be installed without alterations in the province of memory, the management of anteriority, a rupturing of auto-referential humanism, the dissolution of inherited concepts into formally differential nodes – in short, a mnemotechnics for which the materiality of inscription is a pragmatic and desemanticizing point of reference.

We may selectively review (or caricature) several phases in the genealogy or translation of "Bakhtin" to make this point. First, the appropriation of the trope of "dialogue" for an ideology of self and other helped open a controlled and unthreatening discourse of difference in hermeneutic exchange whose primary use was to counter "deconstruction." Secondly, the deployment of Bakhtin's mock-typologies was used to promote a new *descriptive* poetics (despite *the absence of all historicism* in Bakhtin's work). Thirdly, focus on a more extended definition of the "dialogic," viewed against the context of "official language," yielded the Foucaultian Bakhtin of new historicism and cultural studies. It is at this point that the concealed *ressentiment* of ME's agenda at once returns to the ideological closure of the first move and, involuntarily, exposes the dependence of the other Bakhtins on this initial (mis)translation as well. The great value of ME's study may be to have exposed and imploded this narrative construction by displaying the inner logic of *this* Bakhtin all along as neo-conservative, as absurdly shorn and curtailed – a figure that even the leftist "Bakhtin," immeasurably more valuable, intricate and sophisticated, could not quite escape the determination of. Yet what, if anything, supersedes these phases?

Several possibilities emerge which would no longer be possible to unify as a specific agenda (or narrative). The consequences of foregrounding a certain "materiality" to which we have given the chimerical yet transmorphic label NietzscheMarx might include that:

> 1) The dyadic or hermeneutic reading of Bakhtinian "dialogue" – a model installed and defended by the American slavicists – is supplanted by the triadic, disruptive model which involves an overtly agonistic arena of usurpation and defacement. Here the projected and never realized position of speaker is dispersed among a series of effects and agencies. In this model the situation of the personified "third" figure (Thing, inscription, hero, *speaker* by turn) opens a

93

previously closed scenario of meaning to a non-human or material site as well. This scene of perpetual power plays in which no "one" ever unifies the speaker's position literally suspends the reinstallation of any descriptive model.

2) The linguistic "materiality" that is again foregrounded in this Bakhtin has certain consequences associated with a reconceptualization of the "social," a figure that itself now passes through memory, inscription, technology, visibility. For the social, the public, the visible are here linked not to a mimetic reference (the *old names* dismantled by Voloshinov), but to a sheer exteriority from which no interiorist model can return. The materiality of language here represents less a retreat to aesthetic preoccupations divorced from history than a reconfiguration of historical agency. Here, of course, the "aesthetic" is re-defined – along with sign, word, ideology, or dialogue for Bakhtin, and virtually every key term in de Man – and returned to its root sense in conjunction with perception, or where what is called "perception" appears a programmed mode of reading, of what Benjamin calls the "sensorium." It would seem that the ideologeme we still call "modernism," which while pretending to periodize is routinely used to frame (and contain) what is termed a kind of aestheticization, stigmatized through such anti-mimetic clichés as auto-reflexivity which we associate with linguistic functions, might be read as a cultural-historical moment in which sign-systems inherited themselves stood to be purged by remarking the material, non-human *pre*mises of historical "events." If it is useful to shift from the name "Bakhtin" to positing, for heuristic purposes, the more chimerical "Bakhtin/de Man," it is also to examine a few consequences of the system MarxNietzsche.

3) Rather than being at the heart of some interior model of textuality, inscription ("the materiality of inscription" in de Man) appears one name for the site of publicness, of "the social," of consciousness, or the aesthetic. This chain is charted in Bakhtin/Voloshinov. Inscription or, more accurately, *ex*scription resides at the anterior site of authority to be maneuvered about, publicly seduced, or usurped by the stakes for power of "dialogue" – not between a speaker and a listener, but between (at least) two speakers positioning

deferred virtual others as listeners, impersonating the "speaker's" position itself as *strategic* readers of a "hero" (text or inscription) that, in turn, anticipates a rhetorical counter-personification by the simulated, spectral, usurping listener: no one ever quite occupies the first person's position as such (I, the King, Being). In a sense, historical intervention occurs through a mnemotechnic altering of the model or power of a signifying cluster or program. Each possible or gambled future involves the backloop of a katabasis, a visit to the underworld bent on altering an inscription. In this way Donna Haraway has spoken of one task of the post-humanist landscape as "resetting the stage for possible pasts and futures" – and, in her case, one of the tools of this is leveling speciesist discriminations between animal, human, and machine.[16] Yet like Benjaminian *Jetztzeit*, the structure of "dialogue" represents a permanent disruption in the historical continuum. Bakhtin's actual model of "voice" may be less reminiscent of Buber's *I and Thou* than of Avital Ronell's conception of the telephonic switchboard in *The Telephone Book*.[17] Indeed, the strongest use of Bakhtin's categories may not be one that pretends to a descriptive access to history. While such uses have proven fertile, we may well want to ask from now on how *active* participation in Bakhtin's project involves a sacrifice as well: that, perhaps, of the descriptive model. This is already undertaken in anamorphic terms like chronotope, dialogue, carnival, or laughter – terms that must, as we saw with ME's

[16] The quote I have in mind occurs in "Ecce Homo, Ain't (Ar'n't) I a Woman, and Inappropriate/d Others: the Human in a Post-Humanist Landscape': "These are moments when something powerful – and dangerous – is happening. Figuration is about resetting the stage for possible pasts and futures. Figuration is the mode of theory when the more 'normal' rhetorics of systemic critical analysis seem only to repeat and sustain our entrapment in the stories of the established disorders. Humanity is a modernist figure; and this humanity has a generic face, a universal shape" (9).

[17] *The Telephone Book* (Lincoln: University of Nebraska, 1988). One could, indeed, easily see the trajectory of de Man's focus on "reading" as a dissolution of the monumental age of the book rather than its re-fetishization. The dissolution of a hermeneutic system that has fetishized the book can take place through, e.g. de Man's micro-textual release of what – invoked under the name "text" – moves towards a sheer technicity of linguistic memory, networks of relays, transmissions, performative figures. These no longer uphold an era of the "book" as such, without perceiving that as supplanted by some "other" technology or media simply.

monograph, be hysterically *policed* by editorial interests.

4) One of the implications of the phrase "aesthetic" ideology is that the very manner in which the *aesthetic* is defined – itself the cipher for linguistic materiality – underlies various political systems. (Another way to say this is that there is a frequently unexamined politics to how referentiality is constructed and processed as knowledge, information, power, and how perception (*aisthanumai*) derives from this.) For the post post-Marxist "de Man/Bakhtin" the term ideology is not only removed from any field of "false consciousness" or utopian narrative. What we call "ideology" appears not only as the inevitable contextualization of sense on behalf of diverse interests, but a virtual regression and evasion, almost always in terms of mimetic tropes and (for Bakhtin) "subjectivist" or "objectivist" turns.

De Man's "late" text – with its move toward the prefigural, prosopopeia and inscription – may have been misread on the whole through his protracted focus on systems of tropes and undecideability. Bakhtin/de Man – particularly where the latter turns toward the premimetic figures of hypogram and prosopopeia – effortlessly supersedes Žižek by designating the real not as an "impossible" *Ding-an-sich* but as a facticity of inscription *preceding* face or figure. This conception of the power, materiality, and anteriority of inscription – at once de Manian and Bakhtinian – does not only recall the format of Althusserian ideology (or the ISA). If intervention in such an apparatus can only be thought of as interrupting or disinstalling a certain memory grid or system of relay – if contesting these historical implants is one broader implication of "dialogue" – both de Man's focus on materiality and Bakhtin's *trope* of *a dialogics* proffer tools of reading that are, prospectively, pragmatic and technical rather than "descriptive."[18] For instance, de Man's use of hypogram as an elusive site in which inscription precedes and precipitates the effect of apos-

---

[18] The figure of inscription is, accordingly, adopted by those working to efface a self-mutilating binary between the political and theory. An example occurs in Judith Butler's *Gender Trouble*: "within the sex/gender distinction, sex poses as 'the real' and the 'factic,' the material or corporeal ground upon which gender operates as an act of cultural *inscription* . . . The question is not: what meaning does that inscription carry within it, but what cultural apparatus arranges this meeting instrument and body, what interventions into this ritualistic repetition are possible?" (143–146)

trophe – a coming to voice, or face, which the *gramme* simultaneously bars the arrival of – provokes the virtualization of any
discursive or historical location. This, like what Benjamin will
mean by invoking the notion of "states of emergency" (*Ausnah-
mezustände*), or emergence, which break up a fixed chain of historicist determinations in order to re-open, and re-negotiate, a
historial network. The Lacanian "Thing" – Žižek's "sublime object of ideology" – may be defined not as a gothic prosopopeia of
the inanimate (supposedly "uncanny" for recalling where the
human is itself such), but as the facticity of public inscriptions
around and against which discursive eddies coagulate in inverting, anamorphic clusters. For de Man the labor of a figure like
prosopopeia (Voloshinov's "apostrophe") appears less that of a
trope to be identified here and there than a *technique* for preceding
representation, and this to interrupt and intervene in an always
already situated (representational) history, a return to virtuality.
There is even a way in which a new humanism lies in the path of
this post-humanism – though in any case, what "Bakhtin/de
Man" here presents suggests an active rather than mimetic approach to representational-memory. And hence to a conception of
the social, the material, the mnemonic, and the public that dissoci-
ates the idea of the political from being exclusively determined by
a regressive referentialisms which, to some extent, arrested critical culture within the specular detour of the late 1980s. Once this
mnemotechnics is more fully explored, the post-Marxist and post-
deconstructive de Man/Bakhtin may appear, in name, secondary
or even irrelevant.

3

Mnemotechnics: time of the séance, or the mimetic blind of "cultural studies"

[O]ne could say that your study is located at the crossroads of magic and positivism. That spot is *bewitched*. Only theory could break the spell . . .

Adorno to Benjamin, a letter

The archivization produces as much as it records the event.

Derrida, *Archive Fever*

1. The three "cultural studies"

How, today, can we speak of an archival politics that takes into account the reflexive paradox involved in any attempt to intervene in a representational or ideological program? How, in the instance of a "cultural studies" which has superseded the interests of so-called "high theory" with stunning success, can a suspicious regression to precritical representationalism suggest a reinscription in more traditional models that must, now, be interrogated – as though moving back to the subject, back to a phenomenological "body," back to a pan-mimeticism whose political credentials may be more assumed than real, back to a kind of mimetic-humanism? How may notions of the pragmatic, the everyday, or the empirical echo nonetheless with a suspiciously idealist logic – particularly if a true archival politics involves not so much opening a new set of co-ordinates within a received mode of memory management, a mere re-territorializing, but altering how a given archival logic may function, generate time, police hermeneutic decisions?

We will here present an argument *for* "cultural studies" – or at least a way of conceiving it that perhaps remains virtual today. For I would suggest that there are at least three (American) "cultural studies" as constituted in the current scene: first, a sort of initial transposition into *practical* projects of so-called theoretical agendas, followed by a sort of *secondary* revision of this movement (grouped with the label of "cultural studies," given a genealogy, returned to a familiar referential model that precisely was to have been transformed at first), and a third "cultural studies" – a mnemotechnics, virtual and implied by these first two, but still *to come*. The second I will call a cultural studies imaginary or the political imaginary of "cultural studies" – a way this project has been genealogized, appropriated within critical politics, stigmatized and hailed as a "sociological" enterprise. What I will argue for will be, in fact, the "third" way – but of that in a moment.

One can locate a prehistory in the term, then, that continues to delineate what I will call a "mimetic blind" of cultural studies today – that site where, seeming to present itself as a *descriptive* enterprise, it is subtly returned to an "older" representational or epistemo-critical model which (to protect a political imaginary that is programmed by that) argues for a separation of the epistemological from the "political."[1] It is not accidental that one of the ideological gestures inherent in cultural studies (or, more obviously, its American pragmatist wing) is the bracketing of what it calls epistemology or "theory" or philosophy – as though the latter could be ejected in a safe return to the practical and

---

[1] This characterization is at best provisional, if what we call "older" itself conforms rather to what, throughout canons of interpretation, may be called a perpetual revision and often chiastic defense formation before the virtual events that key texts stage. We might advert to how this sense of a historially produced and politically invested signifying order is addressed in F. Kittler's *Discourse Networks* 1800/1900 (1990). Introducing and summarizing Kittler, David Wellbery calls this epistemo-aesthetic regime "hermeneutics" and notes its material mode as an installed management of what Benjamin might have termed the "sensorium": "hermeneutics draws on and ratifies a specific rendering of linguistic materiality . . . [T]his myth appears less as a philosophical hallucination than as a function of instructional practices and technologies. Far from being our natural or human condition, hermeneutics merely results from specifically trained coordination of children's eyes, ears, and vocal organs. It is a discipline of the body" (Foreword, x). He adds: "as long as we continue to operate within the hermeneutic paradigm we are paying homage to a form of language processing long since deceased" (xi).

6789

political.[2] This complex positioning risks being diverted into what I will term *a historicism of the present* – a retro-humanist, retro-mimetic frame oblivious to what we will name, with Benjamin, a "materialistic" basis for such interventions in the historial. These virtual interventions (virtual, since requiring responses, counter-signatures, and implementations that can only be initiated) occur, if and where they do, as episodes of (dis)inscription. Their possibility implies a politics of memory, or mnemotechnics – recalling, if still vaguely, such moments in Nietzsche's *Genealogy*. They presuppose a reflexive, transformative focus on the "site" or place – Benjamin calls this a prehistory, or sometimes *Ursprung* – from which the very protocols of perception, value or decision are mutatingly prescribed. Of the first two "cultural studies" I will be most concerned with the second, its political imaginary, or how the latter seems to reframe and denature the "first" (though there is, perhaps, no real chronology here). This occurs in an aesthetico-political move – that is, a programming of how the senses interpret and are "experienced" – that must be remarked: it narrates an identity of "cultural studies" by dividing it from (and against) the epistemological problematics associated with "theory." This is usually presented as a return to the domain of the practical, the everyday, the lived, the body. This is the *frame* or frame-*work* today – that which links an american trajectory of "cultural studies" to Habermasian communication, or Bourdieu's contextual-institutional historicism, or that pretends to trace it to an origin in a fairly narrow but pointedly anglophone British socio-pedagogical project which "American" cultural studies may really have little to do with, except for the mimetic legitimation offered by the specter (that is, the promise and the remnant) of sociology and ethnography to academic humanities.[3] (Certainly *American* "cultural studies" ritually returns in its British namesake to an *Anglo* paternity by which alien, dialectical, or francophone influences might be purged.[4]) Yet the quest for legitimacy through socio-

---

[2] This is the primary thesis of Cornel West's *The American Evasion of Philosophy: A Genealogy of Pragmatism* (1989), on behalf of multiculturalist politics.

[3] In the case of Habermas, we have witnessed this reverse genealogizing before – what resembles an opportunistic bird laying an egg in another's nest, imperiling the resident's whose eggs hers simulate: what occurs, precisely, with a so-called "Frankfurt school" Habermas had little to do with but wanted the ersatz pedigree and legitimacy of.

[4] Stuart Hall, among the offerings collected in *Cultural Studies*, ed. L. Grossberg, C. Nelson, and P. Treichler (New York: Routledge, 1992), expresses consternation

descriptive figures often returns "cultural studies" to *mimetic* logics and epistemological models all too proximate to the archival establishment of the academy it had, sought to displace. The moments of "cultural studies" I would address involve, clearly, both the politics of naming (or self-naming) and of taking or giving genealogies.

We might propose, to jump ahead, a critique of the second "cultural studies" in the name of *another* cultural studies that is at once virtual yet implied and even promised from the start. One can, no doubt, attempt a mock-description of this "second" (American) cultural studies: an anthology and delta-like alluvial plain of theoretical moves on marginalization, a flat and perhaps mistaken reading of Bakhtin, a recontextualization of the gestures of "new" historicism (absorbing its imaginary occlusion of a theoretical moment) projected onto pop cultural and "present" concerns, the bottom-up rhetoric that already contaminated the pretext of "identity politics" – and yet, however this narrative is constructed, there will always be a *break*, a sudden territorialization and just as abrupt reterritorialization.[5] For rather than being opposed to the itineraries of a language-oriented "theory," "cultural studies" began as a creative redistribution of its concerns. We will address this still other practice, this deferred model or "cultural studies" *to come*, under the category of the *séance*. By séance we will pretend to name a site disruptive of the incipient historicism that has been imposed, today, over the transformative

and non-recognition of the "institutionalization" American cultural studies had taken (285). When inverted to erect the controlling and canonical narrative of a lost "sociological" and anglo-phone origin, excommunicating an American hybridization of "cultural studies," this gesture has the same territorial and regressive potential as any metaphysical hierarchy.

[5] What Benjamin implicates with the term "historicism" leads beyond any definitional practice to return to an epistemological programming mired in a management of reference and time. In his evocation "historicism" undergoes a certain general translation and programmatization, to encompass an over-reaching narrative, referential, and interpretive itinerary. Nonetheless, the emergence of an American redaction of "cultural studies" out of new historicism cannot be overlooked, nor the tepid prescriptions offered for what, minimally, the term implies. See Patrick Braitlinger, for instance, in *Crusoe's Footprints* (New York: Routledge, 1990), where we are reminded that cultural studies "begins with the realization that reading the isolated 'classics' or 'great book' is not possible without also reading the larger 'cultural text' into which it fits" (22), a prescription usually adapted, as in new historicism, to a bottom-up political agenda (cited in Stanley Fish, *Professional Correctness: Literary Studies and Political Change* (New York: Oxford University Press, 1995), 78).

promise of "cultural studies" by a "cultural studies'" *political imaginary*. All séances, invoking the dead, do so to derive information from a still virtual past in order, in diverse ways, to *decide* futures – what today, and always, involves specific geo-political risk (I will conclude these notations by addressing a recent book by Andrew Ross dealing with eco-politics – that is, the way the political imaginary of "cultural studies" contests an uncertain materiality of what will be called, simply, "earth"). Implicit in the "materialistic" logic of the séance is a scene of reading that wills to precede the graphematic determinations of historically installed hermeneutics and referential models; turning the material traces of the language(s), alternative trace-chains, it stands to reshape how the archive reproduces itself and generates "laws."

There is, then, a more diffuse manner in which the epistemological is shaped politically and "experientially" by aesthetic and linguistic decisions that lie behind the familiar or installed claim to a pragmatic, everyday, referential, socio-historicist "politics." It is not without point that where "theory" had been received with routine hostility by traditional studies, cultural studies programs appear funded and, relatively, embraced – though the way this may economically solve, for administrative purposes, the pharmacological problem of inter-disciplinary study may prove short-lived.[6] Despite an ostensible shift in subject matter or terrain – popular culture for canonical texts – the overwhelming priority of the tradition lies in assuring no disruption of a prevailing epistemo-critical regime, reflected in the historicist mode of a familiar archive and its mimetic components. The referent may change, and tolerate whatever rhetorical claims that spawns, so long as the mechanics of reference itself resides, like a law or grammar, at the heart of discursive production. The ersatz empiricism of a British "sociological" model seems less to open cultural studies to historical transformation than supply a long installed mimetic regime with new names and objects to feed it from the contemporary field and mass culture. What results, I have suggested, can be called *a historicism or, let us now add, an archivism of "the present."* This would explain the ease of its em-

---

[6] For an analysis of the autithetical role that "cultural studies" serves in the mutating service industry that the "university" promises to become in assuming a corporate, rather than a statist, ideology, see Bill Readings, *The University in Ruins* (Cambridge MA: Harvard University Press, 1996), 89–119.

brace by too familiar institutions, though the stakes are more extreme. What, after all, is a "present" – what is *its* time – if it itself, in being addressed and collected, is converted (back) into a new-older *archivism* (let us keep the term "older" open for further inspection): such a "present" is, per definition, itself doubly deferred, lost, even as the archaisms of linear time and causal narratives appear re-installed to ensure this deferment under a long (dis)installed aesthetico-political regime or even model of reference (as with the promise of appearing "sociological" *as such*). Rather than engagement and transformation – which implies a shift within the epistemo-political model, in the *sensorium* (which is always already a hermeneutic), we generate another archive. The specter of intervention is defused by a system which the "second" cultural studies (but now, which?) serves unaware.

The political promise of "cultural studies" – its claims to reference, the everyday, effectivity, the pragmatic – may be imaginary to the extent it is programmed by a politico-aesthetic model linked to *historicism* that precludes the very interruption of prescribed causal chains which any politics of the future, "today," must invoke. This brings us to a last problem that marks this territory as strangely *spellbound* (to cite from Adorno's letter to Benjamin, yet also to allude to a film of Hitchcock's dealing with mnemotechnics and the prefigural). That is, that "cultural studies," unlike almost every other critical program we have witnessed – deconstructionism, say, or new historicism, or "identity politics" as such – *seems unable to die*, as though exempt from cycles of dominance and withdrawal. Instead it spreads, absorbing and assimilating styles, persisting *as if without other*, *as if* at or beyond the "end" of a received construct of (critical) history – descriptive corollary to a near or coming global installation of formal democracy.

Any séance that would invoke, or question, the logic of "cultural studies" would encounter this paradox: that it cannot "die," not because – in its *second* format (that already of a perceived repetition, as is, however, the "first") – it eschews a certain effect of death (the allohuman, the material, the linguistic-mnemonic), or because as *a historicism of "the present"* it evacuates that same present in advance, but because it never quite existed – nor could. Because, even in its "first" moment, it remains oriented toward a future transformation of the archival, which in the second revision gets if anything re-installed, totalized and without other.

What is, now, such a historicism of the present, and what interests does it serve? How would the very return to the real, to lived life open, discretely, onto a new *thanatorama* of image consumption, whose immortality or deathlessness was purchased at an unusual price: this "cultural studies" cannot die (perhaps), because in another sense *it never quite existed* – at least, not as what it names or promises, neither as a rupture into otherness nor as a technical intervention in the historial as such. That is, to borrow a Benjaminian trope, it cannot contrive or spectrally stage its event as a "state of emergency" (*Ausnahmezustand*) or emergence, because – failing to put into danger, or gamble, the very models of reference or mnemonic management out of which possible presents and futures are produced – it must return to the very systematic that would permanently defer such rupture. "Cultural studies" appears vital, extremely present, alive; yet as an archive of that present it defers and fetishizes it like a corpse.

So we are brought to the third "cultural studies," which might be thought as antidote to the second and yet *implied or promised in the first*: a "cultural studies" to come, a virtual project that engages not a *mimetic* model, but one of inscription, a mnemonic politics out of which alternate models of reference, causality, the historial, and the "event" become possible. Before examining where and how such a model presents or fails to present itself, where the figure of (dis)inscription becomes thinkable in relation to materiality, we might recall an image Benjamin seems to perversely gift us.[7] It is in fact the non-existence of what is named or desired by "cultural studies," the failure of available models and imposed ideological grids (as sociology, as Enlightenment anthropology, as historicism), that testifies to an alternate political field.

When Adorno, critiquing Benjamin's work on Baudelaire, speaks of breaking a bewitched spot as if between descriptive "positivism" and invocative "magic" – as if, that is, what Benjamin was writing were descriptive *cultural studies* – he recommends a return to something called "theory" to break the spell. That "spot" would be bewitched, or spellbound, certainly, which

---

[7] Judith Butler, in *Bodies That Matter*, seeks to re-establish the problem of "materiality" in a double relation to the metaphorics of inscription and the body, in which the later serves, nonetheless, as a constitutive site. For a review of this trajectory, and a turn toward Derrida's text as a movement (still) beyond this re-inscription, see Pheng Cheah, "Mattering," *Diacritics*, 26, 1 (Spring 1996), 108–139.

endeavors to mount an emancipatory project which parallels, if not feeds, greater conservatism both in the academy and the national political environment generally; that, expounding the cultural topoi of the present, adduces an archivism of that present. Adorno does not fully realize where a less evident theorization resided in Benjamin's writing project, a praxis that will have had from the start different *names*. If we turn, peremptorily, to the term "allegory" as one such name, it is first to acknowledge that it, at least, *seems* dead – and seems to have been before it was even recirculated. Certainly Benjamin, who famously reconfigured the term, seems to have let it recede or at least fold into an dissimulative series of *non-terms* across his writing – for instance, as "shock," as a wholly revised figure of cinema even, and, in the end, as "materialistic historiography (*der materialistischen Geschichtsschreibung*)."[8] The last occurs in the *Theses on the Concept of History*, where the non-term "allegory" seems associated not with representation but an *epistemo-critical* event (a term used in the prologue to the *Trauerspiel*). We might recall, for now, that the so-called "modernist" revision of traditional allegory – itself an icon of mimeticism, a transcendental signified delivered from the coded sign – does not merely entail a *shift* from a pure representational form to one incorporating a reflexive account of a work's conditions of production (or consumption). Rather, in Benjamin's account it goes two critical steps *beyond*. First, collapsing any mimetic logic, it summons an *aesthetico-political model* out of which historical "experience" and the hermeneutic sensorium get produced and configured; and second, it does not proceed to *represent* that, but holds open the possibility of actively deforming and negating the signifying order out of which its own present had been generated – hence erasing the conditions of its own articulation. As Benjamin puts it in the *Trauerspiel*: "[Allegory] means precisely the *non-existence* of what it (re)presents" (*Und zwar bedeutet es genau das Nichtsein dessen, was es vorstellt*).[9] Differently put, it turns upon and reflexively alters the very trace-chains of

---

[8] Walter Benjamin, "Theses on the Philosophy of History," in *Illuminations*, 262; *Illuminationen*, 278. All German citations will be from the latter volume, listed after the English. The primary "return" of allegory in its own right occurs largely around Baudelaire – transposing the figure of the Baroque to that of modernity – and in *Zentralpark*.

[9] Walter Benjamin, *The Origin of German Tragic Drama*, 233; *Ursprung des deutschen Trauerspiels*, 265.

anteriority out of which its own moment would have been projected; warps and dislocates not only traditional mimetic models by marking and curtailing the latter's always *virtual* occurrence as an "event" (virtual, in so far as it requires to be activated, countersigned, selected, instituted repeatedly) but intervenes in the mnemonic order out of which diverse "presents" stand to be produced. (As de Man precises in "The Rhetoric of Temporality," *allegory* as the commentary of (material) sign on signs involves a deformation of *anteriority* as such, and with it any schema of successionist history.)[10] This returns us to the subtle danger inherent in the specter of any variations on the model of "cultural studies" that, structurally horizonless and without other, may be imprinted as *a historicism of "the present."*

There is an enigmatic moment in Benjamin's *Theses on the Concept of History*, a text we associate with the occasion of his suicide at the Spanish border, in flight from the Nazis – a moment invoked less for pathos' sake (death chosen, in a way, over the company of Adorno in New York), than because of how it crystallizes an assertion in the text.[11] For Benjamin *repeatedly* opposes his hyperbolic yet also pragmatic anti-program of historial intervention to what is called the "enemy" or *Feind* – and more specifically, with both a literal and allegorical referent, "fascism." He suggests a war within and between programs of representation

[10] That the relation of de Man to Benjamin has been taken as a routine assumption does not mean it has been calibrated in effective ways. A recent collection addressing itself to history, *Walter Benjamin and the Demands of History*, is introduced with – and against – a certain notion of this link in mind ("the pairing produces intricate problems (5)). This link is not really defined in the "Introduction," before it is quickly turned from with a certain coding of de Man's *Le Soir* episode as focal point ("Does de Man exorcise *Le Soir* by seeing through Benjamin's eyes, thereby acquiring a certain moral subjectivity and authority?" (6)). In fact, that this link is not established or explored widely to date may perhaps reflect less on a blockage, severe, in the digestion of de Man's emergent project than a desire to preserve a certain iconization of Benjamin – and is attested to by the mentioning of de Man, for all that, only once in all of the succeeding essays. It may be, that is, that this interface – de Man/Benjamin – has been another "given" that has been publicly tagged in order to archive or occlude it.

[11] Benjamin's *Passagen* is routinely translated as "Arcades," and has proven an evocative image for a virtual project, yet the term also, clearly, echoes an association with textual passages and the figure of passage, poretics itself: the implication of a site of translation, transport, within a mnemotechnic cultural text is lost with the mimetic translation of "Arcades." This problematic arises elsewhere, as in his commentary on Baudelaire's *passante* in "On Some Motifs in Baudelaire" (*Illuminations*, 155–200).

that extend incrementally beyond his immediate horizons – another war within that before him, upon the victory of which the shape not only of alternative futures, but of a past (he speaks of "the dead") out of which any future would have to be cast, depends. When we speak of "alternative futures" we can conjure this idea with reference to the seeming foreclosure of history which Benjamin encountered (at the time, the nazi conquest), but it would have to stand, as well, for the way in which received interpretive narratives in a historicist ideology preclude alternative modes of thought, or action, including transmorphed conceptions of the non-human or time: prospects that remain key, say, to addressing the accelerated evisceration of terrestrial resources in the machinery of mimeto-capitalism. At this point of decision, a "state of emergency" upon which the stormclouds of Euro-fascism descend, Benjamin does a peculiar thing. In naming this *enemy* he does not concern himself with Hitler, or the nazis, which would be easy and provide much pathos. Instead, the "enemy" has one clear name, and it is that of an epistemo-critical habit: *historicism*. One need only contrast the image of a jackbooted nazi to your usual new or old historicist – in my experience, usually nice people, often left-leaning if a bit passive aggressive – to register the profound scandal of this claim. Historicism, archivism, mimeticism: not just because it narrates events from the position, always deforming, of the *victor*, but because a received (or ceaselessly embellished and hence covered) ordering of "empty" continuous time, a specific machine of representation, works in itself to foreclose of what he will call, in the final avatar of allegory, *"materialistic* historiography." *The latter is epistemo-critical, of a purely aesthetico-political order.* Thus the trope of victory, here, if that is granted to "cultural studies" – and it routinely is – involves less a show of strength alone than a dialectic of violence, of retro-legitimation, perhaps of entrapment.

If at the time of the *Theses* (putting aside that this "time," this definition of time and event, is in question) Benjamin faced the prospect of a foreclosed future and erased past represented by the victory of Euro-fascism, an inevitable question remains. Have we, in our liberal discursive present, in a global political moment more or less marked by the pretext of at least formal democracy, arrived at that future to have been rescued from Benjamin's own "state of emergency" – one established with the defeat of Euro-fascism he could not witness? Or, if he was penned in by the hermeneutical machinery identified by him with "historicism," are *we* – now in a horizonless environment defined not by a historicism of the past alone but by a *historicism of "the present,"* by a discourse whose non-existence does not effect its evisceration of the political in the latter's name – in, if anything, *a more dire historial impasse?* What is the pragmatic use of what Benjamin offers as a counter-stroke to this totalization, a mode of mnemonic and historial intervention called at once *materialist* (but in a manner, as Adorno observes in the letter cited, that has little to do with orthodox Marxian trajectories, including Adorno's own) and a *graphematics* of inscription?

One might ask whether any "decisions" confront us today – a today as if doubly absent to itself, archived, deferred. One thinks of those inherited narratives whose calculable inevitability inform (yet are derealized in) the mirage of a global polis. For instance, were we to generate a facile list subject to an emergent *combinatoire*: a relation to time and resources that, inscribed in our very habits of linguistic usage, heralds the decimating consumption of bio-diversity and bio-support systems (suggesting that how we mimetically think the *bio-logic* is itself part of a self-canceling trajectory), an impending split between a techno-class and its expanding others, the triaging of entire continents within the media (Africa), the accommodation of increasingly routine if episodic genocides, and so on. Such "events" with more or less calculable time-tables stand implicated in the effects of a mimetic epistemotopy of reserves or reference: that is, in a political imaginary and auto-referentialism of the humanist-mimetic model. If one cannot properly séance a ghosted present rendered its own deferred archive, for what never quite existed (a reverse ghost, like "cultural studies," feasting off a promised future existence that does not, for that reason, arrive), we may recall one element that seems to attend any *séancing* that would bring alternate pasts at table with still virtual futures. That is, a certain knocking, as beneath the table, syncopated or in intervals as if from outside, visualizable in the premimetic mode of a recurrent series of bars or slashes at once material and preceding all perception or reading, (a)rhythmic, a system of marking that seems to generate and dissolve mimetic images or narrative. This invocation, we may muse, which accesses the logic of "pure language" in Benjamin's translation essay, does so by immersing the data of every received conceptual edifice, operative or otherwise, in the matrixal configurations which, today, we perhaps too passively affiliate with new teletechnologies (digital referencing, hypertext, email).

It conjures a site precedent to any distribution of representational force and sedimentation – any regimen of identification and anthropomorphism presented as current facticity.

2. Epistemo-political folds

In an earlier aside, we noted that Ernesto Laclau situated one death of the term "ideology" at that site where a dissolution of "extra-discursive" grounds denied to the word any traditional norm against which to measure distortion or false consciousness. At that point the term returns in the hiatus of its afterlife, no longer as concept or word but as a kind of *translational* marker. Insisting on a logic of ex-posure,[12] on the radical exteriorization of all that has been (or will be) coded by interiorizing metaphorics, it remaps mimetic logics, "subjectivist" or "objectivist" edifices (phenomenological, structuralist idioms), and political projections according to the movement of an always exterior trace. Such a movement – which stands to alter the mnemonic or representational grid out of which the previous definitions of "ideology" itself emerged – may first seem to dissolve anthropomorphic and mimetic projections of the fullness of meaning ("what an ideological distortion projects . . . is the impossible fullness of the community" (303)). "Translation" in Benjamin seems to imply this general logic, which involves a moment of semantic evacuation (the dissolution of "interiorizing metaphorics"). It may also seem to impose a certain ethical direction, tracked in relation to a "materiality" more performative than referential. One mock-genealogical way of interrogating this logic – which, at bottom, dissolves various logics of interiorization, or aura – is to excavate, in Benjamin's text, the site from which a similarly recirculated, translated, or ghosted non-figure of "allegory" seems to have briefly sprung.

[12] One such logic of ex-posure is developed with reference to the transformation of hermeneutic protocols in Werner Hamacher's *Premises* (1996).

If what Benjamin calls *"materialistic* historiography" suggests a counter-stroke to the scourge of historicism and even an anti-program of historial intervention – a re-writing of various pasts, *themselves at all points virtual,* to displace the foreclosure and predetermination by imposed trace-chains of accessible futures – the phrase also represents the final avatar in his writings of a site passing behind the terms "shock" and "allegory." How, for example, does this non-term "allegory" – which, let us concede, never took hold, even in de Man's ferocious revival, as if the word simply could not bear it, was already too old, too saturated – anticipate the most material intervention in historical politics Benjamin will summon? We must re-inspect the site where "allegory" emerges, briefly, as an epistemo-political problem, and why it seems canceled in advance of its own circulation – or as the condition of that. That is, why does "allegory" not only emerge in its supposedly modernist phase in the *Trauerspiel* book of all places, an under-read mock-academic treatise (yet this "mock," this complicity, is essential) on texts no one reads? What logic re-circulates within a word that invisibly negates the traditional figure it cites (allegory as a mimetic logic)? What seems clear is the remainder cannot quite do what it will be asked to: pretend to name the entire interventionist-historical gesture of a mnemotech-nics which transposes or converts the logics of mimesis (model and copy, term and referential) from a passive to a pro-active function, and with that temporality, "experience," the mutating structure of the historial, "events"?[13] Even if we supplant the term today with another to reconfigure the non-space it has occupied – I have elsewhere suggested *allographics,* stressing the negational and otherating "action" of material inscriptions on anterior terms – it would not suffice to clear a site which begins, in the *Trauerspiel,* with an act of forgetting.

In the case of Benjamin's *Trauerspiel* the text cannot quite erase

---

[13] By *mimesis* we do not mean so much the double sense opened in Plato – that, on the one hand, of poetic imitation (and a certain third person narration) and, *as if* inversely, the installation of a representational concept of language (paradoxi-cally, perhaps, in the figure of the *eidos,* which may be otherwise read as the phenomenalization of an inscription, or the cancellation of figure itself, even a "primal letter" as remarked in the *Theaetetus*). Rather, we use the term in such a way as to flatten and combine both, converted into what may be an installed regime of interpretation more generally – and what, invariably, legislates as-sumed models of reference. This model, typically, *trusts* in the promise of a descriptive rhetoric that actively effaces the event of prephenomenal inscription.

the traces of this forgetting. Benjamin's use apprehends where "allegory" does not reproduce but absences, alters, defaces, and negates what it (re)presents – where, that is, the impacting of signs commenting on other anterior signs is not passive but stands to alter those signifying trace-chains and anteriority. This is why mimesis, as a bureaucratization of past-management, of the politics of memory, hides behind the trope of "nature" and natural reference. Yet this process becomes all the more imperiled when what is performed allegorizes "allegory" itself, both the term as such, to be sure, but also *the* key precursor text in which this very operation ("first") occurs. This site supplies an opportunity to inspect how mnemonic incursion or intervention – which is always in the archival itself, in how the structure of the promise is managed – might proceed ("might," since such logic remains virtual even when canonized, instituted, subordinated to certain protocols of interpretation). For, contrary to the vague sense of commentators that Nietzsche's work is either secondary to or dealt with hostilely by Benjamin – an occlusion that serves a number of purposes – the *Ursprung*, in its mock-origin (which, after all, is what *Ursprung* or *Ur*-leap connotes) absorbs and repeats, distills and encrypts, the historial implications that had themselves gone unseen, of *The Birth of Tragedy*. Part of the trauma of the *Trauerspiel*, so to speak, which will confirm at once its power and inaccessibility (since it seems, as a rhetorical performance, to find precisely this itself indigestible, and with reason), is the precision of the reading of *The Birth* that it offers – the release of a move, call it "Epistemo-Critical," that *The Birth* puts in circulation and (again) disguises.

To say that *The Birth of Tragedy* is doubly allegorical is not enough, of course, since the term conceals its own allotropic sense – that is, other than tropological, other than figural import. This prefigural site may also be termed apotropaic, one turning the gaze away, before which figurative or ideological investments are cast up. It is not enough that the *Trauerspiel* seems superimposed over *The Birth* – two works on cycles of "theatrical" history into which representation is enfolded, and out of which historical ciphers emerge – or that *Ursprung* repeats and supplants (even reads) the mock-genealogical term *Geburt* (*Ursprung* tends to evacuate the space of "origin" by pointing, instead, to a pre- and post-history – *Vor- und Nachgeschichte* – of the form or event).[14] What is also involved, in Nietzsche's case, is the transformative address of an alloplastic narrative that not only implants linguistic or "literary" forms at the generative source of epistemo-historical cycles (moving as if from dithyramb to dialogue, to dialectic and Socratic decadence, and so on), situated over something called "music," but a total redefinition of the "aesthetic" as *the material* as such, precedent to perception, narrativization, historicization. (Such, in fact, may be necessary to *figuring out* what "materialistic" means for Benjamin, as well as the notion of a historically programmed "sensorium.") The transformation in question will always, precisely as a reformulation of the polis' archival laws, be *epistemotopic*: a matter of inscription, of where the "aesthetic" predicts the status of a historical *sensorium*, always hermeneutic, out of which experience and narrative is projected.[15]

We can suggest why, even today, it is necessary to mute the implications of this declension of "allegory" by calling it *modernist* – a by now familiar containment. For by the term "modernist" is generally (also) meant reflexive, aesthetic, and so on, as if opposed to the referential engagement with the historico-political that precedes and supersedes its interests. By this "modernist" notion of allegory, so called, is meant a text's (mere) shift from the representation of abstract meanings to a work's account, as if reflexively, of its conditions of production (or consumption). Yet this leaves out the decisive shift noted before: that allegory in this usage, which can hardly be called a concept or literary historical mode, does not represent but negates and anamorphically transforms what it (re)presents, offers to alter the inscriptions out of which its own historical signscape is projected. That is, whatever is concealed beneath the term allegory, when it occurs, does so as virtual "event" – and this virtuality must be activated, engaged, resumed, found otherwise, *contracted* to the future in reading, or deferred. In Benjamin's terms, again, it "means precisely the non-existence of what it presents." Differently put, the property of *reflexivity*, so called, is not the suspension of historical reference

---

[14] This sense of *Ursprung* is developed and elaborated in Samuel Weber, "Genealogy of Modernity: History, Myth and Allegory in Benjamin's *Origin of the German Mourning Play*," 465–500.

[15] See in this regard the treatment of how the Furies are used to establish Athens' laws at the end of Aeschylus' *Eumenides* in my "Coda: Post-humanist Reading," in *Anti-Mimesis*.

and engagement in a narcissistic formalism, but the active condition for the alteration of the historial, or a mnemotechnics and
disinscription operative within signifying networks. It presupposes an (a)rhythmic break, in which undergirding matrical relays surface. As Benjamin's text apprehends of Nietzsche's, it is
the (retro) installation of materialistic cultural and linguistic
forms in a then pro-active mnemonics that recasts epistemo-historial "experience" (a term, that is, "experience," which is foreclosed by this fact, as Benjamin elaborates elsewhere). What is
called the aesthetic in Nietzsche – such as in the famous statement:
"it is only as an *aesthetic phenomenon* that existence and the world
are eternally justified (*gerechtfertig*)" (a strange word, suggesting
as it does an *ethics of the aesthetic*, heard as a type of justice linked to
the material trace) – must be understood through the Greek *aisthanumai*, for perception, as the materiality of a linguistico-
semiotic order whose phenomenalizations, as consciousness-
effect, will be narrated in the transformation of theatrical and
linguistic forms – again: from music to dithyramb, to dialogue, to
dialectic and so on. What Nietzsche constructs is a mobile telegra-
phematic and media network, in this case the ur-model of such
installations, out of which historical and discursive worlds are
projected – a remarkable teletechnological system that marks the
correlation between linguistic forms and the programming of
perceptual and historical modes. The discrete installation and use
of such a "model," however, explicates too clearly what is meant
by the aesthetic in Nietzsche – the programming of historical
"experience" by mnemonic and graphematic shifts.

Yet here, where Nietzsche seems to place the "aesthetic" before
the human agent, Benjamin protests – in one of criticism's most
vertiginous performances – that "all sane reflection is at an end"
(103), and in that gesture appears inscribed in this counter-model,
even programmed by it (as is, we might say, later Nietzsche). This
Geburt or *Ursprung* of a counter-tradition to the mimetic and
historicist norm presents Benjamin with the means of writing
under the guise of literary history and literary criticism a self-
canceling "model" for the dissolution of the received epistemo-
critical model of models.

We can repackage some of this now. Benjamin effaces under the
term *allegory* a moment in Nietzsche's text whose "birth" is in
turn disguised under the rhetoric of *music*, or rather, not music as

such, in the first title anyway, but *"aus dem Geiste der Musik"* – a certain spirit or ghost of "music." What, however, is the ghost of *Musik*, at once marking it as anteriority (or dead) and reducing it to a kind of infinite semiosis precedent to consciousness, reading, "history"? It is generally regarded that the opposition of Apollo and Dionysus in *The Birth* has a dialectical function, or in all events, presents the conflictual and contending forces of a histori-cal province understood as an *epistemo-critical* site (both gods have to do with art, a specific way of reading *techne*, and both seem articulated in or associated with states of individuation, imaging, cognition, poetic *form*, history). Traditionally, the "opposition" can appear to superimpose itself on others, particularly where, as seems inevitable, a priority is given to "Dionysus," the originary figure of premimetic music, of nature in a sense or the prein-dividuated, to which Apollo then seems to emerge as a powerful after-event of sorts, a sort of secondary revision.[16] Other opposi-tions, however banal, are hard to suppress in finding analogies to these gods – figuration and logic, content and form, poetry and dialectic, music and mimetic language – even though none is instituted, and the gods often bleed into one another. Yet while later in Nietzsche's writings Apollo disappears, absorbed by the powers of Dionysus as a figure – here one thinks of the late signature as though a general insignia for his whole project, "Dionysus vs. the Crucified" – the apparent narrative of *The Birth* turns on the preoriginary nature of music (marking the study's failed role as a recuperative model for Nietzsche's own supposed "present," offering Wagner as transforming agent). Accordingly, Apollo is the god of distance, of the mimetic and the image – perhaps, we would say of "cultural studies." Yet without re-

---

[16] Citing the "Epistemo-Critical Prologue" of the *Trauerspiel*, Samuel Weber com-ments on how Benjamin uses the trope of "natural history" in a parallel zone: "What Benjamin calls here, in the most oxymoronic sense imaginable, '*natural* history': not the history of nature but history *as* nature, is precisely the discrete, un-genetic aspect of the origin, the split coherence of which articulates itself in a manner entirely incompatible with any sort of linear or even dialectical develop-ment" (473). For more extended and detailed discussion of the figure of "natural history" (*Naturgeschichte*), see Beatrice Hanssen, "Philosophy at Its Origin: Walter Benjamin's Prologue to the *Ursprung des deutschen Trauerspiels.*" Here, it is argued, Benjamin's rejection of "the model of reflective consciousness for the linguistic nature of truth" (812) entails the "call for another form of history, one no longer ruled purely by the concerns or categories of human agency." Han-ssen will link this "natural history" to the concept of "pure language," a kind of pre-figural Apollonian measure, in *Die Aufgabe des Übersetzers.*

hearsing the web of transformations Nietzsche plays upon for diverse ends, there is a clear moment – early in the work – in which this system, on which all hinges, is dislocated. It is a moment in which Apollo, god of form, briefly yet unmistakably *precedes* Dionysus at the site of "music," and Nietzsche's occlusion of this moment harasses the career of the text. It occurs in section II and concerns the term *rhythm*:

> If music, as it would seem, had been known previously as an Apollonian art, it was so, strictly speaking, only as the wave beat of rhythm, whose formative power was developed for the representation of Apollonian states . . . The very element which forms the essence of Dionysian music (and hence of music in general) is carefully excluded as un-Apollonian – namely, the emotional power of the tone, the uniform flow of the melody, and the utterly incomparable world of harmony.[17]

Here the Apollonian precedes, it excludes its others ("carefully excluded as un-Apollonian"), and must be excluded in turn. If the passage recalls Benjamin's inverse dismissal of Nietzsche's purported views on the "aesthetic" (that is, mnemonic or *materialistic*) nature of phenomenal existence, it is doubly odd when, a moment later, we hear of nature and Dionysus in respect to language: "The essence of nature is now to be expressed symbolically; we need a new world of symbols; not the entire symbolism of the lips, face, and speech but the whole pantomime of dancing, forcing every member into *rhythmic* movement." (40).

This precontamination by the "Apollonian" of the natural or Dionysian – as a movement into the materiality of the body, into a symbolic nature in excess of "lips, *face*, and speech" – rewrites the Apollonian non-source of music ("known previously as an *Apollonian* art"). Apollo "precedes" the mock-originary effects of Dionysus by virtue of a strictly *formal*, material difference. Here, momentarily, "Dionysus" has become the mimetic god ("the utterly incomparable world of harmony"), and Apollo the figure of sheerly amaterial materiality, premimetic and non-identificatory. The moment bears analogy to where for Benjamin the aura associated with personification is struck, vanquished with cinema – and where, as an analog to cinema, the intervaled array of aural knocks or parallel lines (like the light-dark-light shadow of a rushing train) emerge, in Hitchcock, as emblem and agent of this

[17] Friedrich Nietzsche, *The Birth of Tragedy*, 40.

disinvestiture and loss of all interiority, identification, or mimetic illusion.

The figure of difference called *rhythm* – the preoriginary mode of "dancing, forcing every member into *rhythmic* movement" – could be heard as a certain knocking, visualized as a series of bars, preletteral to be sure, whose very seriality incorporates an *a*rhythmic space or rupture, even as their repetitions, like *foot*-work, project and parody the allegorical promise of narrative, of revised and managed anteriority.[18] Such feet or legs also carry the trace of anteriority heard in legacy, of the legislation of legibility heard in laws of transmission. What we might emblematically call the bar-series of (a)rhythm represents a sheer formalism at the non-source of music – its *Geiste* – which dispossesses all accrued features of mimeticism, identification, or content before an anti-model (that is, one refusing the very terms of model and copy) of "history" as an allomorphic site of inscriptions subject to incessant prefigural disruption. No doubt this will seem picayune, unutterably banal, a prefigural figure void not only of content but virtually place or "existence," yet its consequences seem indelible. Like the knocking in a séance, this now *ur*-Apollonian *seriality* – implanting formal difference at the preoriginary and material site of a *Musik* out of which the aesthetics of perception (that is, reading) forgetfully and anthropomorphically proceeds – represents (or precisely not, since it cannot re-present), the undoing of "allegory" at the traumatic and catachretic non-site of its contemporary re-emergence in Benjamin, what will be echoed later as the figure and anti-mnemonic effect called "shock." (We might note that if "allegory" becomes to some extent bracketed and transposed into subsequent figures in Benjamin, in de Man it is pur-

[18] While we address, under the sign of Apollo, a "mimetic blind" in historicist models, one could in turn speak of an anti-mimetic blind in the tradition of reading the text. One thinks, here, of the labors involved in de Man's decisive revision of this text in "Genesis and Genealogy," in *Allegories of Reading*, which depends upon citing material *excised* from Nietzsche's published text in order to support a materialistic and anti-dialectical reading. Yet all along the text itself can be seen, *un*excised in the above quote, to say precisely that, a torsion that compels us to produce the text as a different cultural force, or monad. Perhaps the most precise disentangling of this knot, as a detour of close reading, is provided by Andrzej Warminski's "Prefatory Postscript," in *Readings in Interpretation*, xlii–xlvi, where, too, *the same occlusion occurs* – that is, where a renegade reading must be furtively staged that resides on the proverbial surface itself. But why all the hyper-subtlety and dodging? The overt return of Nietzsche's signature to this materialistic "reading" has further consequences.

sued, pressed to the limit and gambled on – to the point where it will no longer function usefully, only to be revived even there.)[19] If Apollo implies or wields a specific blinding effect – presenting himself as the god of images and the mimetic, while his own formalism must be called the dissolver of mimetic models at the site of inscription – one can pretend to see why he is absorbed, in Nietzsche, by and into the more iconic figure of Dionysus, though the latter can no longer be projected upon, merely, as some sort of pagan life-force (particularly given Nietzsche's entirely semiotic notion of a "life" not to be heard, explicitly, as organic, or even alive).[20]

It is interesting that, toward the end of the *Theses*, Benjamin invokes the history of "organic" life on earth – what displaces the anthropomorphic and mimetic notion of history – as a corollary of the disruption called "materialistic historiography," or shock, or "allegory." The caesura-effect of this preoriginary rhythm, this *Ur-sprung* of *Musik* whose apparent return, like the flute-playing heard before Alcibiades' appearance in the *Symposium*, unbinds the historicist "continuum" of causal chains, and with it linear history, opening a séance-effect sometimes called "Dionysus" by the later Nietzsche – a moment out of which alternate mnemonic terms, restorations and erasures, appear summoned (Dionysus, we recall, speaks for some reason for what is called by Nietzsche "earth"). This occurs at a site or present, the "time" of the séance or scene of (dis)installation, out of which such decisions spectrally present themselves. The Apollonian effect of (a)*rhythm* can be momentarily allied to "nature" in the above citation because of a materiality in advance of any *figuration* – an alliance with the "organic" and non-human history of a life or earth not identified with living or dead, but rather an infinite semiosis that is preoriginary yet involves (as Nietzsche projects) a virtual politics of earth. In a way that projects a hermeneutic blind familiar in the canonical readings of *The Birth of Tragedy*, this effect compels in advance a reverse

---

[19] In "Pascal's Allegory of Persuasion" we read: "To say then, as we are actually saying, that allegory (as sequential narration) is the trope of irony (as the one is the trope of zero) is to say something that is true enough but not intelligible, which also implies that it cannot be put to work as a device of textual analysis" (*AI*, 61).

[20] It is Benjamin's "materiality" that Adorno, in his letter, implicitly identifies as Nietzschean. See *Aesthetics and Politics*, 131.

inscription of Apollo (appearing, thereafter, as the ancillary and mimetic god), in turn rewriting what Benjamin will call "allegory" under a name, Dionysus, that must also be misheard – that is, as originary naturalistic life-force.[21] For instance, when we find at the end of Nietzsche's writing the signature "Dionysus vs. the Crucified," that figure seems itself inscribed in a hermeneutic inversion or chiasmifixion of sense – the site of an "ideological anamorphosis" (Žižek) of the Thing-like, material, essentially non-human effects of mnemonic inscription – which might itself be called *the domain of "the Crucified."* Rather than see this late signature, as we tend to, as the fairly banal opposition of a pagan principle of life to the depredations of Christian value systems or the ascetic drive, we may read it as the programmatic opposition of a premimetic effect – of a "materialistic historiog- *raphy*" predicated on the disruptive (dancing) powers of a non-human semio-aesthetic effect at the heart of any *sensorium*, understood as a historically contingent narrative legislation of the senses according to perceptual-interpretive laws – to the chi- asmic province of a hermeneutic that has always already in- verted and socialized value polarities ("the Crucified") in a mi- metological regime. It is this regime Benjamin opposes as "fascist" – that is to say, blinded, programmatic, robbing his- torial agency of its power to decide – as the "enemy," as *histori- cism*.[22] The projected *war* implied by the placelessly mytho- graphic signature, Dionysus vs. the Crucified, may be heard as

---

[21] In fact, the precise reading of the Apollonian in Nietzsche that I have sketched – what remains a dangerously accurate, and still forbidden understanding of that text, it seems – leaves a trace in a note of the "Arcades Project," in *Konvolut N*: "every historical state of affairs presented dialectically polarizes and becomes a force field in which the conflict between fore- and after-history plays itself out. It becomes that field as it is penetrated by actuality. And thus historical evidence always polarizes into fore- and after-history in a new way, never in the same way. And it does so beyond itself, within actuality per se; as a length divided according to the Apollonian measure experiences its division beyond itself." See "N (Re the Theory of Knowledge, Theory of Progress)," in *Benjamin: Philosophy, Aesthetics, History*, 60. The Apollonian figure of *measure*, here linked to rhythm and a "division beyond itself," networks with the concept of caesura that defines, for Benjamin, the so-called "dialectical image," or for that matter translation ("This image is the caesura of the movement of thought" (67)).

[22] Samuel Weber develops a similar explanation of what Benjamin means by linking "fascism" in the *Theses* to a certain aestheticization identified with a mimetic control. In *Mass Mediauras: Form Technics Media* he suggests: "Fascism thus reinstates the aura of the world-picture by means of the very media that undermine it" (102).

opposing an allohuman and (a)material dance of formal and semiotic agents without interior, traces evocative of the allohuman, or earth, to the institutional travesty of a mimetic and humanist hermeneutic – the latter conceived, now, like the Lacanian "Symbolic" in caricature, machinally operative in preinscribing material events in inverse, recuperative, historicizing archival formulae.

The prospect of a "historicism of the 'present'" so horizonless that it presages a benign deferral of its own "present" (or decisions, and hence future) is thus made possible to think, today (yet what today, or whose?), in relation to *an other* that is also allied to the non-human, perhaps to an other "earth" in a particular way. Where does this return us to the geo-political, then? If we ask, today, what a practice for the disruption of received and potentially totalized narrative logics might be we are presented with all too many inherited causal chains, like those mentioned above, whose calculable results seem inescapable within our conception of time. There is no received logic, for instance, on the current biologico-economic front – population, deforestation, evisceration of reserves – that is not, as a pure calculus, catastrophic over any time frame other than several decades (what is already stretching the imaginary of a "historicism of the 'present'"), calculations that, at best, program themselves by partaking of preset vocabularies and medialogies. If we pretend that a certain *technicity*, under the guise of various mimetic ideologies, stands to deplete and eviscerate the functional orders of something called "nature" (and you will see, in a minute, why I choose this example), it may be necessary to rewrite the latter term as informed, all along, by a different *counter-technicity* and *mnemotechnicity* the rethinking of which suggests the site of knocking, of rhythm, out of which the sort of intervention Benjamin proposes can be conjured. (Conjured, though no guarantees of any sort, or predetermination, come with this opening – indeed, their absence is its condition.) We see, perhaps, how a specific epistemo-critical machinery allied with "historicism," in Benjamin's schema, becomes a by-word not only for *fascism*, or implicitly capitalism, but an entire mimetic-hermeneutic order – an order of language or pan-historical ideology that is (also) installed in the site of "nature," under the rubric of the referential or "real." Though operating there as a machinal manager of *anteriority*, the mnemonic, and so on – supplanting for inscription the phenomenal pretense of transparent reference – it may represent, like the church in numerous "third-world" countries or certain political imaginaries in the academy, not simply reactionary interests (*or* epistemologies) but the very enforcement of those.

It becomes clearer why, when the non-word "allegory" emerges for Benjamin over the site of Nietzsche's materialist model of what now can be called (an) aesthetico-political "history," it is also as a figure for what, in the latter's text, will be called a transvaluation, a translation of sign-systems, of orders of reference and value, of the "human" – and this, in a way that presupposes a transformation within the model of mimesis (what every "historicism" resists) from a passive and reproductive machine of model and copy, a mode of *ressentiment*, to a pro-active "mimesis" without model or copy, a site where allographical events or acts negate and alter the mnemonic switchboards and conditions of (re)production, that have controlled or spectrally managed cognitive and referential reserves. In this overly accurate reading of the *Trauerspiel* by *The Birth*, in this impacting and erasure, Benjamin appears inversely programmed by a part of Nietzsche's project (or a reading of it that has yet to be instituted).[23] Implicit in such a proleptic agenda is where logics inherent in the use of the term "nature" appear *ex*posed – as it seems to be in the passage from *The Birth* on Apollo – not as ground of the real, of origin and reference, but as a hermeneutic *Nachkonstruction* (even, as we will see in the case of Andrew Ross, when argued "against"). That term is disclosed to have helped legislate a more or less *passive* mimetic ideology indistinguishable from (and perhaps preceding) a received trope of *capital*, the perpetually re-creation of a "received" model of language and archival logic. Simultaneously, that semiotic topos is recast as a proleptic or pro-active "mimesis," what in fact *nature* – to the degree it encompassed bio-semiotic laws – had all along ma-

---

[23] This hypothesis contests as misleading the commonplace that Benjamin's *Trauerspiel* constitutes an "inversion of Nietzsche" (see Rainer Nägele, "The Poetic Ground Laid Bare (Benjamin reading Baudelaire)," 148. Gary Shapiro, in "Hashish Passages: Benjamin's Labyrinth" (unpublished), has recently noted that the *"Trauerspiel* book must be understood as an anti-*Birth of Tragedy*," which would be true only in so far as the *Birth of Tragedy* must be itself understood that way (that is, as an entirely other text than the canonical-hermeneutic reading takes it to be).

terially implied. For instance, in the very alloplastic forms cascading and morphing in bio-thanatological succession through innumerable insect, plant, and marine species – determining and determined by situational and individuated modes of camouflage, counter-chemical warfare, color and shape-shifting metamorphosis, predatory and anti-predatory strategies proleptically and pro-actively miming inhabitational signs and relays compared to which the ideological conventions of human linguistic reference with their presumption of reproducing "same" referents must seem impositionally violent and primitive.

So there is a double form to cultural studies' *archivism of the present* – the one, as it were, passive and reinscribed, making its place in the family mausoleum of representational projects, the other substituting new terms and conceptual types in a general (if still unreflected) reseeding of referential matrices. If on the one hand it extends a familiar archive, it can also be said to project – according to a *virtual* logic that presumes acts of reading beyond its own mere shift within an informatrix – the ant-like construction of a kind of new mnemonic *labyrinth*, re-networking diverse accounts, images, name-systems, object-systems, interpretive remnants.[24] The logic of this remains in anticipation, necessarily, of a different, more transformatively active sort of reading or mnemotechnics to come.[25] If a reconfiguration of the political – which is always also to say *a politics of memory* – must disrupt the mimetic model of cultural historicism, Benjamin locates the site of this labor in what he calls the "monad," heard as the crystallization of key junctures or traces within a cultural or mnemonic circuit – nodes of relay, or transmission ("Where thinking sud-

---

[24] The great exception to Benjamin's not bringing up "allegory" again is around the figure of Baudelaire, and this to sheer excess, in *Zentralpark* (*Illuminationen*, 230–50), which one might describe as a hyperbolization or allegorization of "allegory" itself – a near implosion. The figure of the labyrinth in this text testifies to the emergence of a new mnemonic grid tied to commodities: *"Das Labyrinth ist der richtige Weg für den, der noch immer früh genug am Ziel ankommt. Dieses Ziel ist der Markt"* (236); then: *"Das Labyrinth ist die Heimat des Zögernden"* (238).

[25] Alternately, any shift from a passive to an active "mimesis" not only alters the definition of "nature" itself, but allows Benjaminian *allegory* to stand as a linguistic-political technique and agency for what, in Nietzsche, may be entailed in the hieroglyphics surrounding the MacGuffinesque passage of "eternal recurrence" – the conversion of a passive, reactive, historicist, epistemotopy of *ressentiment* as though forward, into a different switchboard of relays and possibility. In Benjamin's system this will go by the name of *"weak* messianism."

denly stops in a configuration pregnant with tensions, it gives that configuration a shock, by which it crystallizes into a monad. A historical materialist approaches a historical subject only where he encounters it as a monad").[26] As Benjamin put it in his response to Adorno: "In the monad everything that used to lie in mythical rigidity as a textual reference comes alive."[27] The monad, the site of conversion of temporal threads and itineraries, irreducibly singular in each case or conjunction, appears like a situated non-word out of which diverse referential orders are culturally generated, a node out of which other, differently marked image codes or clusters stand to be produced.[28] The conceit of the "monad" projects the site of a mnemonic node through the rewiring of which intervention can be gambled, what effects by extension diverse relays and routes of tele-transmission by which what is misleadingly called the archive generates historical value, "experience," protocols of decision: alter, let us say, the manner in which a key-node like "Plato" is thought or produced, read him as all along a materialist of sorts, and every

[26] "Theses," in *Illuminations*, 262–3.

[27] *Aesthetics and Politics*, 137. The "monad," in this sense (whose proliferating network becomes a "constellation"), is viewed as a mnemonic-textual node whose alteration stands to modify the past as well as the mnemonic (re)production of "future" sites. It has to do with a mnemo-*techne* that alters the very production of "reference," the *sensorium*. It would seem that the "monad," supplanting Benjamin's revision of the Platonic Idea as an interpretive node, is distinguished by its *virtuality* – both as mode of existence, and of producing futurity.

[28] Commenting on Benjamin's figure of *translation*, Hanssen notes that Benjamin's concept of pre-linguistic materiality – through which a Nietzschean topos of transvaluation now appears to pass – involves a "non-human, non-humanistic history," that is renamed "natural history in the prologue to *The Origin of German Tragic Drama*" (817). Hanssen elsewhere differentiates Benjamin's concept of *Ursprung* as an attempt to "move beyond the theory of the eternal return, which he regarded to be the manifestation of a mythical power of history" (823). But one could counter that this is only a particular interpretation or "mythical rigidity" of this trope – rather on the order of his dismissal of Nietzsche's "aesthetic" prioritization. In fact, the return of a materialistic-aesthetic premise in the *Trauerspiel* – like the alliance between Apollonian *Musik* and *reine Sprache* technically – predicts where, by the time of Thesis XII, Benjamin will be citing Nietzsche's "Use and Abuse of History" as a cipher of "materialistic historiography," precisely a return to the earliest Nietzsche. Hanssen similarly reads Benjamin's *"erkenntniskritisch"* prologue as, literally, a "radical repudiation of epistemology" (820) in the mode of a philosophy of consciousness, which, while true enough, does not account for a reverse inscription, through the prioritization of language, where a different "epistemo-critical" model returns (as can be said, too, of *The Birth of Tragedy*).

narrative and conceptual-historial web dependent on it as key-stone (dawn of the West, father of "platonism") stands to be altered, to pass into the accounts of alternative histories. If a preconceptual agency of language's materiality remains the touchstone of intervention in the historial network, one that dis-figures inherited systems of thinking reference (or cause, or tem-porality, or the earth), how does this impact on "cultural studies" today, or direct us to one to come that, undoubtedly, will assume a different name?

3. Geo-metrics

If we submitted the word "culture" to a general translation and review today, it might appear almost void of definition. Here, however, a slightly altered logic emerges – in the active attempt to rid the term of its ethno-anthropological traces. We might begin to redefine cultural zones according to two questions which seem, in turn, to network others. First, how does an institution or cultural frame produce (and consume), project, legitimate and archivally manage *reference* (and with that, the entire reserve of anteriority) and, secondly and more complexly, how does such order and name, incorporate or occlude a domain of radical otherness – in excess of any mimetic or humanist fold? The second would be itself referenced to a "materiality" neither linguistic nor simply beyond signifying structures. Given this potential return of an other use of "materiality," we might addend to these co-ordinates another question: how do we locate or place, map or situate, the penultimate systemic and mock-referential idea of "earth" – or any historial responsibility toward that instance?

The enigma in Benjamin's catachretic relaunching of the term allegory is that its success (a certain version of "allegory" gets associated with the modernist project) coincides with its pro-grammatic failure (a certain version of "allegory" gets associated with the modernist project). What interests us as a problem is not only that it is self-canceling, but that the nether logic of the term's perpetually *other* sense deranges the habitus of mimetic indices and historicist metaphorics. It does not turn aside from the "pol-itical imaginary" of former practices, but stakes out materialistic if spectral grounds from which that imaginary would be recalibrated – the point from which, for instance, a publicly inscribed political project can be seen, inversely, as another footsoldier in this mimetico-historicist closure. If the elusive implications of the phrase *"materialistic historiography"* entail what might be called an *allographic* opening to a certain outside of a received determination of memory (collective, canonical), this occurs by way of an invocation or séancing of the allohuman that also suggests the evocation of an unpredetermined "time." This gesture or invocation involves not only the dead, including the living dead of a historicist coding marked by the evasion of the performative; not only the archivism of the "present," with its images converted into consumable currency due to their recognizability and circulation, but increasingly a materiality we must in some measure associate (if only through the figure of measure itself) with earth. Among other things, "earth" lies concealed as precept behind every installed model or bureaucratization of reference. The name "earth" – which tends to be routinely anthropomorphized – at the same time may not co-incide with any simple referent, since it might arguably include, as an invocation, the protocols of human reference among its hosted effects. One is tempted, because of Benjamin's iconic status for a representative "cultural studies," to study the effects of juxtaposing what could be termed a Benjaminian trope of nature, or natural history, to the (forgetful) reinscription of what is here called the second "cultural studies" in an unreflected referential model, and the political imaginary derived thereby. To guarantee this rupture by an *other* history – what the *Trauerspiel* perhaps inversely calls a "natural history" – Benjamin evokes the anti-apocalyptic image of "organic life on earth" to displace the anthropomorphic (that is, oddly, historicist, or "fascist"?) perspective in thesis XVIII: " 'In relation to the history of organic life on earth,' writes a modern biologist, 'the paltry fifty millennia of homo sapiens constitute something like two seconds at the close of a twenty-four hour day. On this scale, the history of civilized mankind would fill one-fifth of the last second of the last hour' " (263). While Andrew Ross is, in ways, a fairly idiosyncratic representative of "cultural studies" (which, to date, can take pride in its refusal of policed orthodoxies), it is precisely in his conception of a politics of the politics of the earth that a certain ideological inflexion – call it, the implications of the mimetic-humanist regress – become particularly clear.

Dispersing, for a moment, Benjamin's invocation of non-human life, of organic and temporal processes (*Naturgeschichte*) that explode a nineteenth century conceit of "history" long misplaced as a code word for the real, we *return* – as it were, in a double sense – to a hypothetical present: the *con*temporarily present "present" of cultural studies, horizonless, columbarium-like, institutionally undead. If this "historicism of the present" shares with a naive Apollo a structural blind – an appeal, that is, to mock-referential images unalert to where these narcoleptically reside over a different sort of humanist formalism – we can examine one side of its political imaginary in the context, nonetheless, of how one master-referential is patrolled, "earth." This, with awareness that any invocation of the earth, today, confronts in its generality the issue of the material, the non-human, of possible futures and non-futures, of the geo-political and the aesthetico-epistemic, of the pre- and post-catastrophic that frames the very achievement of the prevalence of formal democracy in a mimetico-political imaginary free to focus on "liberation": that is, the playing out, nonetheless, of a dialectical narrative's utopic, yet seemingly techno-friendly purview.

This emerges in Andrew Ross' *The Chicago Gangster Theory of Life – Nature's Debt to Society* (1994), a sort of crowning symptomatic of one face of cultural studies' status or state (state, in the strong sense of discursive legislator of norms). Basically, Ross presents an ideological dressing down of contemporary eco-politics on behalf of the emancipatory class struggle – locating in the former a new threat to the dominant code of the "social," particularly when challenged by the former's non-anthropocentric rhetoric: the compulsion to strike at what threatens the mimeticism of Ross' own discourse is what makes the performance symptomatic. Ross' book, whose complexities I can not hope to treat briefly, is a hieroglyph of the times – since here, in the name of a left-identified stance, of "the social" and "liberation" (of which more in a moment), Ross revives the "struggle" of the oppressed against the rhetorical fascism of the new class enemy, the ecology movement. Let us leave aside what vapors account for this choice of enemies, what allows Ross to point his flâneur-like – or at least Soho-strolling – artillery at this latest perceived threat to what is in the end less the "social" as such than a humanist epistemology of the image, a displaced para-Apollonian investment that projects its mimetic imaginary onto the trope of "nature" itself. Echoing by inversion Benjamin's invocation of a "modern biologist" to dismantle historicist fascist-humanism, the metaphor of Ross' ire – from which the metaphor of his title is taken – is the biologist Dawkins' "selfish gene" theory, which he broadly assimilates, by an obscure metonymy at best, with eco-rhetoric. In this neo-Darwinist genetic determinist rhetoric Ross perceives the echo of histories of oppression justified by appeal to nature: indeed, filled with factoids garnered from diverse pop cultural sources (the presence of these consumables constitute one of the programmatic appeals of Ross' writings), what spurs Ross' attacks on eco-apocalyptic rhetoric is the mock-authority that the non-human factor puts in play – its corrosion of the "human," or a familiar left political imaginary. Ever working by analogy, the coincidence of the GATT agreement to a discourse of eco-scarcity assures that the latter is designed to further disempower the working class ("The planetary concerns of ecologists were pursued at the same time as capital's move to break free of the labor-friendly constraints of national Fordism and enter into GATT's capital-friendly global phase of operations" (14)). A ventriloquized "nature" spurs Ross' recollection of past rhetorics of oppression that appeal to natural legitimation (racism, sexism), and the romantic struggle is revived in the most gratifyingly manipulative of tones: "*we* may soon be engaged yet again in the struggle to prevent nature becoming the referee of our fate" (5).

Of all the real class enemies in the age of Gingrich to go after with double-barreled glee, why does Ross choose *the Greens* – a move which at least has the perverse inevitability of being instantaneously co-opted by some of the retro forces Ross would pretend to indict (yet in fact appears preinscribed in)? The *authority* of this non-human other that triggers the rhetorical alarms of class defense ("wholesale revival of appeals to the authority of nature and biology" (5)) may be projected onto an assumed or standard trope of "nature" to begin with – a term Ross never questions. Indeed, like the title, in which the words "theory" and "gangster" are coupled as a concept of "life," the enemy will turn out to be at least double, and in a way Ross cannot give focus to.

Ross relies heavily on an unreconstructed nature/society dyad, however reversed ("Nature's Debt to Society" is the sub-title), in which something called "nature," nonetheless, gets subtly recast – and rebuffed – as a claim that does not recognize its "debt" for having itself been (or seemed) constructed by the social, as a logic of the non-human. Nature in fact splits at this site, is emptied, ventriloquized in *sotto voce*: it is traversed, as it were, by numerous constructs or personifications within Ross' mock-arcades style. On the one hand, it represents inscription before the investments of a mimetic discourse – the facticity of anterior traces projected onto the absurdist image from which the book's title derives, gene-theory; on the other, it suggests a counter-double of material inscription, its *phenomenalized* code. That is, the projected "authority" of nature Ross rebels against in the name of class struggle – yet which he in a different way reaffirms and performs – remains that of a certain mimetic machine, a referential program Ross cannot free himself of without his way of constructing a political imaginary unraveling. There is, therefore, a double "nature" in his sights which cannot be shot at, largely, without a self-wounding effect. This is reflected in the move whereby, setting up eco-apocalyptic rhetoric as itself co-opted by ruling class interests (the rhetoric of scarcity, say, enforcing labor's disempowerment), he ends up defending those same interests when challenged by the former, like a junk science witness at a Republican committee hearing on tobacco or wetland development. What seems less at issue is the projected "authority" of a non-human other that cannot be read within the social narrative of a utopist liberational gesture that is already heard as programmed and nostalgist from within the left academic establishment. The question has never been, as Ross pretends, that of an iconic "nature" which gets vilified if it is not read as a humanist, socio-ideological invention (he reminds us: "ideas that draw upon the authority of nature nearly always have their origin in ideas about society" (15)). What persists, instead, is a kind of *mimeto-humanist* revanchism (Ross suspiciously notes the "charismatic fauna" (6) of nature television and help-the-rainforest type appeals, adding: "Humans rank low on that scale"). That is, an investment in a too familiar model of meaning and narrative management, as well as the marketability, at which Ross has always excelled, of the pop image as uncontested thought-commodity. One need only compare his touristic launch-point as global diagnostician (at "a resort hotel on Fiji's Coral Coast" (21)) to the rawly implicated "third world" time-

traveling construct of Alphonso Lingis in *Abuses* to discern transformative options which the genre of allographic self-inscription
presents – or the yuppie and media-cocooned coding of Ross'
flâneurism. Ross' ambivalent demonization of the Greens involves
several subtexts, it seems, that participate in several mystified
binaries. The Greens will be *analogized* to biological determinism
in order to be opposed, in turn, by the greater program of social
liberation; yet beneath this lies an alliance of Ross' linguistic
premises with the multinational representational interests that
sustain his own epistemotopy – and beneath the scare-figure of
the bio-determinist lies an entire order of materiality that subverts
those "representational interests" in non-mimetic logics allied, in
this political imaginary, to a putatively gangsterish or coercive
theory ("The Chicago Gangster *Theory of Life*"). Has "theory," at
this juncture, been again transposed into a cipher for a material
other to mimeto-humanism – now allied, however, to what lies
behind the politics of a ventriloquized "earth"?

What is called "nature," to condense matters, becomes an icon
as ventriloquized by Ross as anyone, doubling for an "authority"
(always also from the past, like the terrorist "selfish-gene" of
Dawkins) that is, nonetheless, obscure, "theoretical," at all events
double, and the double of its own doubleness. This emerges not
only in the reversion to consumer marketing that Ross makes the
token of his advice to eco-apocalyptics: that is, to get out of
scarcity rhetoric, and self-denial, to be "sexy" ("The ecologically
impaired need to be persuaded that ecology can be sexy, and not
self-denying" (15)) – what, after all, works for him. In fact, I will
suggest, one machine of "nature" in Ross' contracted political
imaginary lies within his own discursive network. As the other of
a "social" which must be re-installed, it is in fact a troubling trope
– indicative of an *other* historiality which stands to dispossess
Ross' discursive enclave, image-consumerism, and left-lite
stance. One of its manifestations may be less the cover for neo-
capitalist strategies hiding behind the rhetoric of earth, as imag-
ined, than a machinal effect that in fact goes to the heart of Ross'
own embattled mimeticism. In short, without being marked – and
this perhaps is the pathologic core of Ross "political" gesture –
nature also names the mimetic ideology that sustains everything
in Ross' rhetorical stance, every investment in class analysis,
mock-historicism, and the cultural commodity whose promotion-

analysis remains his entrepreneurial (i.e. cultural) capital: nature, amidst else, is the trope for a mimetic disposition of language that manages (and defers) the transmission of anteriority, rewriting trace, mnemotechnics, and ideology (again) as the transparent referentialism of commodity analysis. Or rather, is both its other (gene-theory) *and* that – the non-mimetic other and the machine that upholds his mimetic investments (that suspects its image in that other). As a mimetic machine implicated not only in the evisceration of the subject under discussion (earth), but a growing fault within his own discursive position that no rhetoric of "struggle" can quite efface, the authority of "nature" has a double face: on the one hand, it mimes a non-human supplement associated with theory (we can forget about biologism for the moment), or a historiality unmastered by available left-academic narratives; on the other hand – and more interestingly it names the historical-discursive enclave that Ross' gestures, which mark their own fault, are themselves uncomfortably programmed from, an "authority" sufficiently displaced, and irritably experienced, so as to be rebelled against, if only in the hallucinatory form of Greens (one thinks of Macbeth's attackers holding branches before them).

What lies, so to speak, *behind* this "nature" – which, we will see, has (always) been itself an ideological trope, and not just as used by oppressors and ruling-class interests – is less the specter of inscription, of a *materialistic* double to the biological non-human other, than what already occludes and obfuscates this site in the controlled image-culture Ross partakes in. That is, one in which chiasmic reversals ("crucifieds"?) of hermeneutic terms precede and direct the scene (for instance, "nature" concealing a linguistico-ideological machine, "technology" a type of retro-humanism, and so on). A certain "allegory," or de-naturalized Dionysianism stands to dismantle this site. We are now in a position, however, to draw a larger hypothesis, which cuts through the politicizing manipulation and failed exorcism of terms like "modernism" and theory: that this movement or passage – for this has been the suppressed element of Benjaminian (or Nietzschean, or de Manian, or Bakhtinian) allegory – invariably involves a translation effect that, paradoxically for some, *depends* on the co-privileging of a material trace of "language" whose reflexive performance and implementation spur a transition not back to some icon of

auto-reflexivity (that suspends an "older", and frankly destructive, even "fascist" referential machine), but as if forward, pro-
active, outside of a mimeto-anthropomorphic foreclosure: a foreclosure that continues to hold diverse "futures" hostage to the
violence of entirely political erasures which it demands. That
"materiality," on the contrary, has come to represent the token of
a bridge-site to allohuman technics that stand to re-wire the rhetoric of the virtual, decision, anthropomorphism (ocular-centrism,
identificatory tropologies), indeed, the event. It represents, in fact,
a point toward which the narrative production of recent phases of
"theory" and historicist reaction, down through cultural studies,
stand to re-converge in the mnemonic redefinition of "materiality." One can add the hypothesis that the politics of theory – of
theoretical positions, and of the word "theory" – which a rhetorical edifice like Ross' is a late symptom of, has led to a reification
and invisible neutralization of the "political," to a politics "in
theory" marked by an invisible reliance on a repetitive discursive
allocation and machine.

Some of this comes to the fore over the notion of the *image* itself,
the locus of the suppression of the epistemo-critical, and subsequently Ross' metaphoric use of technology – which he presents
himself as a (invariably humanizing) promoter of.[29] The deferred
"war" of this encounter may not be other than what Hitchcock
inserts in his "political thrillers," where a denatured "light"
(riven, intervalled, a pyrotechnic) occupies one of the sites masked
as an anthropomorphized "nature" in the example Ross projects.
Such espionage emerges, for instance, when Ross gives attention
to Sontag's indictment of image-culture in *On Photography*, which
takes the form of questioning a destructive culture of image
consumption's effects on the real: "In *On Photography*, a book
about the 'ethics of seeing' the world through the voracious filter
of image consumption, [Sontag] argues that the world is con-
sumed and used up by our appetite for images . . . In Sontag's
view, the world has been reduced to a set of potential photographs
. . . and large sectors of its population have become 'tourists of

[29] A similar reassertion of the humanistic space into which the "techno" can be
faultlessly introduced, without interruption, remains a subtext of Ross' putative
valorization of the "techno" – that is, as other than underlying *technicity* – in his
"Hacking Away at the Counterculture," in *Technoculture*, 107–35.

reality' as a result" (172). At the heart of Ross' objections is a desire
to preserve the figure of the "image" from epistemological complicity and agency – as, implicitly, with the transparency of language, even where marketed as pop commodities on par with any
Soho curio shop's commerce in eco-exotica. At root, again, is more
than a covertly "natural" concept of the image (and its attendant
ocular-centrism) that Ross champions – and this, under the inverse
rhetorical feint that the image is being attacked as a figure of
technology, which in turn has to be defended by himself (the
ideological disinvaginations are, at least, double). Attacking nature to defend another nature, only renamed as technology (and in
fact retro-humanist, which may not in the end be "Marxist," or
even *technical*), and this again to attack yet another "nature" that is
in fact the same mimetico-machine inhabiting that socio-humanist
model (as its empowering apparatus and as its dispossessing
pan-historical agency), Ross' objections imply an interesting verti-
ginousness – a loss of representational ground (or earth) – weakly
registered as rhetorical confusions, crucified targets for an inherited posture of "struggle" for which having a rhetorical other
remains a constitutive prerequisite. What Ross appears blind to –
and precisely in the site of the (mock-Apollonian) image, in the
heart of this mimetologic – is that the epistemological critique of
the destroying agency of the image presages an altered aesthetico-
politico thought that is, implicitly, materialist, but not necessarily
anthropomorphic at all. Thus Ross' defense of the image merely
pretends the latter is attacked as technology as such, when in
structing that "images of ecology today are also produced, con-
sumed, and used in ways that can help to counteract the destruction of the natural world" (181), reminding us "how images can be
used to activate popular support" (174). But this apparent recuperation of a supposedly villified technology – not the point of
Sontag's undeveloped position – inverts another polarity (and
here, despite Ross' attack on ascetic rhetoric and promotion of
"hedonism," he is firmly allied with "the Crucified," as unrevised
Marxian narratology tends to be). At this spot, that is a *faux*
technology which Ross sees as his job to remind us is liberation-
friendly, but which then becomes diminished and assimilated to
the retro-humanist "we" of this argument, over against a more
problematic *technicity* that, in fact, dispossesses the political im-

aginary of Ross' culturalist stance (of which more in a moment). Ross' media valorization of "techno" seems to follow the pattern of reaffirming the priority of a human (semantic) order before its framed incursion – like the acknowledgement of a materiality of language that does not alter a familiar model of meaning. Ross' "technoculture," in short, appears another ruse to suppress a more transformative technicity that bars the very interiority Ross' unreformed political "we" requires for its self-dramatization and appeal. Bewitched?

We return to the enigma of a doubly ventriloquized "nature" (or earth), the elusiveness of which emerges in the soft-outline of Ross' political imaginary.[30] That is, it must be egalitarian, it cannot address scarcity (since that is politically tagged as rhetorically co-optable), it must excise the non-human (reduced to a resubordination of the animal), it must ostensibly oppose self-denial. This though the excoriated non-human of which the biologist's "selfish-gene" serves as trope – a determining agency anterior to and unsubjected by Ross' centered "we" – can be represented as what precedes tropes precisely: the virtual site of inscription, a materiality by the ideological inversion of which (or, should we wish to put de Man's more clinical term into play here, *phenomenalization*) Ross' restored iconic community operates, nonetheless, covering an inhuman machine of consumption. One must dissociate the rhetoric of geneticity from the figural function: a *gene*, after all, even a selfish or narcissistic one, is not necessarily genetic, but rather a relay, a mutating *techne* of communication, a force of inscription. Ross' "politics" remains a verbal construct, undangerous to discursive power structures, blind to *geo*-political realities outside of, well, Soho: "A world of common prosperity, for sure, where social fulfillment is experienced individually as well as collectively . . . where public goods are no longer considered to be in short supply or in lavish excess, neither indigent nor affluent, if only because they would now be taken for granted and assumed to be a normative part of our daily, social environment . . . where forms of cross-species justice have replaced misanthropic 'laws' of nature as ecological rules of thumb" (273). If the anti-

---

[30] What Laclau calls the "constitutive distortion" of ideology in its posthumous sense – the projection onto a figure or object of "the illusion of fullness and self-transparency that it lacks" (301), or "the impossible fullness of the community" (303) – seems almost parodied here.

ecological analysis plays into the multi-nationals' interests in the process of preserving, for Ross, the priority of academic left-utopist rhetoric – that is, the unimpeded space of a privileged discursive posture – it is not accidental that the co-optation of the latter by traditional historicism presents a parallel political b(l)ind.

This mimetic blind, in Ross' discourse, emerges momentarily behind the attack on a mislabeled "authority" of *nature* – mislabeled, since at one point this names, precisely, the mimetologic machine dictating Ross' rhetorical moves. The "nature" Ross wrestles both with and against may be a web cast by this mimetologic when pretending to a concept of *phusis*, reference, or origin. One has only to look at the casual PBS Nature or Discovery Channel programs whose "charismatic fauna" Ross jousts with or at to discern a very different nature: not a scene, that is, turned toward the past, to legitimize the promise of a mimetic regime of model and copy, referent and word, "social" fact and ideological reflection, but, all along, and across earth, a proactive mimesis of infra-environment camouflage, metamorphoses, chemical warfare, strategic imitation, counter-signatures between species, predatory and counter-predatory ritual that moves "forward" across diverse temporal planes and backloops by *re*marking technically anterior positions – the zoographic modus of all fauna, all flora, as in the hieroglyphic mimeto-phagic choreographies between species of the rainforest or coral reefs.[31] That is, that what we call *life*-forms appear to transmutate forward, in an apprehension and inscription of surrounding forces and sign systems, in which mimicry serves diverse strategic roles – not to reproduce, according to a remarkably primitive human assumption about *its* language, stable *copies* of a same real. "Nature" in its chemical wars and camouflaging was already allomimetic, virtually linguistic or semaphoric, traversed by what is certainly an extra-terrestrial *technicity* – there is nothing specifically "earthly" about the trace – that interfaces life and death in a fashion which rewrites the hyperbolism of the former as a semiotic effect rather than a bio-logics. (One may accuse Ross of a perverse violation of cosmic PC here – that is, of being *bio-centric* on behalf of a more

---

[31] This – in its political guise – seems not unrelated to the trope of a (holistic) "nervous system" Michael Taussig tries to install as an allo-plastic and material-istic grid. See *The Nervous System* (New York: Routledge, 1992).

generally mimeto-historicist death drive.) This *other* "nature" tells us something different, of which Ross' modern biologist was a distracting parody but of which Benjamin's was certainly an explosive cross-temporal reminder of the parenthesis of the "human" today. Nature has never been other than this radically material effect of a *technicity* that can be called presemaphoric – of a "life" (gangstered or theoretical) that can be grasped as the semiotic-hermeneutic effect of a viral materiality neither alive nor dead as such (in organic terms).

This reminds us, today, not only of a necessary dislocation of the anthropomorphic or humanist trope but that the interface of life and death effects, the conversion of a mimetic regime to a proleptic or active mimeticism without model or copy, solicits and is solicited by a rethinking of "earth" – and, more immediately, a "materialistic" political imaginary – by which temporality must appear (*actively*) reconfigurable, distanced from causal models that remain enchaining and obfuscatory, and which may itself be viewed as an *extra-terrestrial* phenomenon, as can the effect called life. The "gangster *theory* of *life*" – a specifically named *theorization* of "life" – which Ross indicts and attempts to occlude is not biological eugenics nor the ersatz "authority" of a (nonetheless inarguable) eco-apocalypse, but what he rightfully perceives as the gangsterish disruption by a non-human factor of the privileged domain of retro-humanist apolitics' last (or most recent) re-imposition – even as a fetishization of the "social." (But the "social" has always been allied to a public exteriority, itself allied to readability and inscription; whereas the mimeto-humanist – even in the domain of social emancipation narratives – depends on a reinvestment of interiors, a mock private site or programmatic content, self, rhetorical "we.") What emerges, however, is not quite the same as opening the "social contract" to a third party, "nature," a non-human nature as Michel Serres proffers in *The Natural Contract* – a nature that, still anthropomorphized in a legal metaphor, even in the posture of a *parasite*, is not yet thought as an ante-natural and archival site traversing culturally constitutive divisions of living and dead.[32]

From a perspective we can still only name "materialistic" with all sorts of conditions, the labors of "cultural studies" have yet

---

[32] Michel Serres, *The Natural Contract*, trans. E. MacArthur and W. Paulson (Ann Arbor: University of Michigan Press, 1995).

another polar function, distinct from its official eudaimonist promise – that is, to liberate and transform contemporary culture. For if on the one hand the supposition of a historicism of the present appears contaminated (politically) by an incipient archivism, the inverse side of its columbarium-building is the artificing of a newly *labyrinthine* network of cross-referentials, an artificed memory grid beyond itself. Behind the retro-humanism of cultural studies, this information grid is being constructed, awaiting, however, another force or charge that it cannot foresee in its own terms to activate its switchboard *otherwise* – to reapprehend this new descriptivity as a switchboard, a sequence of potential *monadic* nodes, sites of virtual (dis)inscription (and the *virtualization* of once installed inscriptions). It would be here, again, that the time of the séance would emerge or be invoked – a "time" divested of the pretense of presentness. A time that is assertively "out of joint," as the predicate for subordinating the icons of past aesthetico-epistemologic regimes to other – indeed, allohuman – players. "Literature," the archaic yet ritual pre-site of this séance, of which the katabasis is a favored and reflexive moment starting with Homer, simulates that scene in which the ante-natural Dionysian-Apollonian trope of (a) materiality emerges – formal, semaphoric, irrevocably banal, dismantling all mimetic surfaces, putting temporal elements in substitutive rearrangement, "allegorical," a knocking or measuring effect heard, beneath the table, and as if outside.

If historicism as an archival politics stands to be disrupted by Benjamin's counter-strategy – the names for which traverse allegory, shock, materialistic historiography, or something entirely tentative like *allographic mnemotechnicity* – it is not with any pretense to the former's desistence as a viral code for the currency of "facts," knowledge, or ideology critique. What one can point to, though, is the programmatic rethinking of an allohuman technicity that voids metaphoric systems of *interiority*, upon which the humanist columbarium subsists. Such an allo-terrestrial principle may be posited as the *third* term preventing binary closure, which Serres unwittingly summons in his *The Natural Contract*. Only it is also and at all points a semiotic effect, a trace, according to which prosopopeias such as gender and race can begin to be performatively situated or reinscribed. No doubt, doing so in relation to "literature" or reading remains only one privileged site of such mnemotechnics, for altering installed hermeneutic nodes out of which image culture (and identity-effects, or for that matter "presents") continues to be optioned and contracted. To assume that the present can be rendered an archive for historicism's techniques, however, does not guarantee a prioritization of a life we have yet to successfully theorize. Such a labyrinthine memory grid as a potentially "new" set of referential relays and nodes (or monads) could be seen to reclaim that cultural studies to come foreclosed by "cultural studies" as a political imaginary. This, to the extent it could alter the premises from which non-mimetic referential orders can be launched, alternative chronographics tested.

I have suggested as heuristic fiction that there have been two cultural studies – the "first," a host (which is not one), and a "second," a parasite that pretends it is the legitimizing host – and that we might, rather, focus on a third. That cultural studies to come had been implied by the first and cut-off, bracketed, by its reinscription in a potentially depoliticized political imaginary, a traditionalist epistemo-critical model of reference virtually auto-referential in its extended anthropomorphic and historicist prem-ises. Only by turning back through a spectral "materiality" is the foreclosure implied by that programmatic regress possible to confute, since it solicits the site of installation itself. Indeed, we saw that in this gap between intervention and reinscription a mimetological war is opened, fought in critical and more general writing styles, in "allegorical" thought as the rendering virtual of fixed or received and coded histories, in which the stakes may well be the same as they have always been in wars: the cast and viability of alternative futures. (For the Benjamin of the *Theses*, this *war* has not ceased to be lost.) We might redescribe a genuine labor of "cultural studies," today, across diverse projects of re-description, as contributing to the conversion of an archivism of the present into a proactive mimesis through putting in place, often despite itself, a new mnemonic and nominal *labyrinth*, the ant-like stitching and cross-referencing of a memory grid to be assembled not by any theoretical gesture but the gradual sup-plantation of new matrices of nomination that anticipate such a stroke, caesura, or shock. Such a site, like that noted by Adorno in what is a clear misreading of Benjamin's performative or allographical project, would move beyond the positivism of a *faux* sociological real, magically promised by and to a now ancient mimetological machine. Like any *séance* there is a perceived *knocking* here – one at the very site of any emergent phenomenality as such. The knocking answers and asks certain questions – as if syncopated, aural, material above all, a series of semiotic intervals without origin (*Ursprung*), of and before any perception yet necessary to it, at and before (accordingly) where reading or writing constitute themselves amidst chance determinations, virtual coalescences. As if pure form, (a)*rhythmic*, the supplantation of an Apollonian moment not after but before the site out of which the rhetoric of the Dionysian emerges, by then regaled in mythemes and natural flourishes. Traversing determinations of living and dead, emerging from, and extinguishing in advance, like (dance) steps, as anterior traces; rupturing any mimetic surface or code – which it must, compulsively and against its protrusions, generate.[33] Such "materiality," insistently *banal*, like an infinite semiosis, like a foot, may be troped, nonetheless, as the non-human at the moment where the material signifier itself is focused on and passed through first as signified. It would counter and counter-sign all "historicisms." Recalling Benjamin's "materialistic historio*graphy*," it might inflect alternate models of time and mimesis out of which a third "cultural studies" under other names might emerge. Such might, in the process, retro-transform the networks and political imaginary put in place today into a new labyrinth out of which "events" may be stamped, a network virtual and inactive so long as its figures are apprehended, however, as an archivism of an (absent) "present."

It would seem that if the second "cultural studies" cannot die because it never strictly existed, and cannot be encountered even as a specter because it does not even know this situation obtains, it is not, necessarily, because it is on the side of lived "life," the everyday, *praxis*, the present, "liberation," and above all *transformation*. If, rather than promoting a left political imaginary by simply changing the canon and permissible objects of research before the cowering traditionalist, the second "cultural studies"

---

[33] This alteration can be visualized in Hitchcock's use of the bar-series motif across his screen – as though / / / – or, aurally, as a serial knocking, both of which recur in ways that suspend the pretended contract of the mimetic screen image, simultaneously resolving the movement of such into diverse signifying agents.

seems used by the latter to neutralize any alteration of the epistemo-critical order, are we in any position to ask what, "today,"
constitutes historial intervention? The question may be reframed:
can there be an (extra or hyper) "terrestrial" politics if the political
is conceived of still and only mimetically – if it is inscribed, in
advance, in a massive deferral, the time-policing modes of historicism as such, where "nature" becomes a false name or referent for
this site of memory-management and perceptual (that is, aesthetic) pre-orchestration in ritually unproblematized modes of
reading (that is, processing sign and force chains) – or is it not time
(though, one must immediately ask, what "time"?) for an anti-
mimetic political exploration?

There remains a point to add. What we have characterized as an
"older" epistemological model to which cultural studies may
recur can only be read as such from within a specious narrative
frame. It, that model, never really was "older" to begin with – was
always retro-inserted, the hermeneutic or secondary revision inversely sprung up to occlude the trauma of an event (or text).
Instead of any earlier model that stands to be moved "beyond"
we might speak rather of a persistent hermeneutic fold that is
encountered again and again, and has all along constituted a
cultural tendency within canonical communities responding to –
appropriating, interiorizing, effacing – the irruption of an event,
an event always registered on the level of a breach and inscription.
That hermeneutic fold which recurs to anthropocentric and mimetic models may appear defensive, like the Lacanian Symbolic's
need to efface any protrusion of the so-called Real, but it is always
staged over and against an exposed and virtually "materialistic"
import present in – and defining – that event. Kant may appear to
us through "Schiller," but the very nature of that instituted reading tells us more about the import of the Kantian disruption than
the "interpretation" itself. It is the same fold, in a sense, which
converts Bakhtin into the conservative humanist, Hitchcock into
the auteur, Benjamin into the the Marxist, "history" into historicism, Plato into the Platonist, or de Man into "de Man." Accordingly, it would seem that even the counter-narrative offered
above, which leads us toward a cultural studies to come, cannot
base itself on any developmental or progressive movement. One
is tempted to add, or reiterate, that the battles over possible

"futures" are likely to occur not over the specular politics of one suasion or another, but in the models of reference that are installed or disinstalled, out of which different programs of agency and the "human" proceed.

❖❖

PART II

Expropriating "cinema"
– or, Hitchcock's mimetic war

❖❖

4

Beyond "the Gaze"

If, then, we are really to tell how the world was born, we must bring in also the Errant Cause and in what manner its nature is *to cause motion*. So we must return upon our *steps* thus, and take up again, for these phenomena, an appropriate new beginning.

Plato, *Timaeus*

I held the lantern motionless. I tried how steadily I could to maintain the ray upon the eye. Meantime the hellish tattoo of the heart had increased. It grew quicker and quicker, and louder and louder every instant . . . It grew louder, I say, louder every moment! – do you mark me well?

Poe, *The Tell-Tale Heart*

There is a curious relation between film theory and Benjamin's much-cited essay on "The Work of Art in the Age of Technical Reproduction": while the former has rendered the latter canonical to the point of appearing an icon, it does not seem to have digested, and perhaps even forcibly effaces, two of that essay's major interventions (and let us defer asking whether such "canonization" is not, too familiarly, a technique of just such effacement). First, that where in that essay "cinema" is said to occur as and after the obliteration of what is called *aura* – by which, amidst else, is meant a tendency toward anthropomorphism – the emergent materiality implied by this remark is effaced in a tradition guided by logics of identification, mimetic interpretation, and Oedipal logics. This supposed loss of an aura allows Benjamin to open a line of thinking in which the *techne* of "cinema" parallels in his own writing the loss of "experience," a mnemonic break allied to "shock," and finally the most extreme implications of the word allegory: that is, where the mechanics of motion pictures (success-ive shots) mimes the allegorical relation of figures to successive anterior signs while positioning cinematic projection as a parallel to how inscriptions may be phenomenalized, how a "sensorium" appears implemented. That light itself, in this model, originates over a space of marking, as an effect of writing (photo-graphesis, we might say), and is in direct contact with key uses of sight going back to the *eidos*, as figure of knowing/seeing. As the ocularist tradition here described subsists in the evasion and occlusion of this aura-less marking that precedes and suspends any anthropo-morphism, any project of mimetic identification, it invokes a privileged model for probing how the term ideology too might operate. It can be argued that it is over Hitchcock's work that these two trajectories collide: that of a Benjaminian and materialistic practice of "cinema" which, precisely, appears to mark itself as a project of radical intervention, and a hermeneutic tradition (in-deed, auteurism was spawned in relation to him) reliant on theo-logical, identificatory, and mimetic motifs that run counter to this project. In a way, the "materiality" of Hitchcock's practice marked perhaps by a figure of *mother* that laces his text (the premier example of which is in *Psycho*, of course) emerges in a resolute use of premimetic systems of puns, anagrams, sound, and networking inscriptions that render the installation of a different reading model one of its invasive aims. To some degree, the recent emer-gence of Žižek's work on Hitchcock presents a perfect snapshot of this scene: one of a psychoanalytically inspired criticism (like so much in film theory) poised at the point of exceeding the auratic and theologico-mimetic tradition of interpretation, only to be folded back into it at the last moment – becoming, indirectly, a stepping stone nonetheless to a site where a more materialist "reading" may be opened. Like *Psycho*, which links the issues of an obliterative mnemonics and "mother" to America itself, it may be interesting to address this ideological cluster and site – in which the names Hitchcock and Benjamin might be unexpectedly brought together – as an "American" problematic.

It may not at first seem clear why Slavoj Žižek's work should appeal to Americanists,[1] since the Slovenian Lacanian is steeped

---

[1] An earlier version of the essay from which the present chapter derives was first published in *American Literary History*.

in a post-Marxist Hegelian discourse saturated with the sort of high Euro-theory formulae (the big Other, *extimité*, the "gaze") which neo-pragmatism, for instance, often shies from. Whether we are now at the point where "neo-pragmatism" has exposed itself as a retro-humanist ideology primarily marked (like new historicism) by its evasion of linguistic theory – and, for that matter, what might be called "originary" pragmatism – under nationalistic rhetoric does not exempt us, today, from sifting through the conceptual detritus that still occupies, if not clogs, the market-place. This may be particularly true in the case of cinema, or what has been called "film theory," which, despite its often neo-Lacanian programs (in conditional senses), has shared with that retro-humanist episode a covert subjectivist, identificatory, Oedipalist, above all mimetic and, in the end, ocular-centric bias that has inscribed much of its labor within certain metaphysical circuits, and made the moniker ("film *theory*") somewhat oxy-moronic at times. Nowhere has this bias been as evident as in the auteurist critical traditions – running from the theologically inflec-ted (Rohmer and Chabrol) through feminist work (Mulvey, Mod-leski) – that engulf the name "Hitchcock." Like Bakhtin's incarcer-ation by the Bakhtinians, or Plato's platonism, Hitchcock's oeuvre draws this counter-enforcement of mimetic ideology to itself at its point of greatest danger. This, though it can be claimed that precisely that text goes furthest of any in emptying, and violently transforming precisely that hermeneutic tradition through a sys-tem of marking that prioritizes the linguistic and material signifier over perception – including that whose residue can be heard in the construct of "the gaze," even where applied (Žižek) to a non-human site. Yet aside from Žižek's utilization of American film and popular culture to map out a populist Lacan in works like *Looking Awry* and *Enjoy Your Symptom!*, this "postmodern" theo-rist appears something of an American phenomenon *avant la lettre*.[2]

I will first explore this prospect by examining Žižek's reading of

[2] Žižek's most relevant works in this area are *The Sublime Object of Ideology*, hereafter cited as *SOI* (1989); *For They Know Not What They Do – Enjoyment as a Political Factor*, hereafter *FTKN* (1991); *Looking Awry: An Introduction to Jacques Lacan Through Popular Culture*, hereafter *LA* (1991); *Enjoy Your Symptom! – Jacques Lacan in and Out of Hollywood*, hereafter *Enjoy* (1992); and, as contributing editor, *Everything You Always Wanted to Know About Lacan . . . But Were Afraid to Ask Hitchcock*, hereafter *Everything* (1992).

that most problematically iconic of "American" film-texts, Hitch-cock's *Psycho*, and his use of Hitchcock in general. In this examin-ation, however, I will have two aims. The first will be to determine where Žižek's deployment of *late* Lacan – for instance, his focus on the concept of the Real or "the Thing" (*das Ding*) to mark a radical exteriority that structures ideology and the subject – impacts on a rhetoric of the self which has long seemed endemic to American-ists. To raise this question is to acknowledge a parallel between "American" cultural logic and so-called postmodern aesthetics marked by Žižek's use of (American) popular culture ("In post-modernism, this 'apparition' of the phallus is universalized" (*En-joy*, 129)). Once we allow, however, that Hitchcock functions as a partial index to postmodern aesthetics (the theoretical "'post-modern' phenomenon *par excellence*" (*Everything*, 2)), the question arises as to whether Žižek indeed lies "beyond" the models of identification, inter-subjectivity, and narrative that he critiques in Hitchcock's name, or whether Hitchcock's text does not exceed, in the end, the Lacanian hermeneutic that Žižek deploys. For if one of the fascinations of Žižek's work in popular culture is his use of Hitchcock as a master-text, by using Hitchcock mostly to *exemplify* late Lacan a profound foreclosure of that text also occurs. In pursuing this we will return to the problem that Žižek seems to occlude when addressing Hitchcock: that of *language* itself, and whether Hitchcock ultimately deploys a model of *reading* that precedes any metaphorics of "the gaze." I will propose that rather than trying to pass "beyond the wall of language" (Lacan) in quest of a psychotic kernel that obliterates the dead hermeneutic discourse of the Symbolic, we must ultimately substitute for a now familiar rhetoric of "gaze," at least in the case of Hitchcock, a more eviscerating and problematic paradigm of *reading or marking precedent to and productive of seeing/reading itself* – and that of material signs, graphics, marks, sounds, or puns (visual and au-ral) that disperse any symbolic hermeneutic in advance. What emerges here is not just an adjustment of interpretive strategy, a refinement of film "theory," since the ideological investments in a given reception of Hitchcock to date stand to be transfigured (including the rich vein of feminist treatments) by a far-reaching reflection on materiality, memory, and the event – indeed, a rewriting of the aesthetic – that emerges as having driven this "cinema" from the first. To examine this one could turn to another text of Hitchcock's to juxtapose to *Psycho*, one that could be called if anything more postmodern or even poised at the point at which that term seems self-cancelled, *Sabotage*, which I will address in the next chapter. That film, routinely dismissed as minor, may prove to resist the oculist, identificatory, and Oedipalist tradition of Hitchcock "interpretation" – of which Žižek's approach will prove, despite its intent, to be the last avatar, the death knell – and present access to a "materialistic" and linguistic premise for approaching this oeuvre. For the moment we will examine Žižek's theorization as a limit attempt to restitute an interiorist poetics that, seemingly counter to "American" neo-pragmatism, tends only to invert (and sustain) that model, in order to ask where Hitchcock's practice exceeds the hermeneutic and mimetic strictures of "film theory" – and this in a materialist, transvaluative, and post-humanist fashion.

1.

It is interesting, first, to make a detour of sorts using Žižek's approach as example – one that seems to bring together a discourse on ideology, the "sublime," and materiality with an innovative use of Hitchcock as master-text.

If we ask where an Americanist ideology of the self stands to be impacted by Žižek's critique, two sites come to mind at once: American neo-pragmatism (as represented, however differently, by Rorty and Cornel West) and the question of the American "sublime" itself. Like Žižek's project, neo-pragmatism sees itself as a critical move "beyond" post-structuralism – or what it sometimes calls "theory." Yet unlike neo-pragmatism, which does this in a sense by expelling "theory" as the continental *other* in order to reconfigure a domain of specifically American interiority, Žižek insists that all such interiors are ideological fictions busy effacing the radical exteriority that forms their "kernel."

For Žižek a great deal rests on the distinction between a Lacan of the middle period (represented by the Seminar on the "Purloined Letter") and the *late* Lacan, since the latter shifts from addressing the play of the signifier and inter-subjectivity – the parallel of modernism and, for Žižek, post-structuralism – to addressing the proto-psychotic relation to the Real which lies beyond the interpretive machinery of cultural narrative. The middle Lacan concerned with the role of the Symbolic order (cultural rules, the name of the father, the circulation of the signifier, inter-subjectivity, and the law) is for Žižek supplanted by this *late* Lacan whose focus on a Real addresses an absolute otherness "beyond the wall of language" (Lacan). On the one hand, Žižek's focus on late Lacan involves a discrete revision of "the gaze" as the term has been used in American film theory and gender politics: revising a tendency to subjectivize this term, as occurred in Laura Mulvey's influential indictment of a "male gaze," Žižek reminds us that "the gaze" in Lacan is, in the first instance, non-human, a site of personification of the inanimate Thing (*das Ding*):

> what lies beyond is not the Symbolic order but a real kernel, a traumatic core. To designate it, Lacan uses a Freudian term: *das Ding*, the Thing as an incarnation of the impossible *jouissance* (the term Thing is to be taken here with all the connotation it possesses in the domain of horror science fiction: the "alien" from the film of the same name is a pre-symbolic, maternal Thing *par excellence*). (*SOI*, 132)

The Thing as a non-historicizable site or protrusion is what the discourse of the Symbolic attempts to "gentrify." Since film theory or Hitchcock interpretation had come to rely on habits of identification and authorial surrogacy, Žižek's claim to an *otherness* beyond this discursive field parallels the move from post-structuralism to his supposedly more radically grounded post-Marxist ideology critique and discourse of "the Thing." (Žižek links limitless "interpretation" as such to the Symbolic.) Thus the distinction between middle and late Lacan becomes paradigmatic: if the "beyond" of the pleasure principle represented for middle Lacan the assimilation of the subject to the Symbolic order and the law, for Žižek's the late Lacan the Symbolic turns out to be that "pleasure principle" for which any "beyond" is now the unassimilable effect of the *Thing*, around which (absence) the subject organizes an enjoyment (*jouissance*) in which he/she alone appears ontologically grounded.

One example of this move that is interesting for us will be the "subject beyond subjectivity" (*Everything*, 255) that Žižek locates at the core of Hitchcock's *Psycho*: "The ultimate socio-ideological lesson of *Psycho* is therefore the collapse of the very field of intersubjectivity as medium of Truth in late capitalism (*Everything*,

262). If in the neo-Lacanian parable the Symbolic entails an initial "death" by being the domain of automaton-like formula and narrative, "life" is an effect of the (dead) automata of the Symbolic that would undergo a "second" death with the irruption of the Thing – the "obliteration" of an entire signifying order. It is not surprising, as we will see, that Hitchcock is so useful at this juncture, since in effect his text can be said to void the entire "interiorist" and identificatory tradition on which this largely recuperative – that is, romantic, subjectivist, ideological, non-material – concept of the "sublime" has resided (a point I will return to below).

It is Žižek's construction of late Lacan which brings the figures of neo-pragmatism and Americanism into play, particularly where the former sees itself too as superseding "theory" (Žižek's "post-structuralism"). We can now address why Žižek's analysis solicits an American response, particularly if American popular and film culture seem the field in which this Lacan is best exemplified. Since for Žižek the radical grounding of historically contingent truth occurs through the machinations of a prefigural "Thing," one might ask where this radical sense of contingency differs from Rortian relativism? But this is not Žižek's primary intervention, which instead takes place at the very construction of the subject. Rather, what might be called the ideology of "neo-pragmatism" suggests where Americanism both manifests and evades that proto-psychotic encounter with radical exteriority – the *extimate* – which Žižek tracks. Certainly, it is interesting that the word "Thing" is itself one translation of the Greek word *pragma* which we find at the root of "pragmatism," and it suggests a curious inversion in the current Americanist use of the term. Specifically, it suggests that if a certain classical "pragmatism" concerned itself with a type of radical materiality not dissociable from that of language – a premise that is obvious from Protagoras through Peirce – then "neo-pragmatism" may in fact involve less a reclamation than a subtle evasion of that tradition. This prospect makes a work like Cornel West's *American Evasion of Philosophy: A Genealogy of Pragmatism* (1989), which returns to a theological self as the basis for a communitarian ethics of multiculturalism, the more curious. A project like West's, which certainly sees itself as a move from Rorty's *faux* interiority or "irony" into the exteriority of the world and multiculturalist politics, has an irony of its own.

It is curious not only for attempting an all too classical "geneal-ogy" that usurps for left academic multiculturalism the legiti-mating pedigree of the (white) fathers, but for involving, despite its appeal to the political, a regressive return to subjective interior-ity.[3] What emerges is that the "neo-pragmatism" of Rorty and West, in seemingly opposite ways, represents a monumental re-gression within and in the name of the American agenda. If, as Žižek implies, a certain Americanism is manifest in "post-modern" popular culture, and *Psycho* in particular, it supersedes the domain of the Symbolic in a kind of psychotic or anti-Oedipal poetics. If so, Rorty and West may represent the attempt to return to a defensive posture in this regard, inscribing themselves in an Americanist rhetoric of the self that is the classic evasion, and this not only of "philosophy" (West's trope for epistemology and linguistic materialism) but of what Žižek calls the *destitution sub-jective* (Lacan's phrase for the emptying of the subject as well as a certain model of inter-subjectivity) – a destitution, precisely, that echoes Emerson's original refusal of History and that empowers American aesthetics.

Thus *Psycho*'s move beyond what Žižek calls the "pragmatic-hermeneutic inter-subjective model" represents a political inter-vention, in so far as it dislocates an entire tradition of interpreta-tion that could be called (academic) "America's" defense against its own inner history and logic. It would seem that Žižek exploits an implicit opposition between humanism's rhetoric of interiority (on the right and left) and a *rhetoric of exteriority* which bars any return to models of expression, meaning, or inter-subjectivity. Among other things, the subject rewritten as "the gaze" of the Thing as exemplified in *Psycho* "is what the pragmatic-hermeneutic inter-subjective approach endeavors to neutralize at any price, since it impedes the subjectivization/narrativization, the subject's full integration into the Symbolic universe" (258). It is not accidental that Rorty's attempt to preserve the "private" space of the pragmatist takes the form of abjecting the Euro-theoretical "other" (Nietzsche, the French, "theory"), and does so in order to recreate as "American" a space of affirmed interiority,[4] or that West, in appearing to reverse Rorty's *faux* interiority by

---

[3] I analyze this problem in "Too Legit To Quit: The Dubious Genealogies of Pragmatism," chapter 4 in my *Anti-Mimesis*.

[4] Richard Rorty, *Contingency, Irony, Solidarity* (1989), 158.

linking the subject to political communities, does so by restituting a communitarian theological self under the auspices of the political – that is, by affirming a model even more rooted in a *faux* interiority, one that invokes, moreover, an impersonally *voiced* and strangely autocratic political program (West's "prophetic pragmatism").

In contrast to "neo-pragmatism," we might pun, Žižek's *Thingism* retains Lacan's focus on a radical exteriority that exceeds the recuperative inter-subjective model and remains a counter to it. Much in Žižek's analyses of ideology (or "ideological anamorphosis") gives the promise of a new politics, yet the psychoanalytic model can be said to do this only in a covertly *aesthetic* way. That is, by altering the manner in which we read epistemological investment and desire, we alter the options for dissolving ideological formations. Žižek's analysis of the "sublime object" projects intervention less by demystification than aesthetic disinvestment ("whereby the ideological anamorphosis loses its power of fascination and changes into a disgusting protuberance" (*Enjoy*, 140)). If Žižek's analysis of the "Nation thing" raises the prospect of political critique (nationalism viewed as "the privileged domain of the eruption of enjoyment into the social field" (*LA*, 165)), it partakes of the ironic fatalism of specular psychoanalysis.[5] Instead of pointing toward a politics available in the mode of a new mimetic agenda, Žižek's project appears rather staked in the transformation of *interpretation* – a site that reweds politics to epistemology, that is to say, the very model of "philosophy" purportedly *evaded* by the "pragmatism" of West's title.

While Žižek approaches the vast samples of American pop culture with vampiric urgency, eager to assume the particular unrecoverability of American psychosis as his example, the Americanists busily abject that same American logic under the guise of the Euro-theoretical-"other." What Žižek has in common

---

[5] Elizabeth J. Bellamy, in "Discourses of Impossibility: Can Psychoanalysis be Political," may miss the implications of a shift in the very definition of the political when she remarks that what "gets occluded (sublated?) in Žižek's modulation from Laclau and Mouffe's 'impossible' object to his own 'sublime' object is the 'impossibility' of politics (that is, the very real antagonisms, shifting alliances, and negotiations of real political struggle)" (33). A somewhat more complex picture of Žižek's relation to the "political," which is equally skeptical, occurs in Rey Chow's "Ethics after Idealism (1993)."

with the neo-pragmatist – an attempt to narrate a step "beyond" post-structuralism ("theory") and the endless metonymy of the signifier – may be conceived either as a return to the enclosure of a self (Rorty, West) or, more interestingly, as the appeal to a non-historicizable exterior (the Thing). Žižek appears to represent a limit logic implicit in the subtext of "America" itself, before which the Americanist's ideology of interiority or self-hood always re-coils. If a privileged work for undoing this ideology is Hitchcock's *Psycho*, there remains a less visible aspect of Žižek's text that should be addressed.

When Žižek reads *late* Lacan as superseding middle Lacan, as said, he narrates a move "beyond" the realm of the Symbolic and toward the Real. This movement beyond the play of the signifier, metonymy, post-structuralism, and modernism, however, takes an odd or quasi-ironic form, since the latter site itself insists on the suspension of *narrativization* – the Symbolic's renowned tech-nique of "gentrification" or recuperation. Accordingly, through-out Žižek a narrative is structured by repeated invocations of the Hegelian trope of the "negation of (a) negation" ("the whole point is just that we come to experience how this negative, disruptive power, menacing our identity is simultaneously a positive condi-tion of it" (*SOI*, 176)). Time and again, a given first term – "middle Lacan," modernism, metonymy, the signifier, the Symbolic, the inter-subjective, desire, the symptom – will be superseded by a putative *second* – "late Lacan," postmodernism, "metaphor," the "sign" (which, unlike the signifier, produces the "answer of the real" (*LA*, 34)), the Real, the "subject beyond subjectivity," the drive, the *sinthom*. The "negation of negation" becomes Žižek's means of controlling a representational economy and it has its rhetorical dangers. We can see its logic working, for example, when Žižek notes that Lacan's vacated and depthless subject is not a postmodern subversion of the subject of the Enlightenment, but that it all along defined the very logic of that familiar topos. That is: the reader may think that the Lacanian subject (as the second term) involved a negation of the Enlightenment subject (first term), but this is a false narrative, since the former really precedes and constituted the latter in its forgetfulness. It is a system that is also polemically in evidence, in Žižek's contain-ment of Derrida: "The impossibility (of identity) unearthed by Derrida through the hard work of deconstructive reading supposed to subvert identity constitutes the very definition of identity" (*FTKN*, 37).

If the "negation of negation's" economic and recuperative role as a managing trope exacts its price, that becomes visible when one finds dispersed throughout Žižek a series of apparent binaries that are managed similarly as the very premise of this discourse. In each case – modernism/postmodernism, "post-structuralism" (or middle Lacan)/late Lacan, symptom/*sinthom*, signifier/sign, desire/drive, the Enlightenment subject/Lacan's subject – the result is a spatial or anamorphic logic staged as a temporal narrative. That is, again, the "second" term (postmodernism as the focus on the kernel of the Real) supersedes the earlier (modernism, in which the disruption of the marginal is experienced as a subversion), yet, as with Lyotard, the "latter" term always preceded its "predecessor" (the kernel of the Real was only impossibly "gentrified" by the Symbolic). The result is a sort of double effacement, which resituates Žižek's positions at the limit of – if still with*in* – the terms they dramatically invert and empty. This is how the Symbolic or language can appear to be surpassed, moved "beyond," while the description of such movement may involve regressions to seemingly precritical terms (identification, subject, metaphor). This seems the case, for instance, when Žižek reinstitutes terms of immediacy or even identification to point to this site (in *Psycho*, for instance, we are said to *"identify with the abyss beyond identification"* (*Everything*, 226)). We witness this again when "the gaze" becomes the absolute limit term of a personified otherness of "the Thing" beyond subjectivity, yet uncannily turns out to have structured the subject – the Enlightenment subject was all along a cyborg, a vampire, a monster. This movement is connected to the often traditional nature of many of Žižek's remarks on Hitchcock, moments when we seem to see the vampire (a figure with whom the slovenian clearly identifies) forgetfully stooping to take his *jouissance*, draining the cultural corpse of its representational pleasures. But Žižek's invocation of the subject as the hoary undead, meant to shock in uncanny fashion, wears by dint of its mantra-like use, becoming another retro-gesture, a reinscription of a kind of identity (and valencing of "life") that depends on the prosopopeia of "the Thing" repeatedly. He flirts with, manipulates, exploits, and effaces this dominance of the material over the "living," the pre-inhabitation of figural "death" (as inscription, mnemonics, or the projector) that Hitchcock marks routinely in advance of his opening scenes (the example of John Robie's fake suicide, of being a celebrity of the "Underground," or even the post-credit walk of the black cat from *To Catch a Thief* come to mind). Unlike Žižek, who seems transfixed with joy at the ersatz unveiling of "mother" as the personified undead subject, Hitchcock repeatedly marks the death of all his screen figures in advance of any narrative; the collapse of death and the pretense of cinematic "life" not only emerges as the model of semiotic consciousness (or actual life) as such, but one premise by which the text as text usurps alternate temporal logics and poses itself repeatedly (often in the plots of espionage) as a historical act or intervention.

It is interesting that the demise of a certain ocularism seems to occur about the figure of "gaze" precisely. While Žižek appears precise in indicating the special place "gaze" and "voice" occupy for the late Lacan ("the exactly opposite way" of Derrida (*LA*, 125)), a place in which "the eye and the gaze are constitutively asymmetrical," it is the clash between the promising rhetoric of "the gaze" and the place of language in *Psycho* that returns us to the American sublime. Not only does Žižek almost never concern himself with language or dialogue in a Hitchcock text, but *his evasion of language marks a blindness and re-idealization of sorts*. For if the encounter with the "impossible Thing" lies beyond language, subjectivity, or interpretation, it still manifests itself in figures that materially *signify* in some form. Žižek accounts for this space that both is and is not a signifier by way of the Lacanian term *sinthom*. In psychoanalytic terms, it supplants and transposes the *symptom*. Rather than being, like "symptom," a term of the Symbolic generating endless interpretation, the late Lacanian *sinthom* emerges as the uninterpretable and thing-like effect one cannot interpret but only identify with or "enjoy." This is the postmodern effect as Žižek sees it. Among other things, the movement from the signifier (or metonymy) to what is called by Lacan the "sign" – or metaphor, what promises the "answer of the Real" – is portrayed as a move from "language" to a certain *beyond*. This ontological rooting of the subject through *identification* with his or her impenetrable "enjoyment" (*jouissance*) is an identification with the *sinthom*: "symptom, conceived as *sinthom*, is literally our only substance, the only positive support of our being, the only point that gives consistency to the subject," and "the final Lacanian definition of the end of the psychoanalytic process is identification with the symptom" (*SOI*, 75). Žižek's recurrence to conventional interpretation is in evidence in his auteurist rhetoric and investment in a "theological" reading. Examples would include his reading of the end of *The 39 Steps*, as following the routine "production-of-the-couple" narrative (*LA*, 100–101)), or the recourse to intersubjective or Oedipal platitudes (his reading of the end of *The Birds* (104)) or to Lacanian didacticism (his remarks on *Rope* as lesson (*Enjoy*, 37)).[6] Yet this would be Kierkegaardian "leap" out of the aesthetic domain has several interesting by-products, including the fact that the identification of the subject with his or her *sinthom* as the new "end" of analysis topographically overlaps with a site of (reconciled?) psychosis – and here a reading of *Psycho* with Norman Bates as anti-Oedipal hero emerges. When we move from metonymy only to return to "metaphor," or from the "symptom" to the Lacanian neo-logism *sinthom* (*sin*, synthetic, St. Thomas, "man"), we have in fact moved not "beyond" language but back (again), at least as simulacrum, to a precritical understanding of language: metaphor requires identification, the *sinthom* operates like an inert *symbol*. If Hitchcock inaugurates a post-humanist discourse that has yet to be addressed, what emerges as an American sublime *beyond* the models of identification and narrativization would occupy an anti-Oedipal or proto-psychotic space. Yet in returning to a figure of the "gaze" that is a personification of the (dead) Thing, Žižek overlooks where Hitchcock may have other ways of accounting for the generation of his text – ways that are material, linguistic, and prefigural. Before we explore, however, where Hitchcock exceeds any rhetoric of "the gaze" by inserting a model of *reading* in his text (*as* memory, machine, mother, or marking) that exceeds *both* the subjectivizing trends of Americanists and so-called "post-

---

[6] Žižek implies that the appropriation of "the gaze" as a subjectivized category (or blank panopticon) has been a misreading – a fact that has drawn critical attention of late. For recent critiques of the deployment of "the gaze" in film studies, see Craig Saper, "A Nervous Theory: The Troubling Gaze of Psychoanalysis in Media Studies," *Diacritics*, 21, 4 (Winter, 1991), 33–52, and Joan Copjec, "The Orthopsychic Subject: Film Theory and the Reception of Lacan," *October*, 49 (Spring, 1989), 53–72. Of course, the source for the classical adaptation of "the (male) gaze" for feminist theory remains Laura Mulvey's "Visual Pleasure and Narrative Cinema," in *Visual and Other Pleasures* (1987), 14–26.

modern" epiphanies of Žižek, we must examine how the reading is constructed.

2.

The test of this failed hermeneutic apparatus, of course, is in the encounter with Hitchcock's text – and though much more is at stake than an "interpretive" tactic, here, the machine of "exemplary" takes on the films that Žižek offers yields mostly conventional transpositions of some Lacanian formula, missionary translation work. We must now survey the consequences of an alternate, allographic approach that does not return to the cartesian and oculist fold – constituted by an evasion of the materiality of the mark, first of all – one that is less predicated on a machine of reversal and example than the agency of unmarked signifying and citational networks. Hitchcock, in this, remains one of the most powerful implementations of the riddle Benjamin cast by connecting destructive "allegory" with the mnemotechnic of cinema.

In framing his reading of *Psycho* Žižek situates himself first both within Chabrol and Rohmer's discussion ("the theological dimension of Hitchcock's oeuvre" (*Everything*, 211)) and Rothman's equally auteur-identified rhetorical approach. These are, after all, positions rooted in subjective identification that will be threatened by the "gaze" in *Psycho*'s embodiment of the subject's depthlessness. Žižek discretely sets these models up for a conversion, knowing that the dominant traditions of "interpretation" which he would go "beyond" are situated in precisely such terms of authorial surrogacy. Žižek dislocates the "gaze" from any subjective position, turning it into the site of absolute strangeness that is precisely inaccessible to the eye in the field of otherness. He stresses that for the late Lacan "the eye and the gaze are constitutively asymmetrical" (*LA*, 125). "Gaze" is shifted from securing a general field of subjectivity to emptying and re-inscribing that as the prosopopeia of a radically exterior site (the Thing). Yet even when so revised, "gaze" retains the inevitable traces of transparency, immediacy, and power that adhere to metaphors of the visible going back to Plato, or for that matter Emerson. Thus *Psycho* is seen as a text in which we "*identify with*

156

the abyss beyond identification" (*Everything*, 226). To this degree, we might distinguish between Žižek's regressive notion of Hitchcock's rhetorical relation to the spectator ("one is even tempted to say that Hitchcock's films ultimately contain only two subject positions, that of the director and that of the viewer" (218)), and his intuition of the presence of allegory in a proto-Benjaminian sense which contains "the strongest 'ideologico-critical' potential of Hitchcock's films" (219). With Žižek, for whom the birds in that film appear pure representatives of the invading Thing, what is at stake in "the psychotic core of Hitchcock's universe" (241) is a text oriented by the move "beyond the wall of language" (256). Hitchcock's material theorization of language – to date all but ignored, not surprisingly, since it resists *both* the subjectivist *and* this appropriation – remains occluded in this conventional move.[7]

The at times rote rendition of Lacanian dogma ("'reality' is the field of symbolically structured representations, the outcome of the 'gentrification' of the Real" (239)), or the vaudeville stage-directions for the uncanny ("this very coincidence of our view with the thing's gaze intensifies its radical Otherness to an almost unbearable degree" (252)), seldom interfere with the seductive-ness of Žižek's analyses. One of the pleasures of exploring Hitchcock at this stage, however, is the way in which a penetration into the *detail* of the text seems to emerge, so that some odd moment in one film or another leaps out to generate webs of commentary, and it is here that Žižek will seek to redeploy the trope of the *sinthom*. When this happens in sanctioned Lacanian terms – the location of the "blot" in the ship hulks at the ending scene in *Marnie*, or Doris Day's disembodied "voice" pursuing the son up the stairs in the second *Man Who Knew Too Much* – the analysis may be dramatic, yet so bound to the economy of an example that we get only short darting glosses. In fact, Žižek is so wedded to the subject's "impossible point of absolute strangeness" (254) that *he ends up remaining quite mimetic or traditional in many respects.* Yet it is within *language* as Hitchcock theorizes it (as a dismembering scene of material figures, prefigural sounds, graphic puns and repetitions) that the Cartesian subject may be predissolved, much

---

[7] For commentary on this, see my "Hitchcock and the Death of (Mr.) Memory," chapter 9 in *Anti-Mimesis*.

as Hannay opens *The 39 Steps* as a body already headless, that is, with the viewer's penchant for "identification" also already barred.

A tension in Žižek's theorizing becomes apparent when he tries to import the concept of *sinthom* into Hitchcock. We recall, again, that the *sinthom* is a "symptom" transposed beyond interpretation or the chain of signifiers. While it operates as a sheer manifestation or protrusion, it is also a kind of master-sign that nonetheless grounds or ruptures all signifying chains. One might say that, being opposed to metonymy, it subtly operates as a sort of radical or imploded metaphor without being called such. Žižek openly privileges metaphor over metonymy in Lacan's name – the very function that the *sinthom*, however objectalized, represents in pretending the end all signifying chains.[8] Thus he offers a chapter in the middle of his collection called "Hitchcockian *Sinthoms*." Here he begins to identify motifs that every connoisseur of Hitchcock has been entranced and hermeneutically violated by – figures that traverse various films, breaking context, abrupting narrative interpretation, generating parallel universes of sense ("The postmodernist pleasure in interpreting Hitchcock is procured precisely by such self-imposed trials" (127)). Žižek's list seems, for that reason, unaccountably modest (the glass of milk in *Suspicion* that re-emerges in *Spellbound*, the woman with glasses, the person suspended by another hand); indeed, so much so as to indicate a blockage. It represents the irreducible heart of Hitchcock's poetics and yet, for Žižek, denotes a site that must also be contained. For if such transtextual figures (and what are they up to?) are pursued by Žižek it could entail replacing the rhetoric of "gaze," together with its implicit accent on immediacy, with a dismembering but irreducibly material model of *reading*. What is bizarre, in fact, is that this chapter, announced by its very position as the central theoretical contribution of the book, breaks off *after three pages* – indeed, trails off in parenthetical murmurs about the first *Man Who Knew Too Much* that are almost unconnected to the thesis mentioned and, if anything, return to traditional interpretive patter about the family and so on. Why, indeed, does the *sinthom*, so

---

[8] Žižek's main modification is to posit that "metaphor" as itself over an empty site: "The 'original metaphor' is not a substitution of 'something for something-else' but a substitution of something for nothing . . . which is why *metonymy is a species of metaphor*" (*FTKN*, 50).

central to Žižek's system, seem to betray him in the reading of Hitchcock? The answer perhaps rests in the fact that the "symbolic" value of this emblem (advertised as the end and *"limit of interpretation"* (126)), is *ruptured* by the very mechanics of repetition that it is inscribed in or produced by ("details which persist and repeat themselves") – what recalls the operation of Mr. Memory in *The 39 Steps* who can banally repeat only "facts," but is also called *"re*marking," in a position to accord this system of re-marking a sublime status (the formula for the silent flying war-plane):

How, then, are we to interpret such extended motifs? If we search in them for a common core of meaning . . . we enter the domain of Jungian archetypes which is utterly incompatible with Hitchcock's universe; if, on the other hand, we reduce them to an empty signifier's hull filled out in each of the films by a specific content, we *don't say enough*: the force which makes them persist from one film to another eludes us. The right balance is attained when we conceived them as *sinthoms* in the Lacanian sense: as a signifier's constellation (formula) which fixes a certain core of enjoy-ment, like mannerisms in painting . . . So, paradoxically, these repeated motifs, which serve as a support of the Hitchcockian interpretive de-lirium, designate the limit of interpretation: they are what resists inter-pretation, the inscription into the texture of a specific visual enjoy-ment. (127)

Yet they do not end in the detail of "a visual enjoyment," or its myth, since they imply an *active and perpetually transformed* site of reading between emblems, scenes, actors reappearing in different roles, sets of signifying configurations or their erasure which are utterly critical to the postmodern aspect of Hitchcock. They are turned aside from, I would suggest, because as secret agents of signification they dislocate the sort of rush to negative immediacy that is Žižek's favored lure "beyond" subjectivity.

In the first *Man Who Knew Too Much* the allegorical problem Žižek is avoiding is not hard to find. If, as he notes, the "rhythm of the entire film is regulated by a succession of shots," he rightly mentions that scene in which Louis Bernard, shot on the dance-floor, must look down beneath his lapel to see the bullet-hole before he proceeds to *act out* dying, "as if the detour through consciousness is necessary for the shot to become effective" (127). The problem is that "knowing too much" does not primarily allude to knowing something about some element in the plot, but to a cognitive excess that is also a deficiency, and to a "knowledge" of simulacra itself which is also one of "my" death. Hence, not only is Louis Bernard's look one of deferred (re)cognition, later repeated in the blank and uncomprehending look of Abbott's nurse when shot and dying. It is also an excess or rupture between two rhetorical levels that leads to a recurrent *loss of consciousness* in the text: the fainting of Jill, Lawrence being knocked out, Clyde's being hypnotized with a black marble (in which the phrase "black out" changes pronunciation to "blank out," attaching this loss of consciousness to the momentary conjunction of white and black, as on the whiskey sign at Piccadilly Circus). All of this returns us to the first "shot" of the clay pigeon which Žižek mentions without grasping that this black disc is also a *black sun*, a trope of sheer simulation crossing the sky repeatedly. Accordingly, we see one allegory that inhabits the "plot": to assassinate the ambassador Ropa (a name that evokes the Hitchcockian "rope," emblem of narrative time and the suspension of binaries, hanging or "death") is to get out of linear or narrative time, to get out of the simulacrum-of-language that is also what the black sun denotes. It is not for nothing, then, that the spies' hideout is the *false* Temple of the Sun Worshippers (i.e. a movie theater), or that this black sun migrates in the film through black marbles, feet, and even chocolate (or, in *Secret Agent*, through sheer material sound, black dogs, excrement, chocolate again, machines, and finally coded writing). This unrepresentable "excess" is a prefigural materiality that exceeds yet effects "death" as the erasing predicate (and barrier) of knowing. Similarly, it is not for nothing that the Alpine scene at St. *Moritz* is one specifically of conflicting languages, tongues which erase one another when simultaneously spoken at the same time: Italian, German, French, English, Swiss German – a scene of *Babel* in which "voice" is understood primarily or only as translational sound (Hitchcock tells Truffaut of dialogue, moreover, that it is so much "sound" to him).

The purpose in going over these associations is to underline the site in Hitchcock's text that the rhetoric of the "gaze" must remain barred from or blind to – and, on the other hand, generated from as an effect. The *sin* of the *sinthom*, like that of *symbol*, lies in pretending to a synthesis that the cinematic text simply refuses. It is not accidental, then, that when Peter Lorre practices for the assassination it is against the technological backdrop of a record playing the "Storm Cloud Cantata," in order to intervene at just the right instant or repetition: it is, then, the doomed intervention not only at a moment designed to shoot down the black sun (destroy, impossibly, the simulacrum of language with the single camera shot), but repetition, *memory itself as machine*.[9] This is also why this film's remake, the 1956 *Man Who Knew Too Much*, opens with an odd title-text evoking silent film, projecting how an "American family" will be rocked by a single "crash of Cymbals." That is, where the fact of sheer sound preceding any notation or music, a *crash*, is also the rupture of any conception of symbol. And this is also why, when Louis Bernard is killed this time, it will be on his knees and in black face – that is, in a position that covertly cites Al Jolson's "The Jazz Singer" (what Doris Day is in the film), the first "talkie," a citation in which the agent's imparted excess of whispered knowing is that of the origin of "voice" marked as superimposed onto the muteness of silent film – knowledge of the "voice's" non-situatedness. What is interesting, then, is that as Žižek moves into a theory of the *sinthom*, which should be the means of containing the problem of language, the whole operation jams. The very step he takes toward a theory of that which is beyond theory is converted, uncannily, into its other: a return to mere characters (the family), to familiar inter-subjective categories and causal narrative, finally breaking off this chapter. Nowhere is this more apparent than when, in isolating what might be called the signature-effects of Hitchcock, Žižek attempts to convert these into post-Symbolic protrusions which, shed of linguistic agency, nonetheless would be the matter on which all "interpretation" hinges: Žižek, by hoping to circumvent material language or inscription, opts for a site in which what are undoubtedly language-effects should be addressed as things. His attempt mysteriously jams after three pages though. It is simply broken off, abandoned, yet by that fact it points beyond itself. We may call that site which it points to (recalling the deictic gesture of finger-pointing in *Blackmail*) one which Hitchcock nonetheless

---

[9] What Mr. Memory in *The 39 Steps* tells us – as a stand-in for the camera (what also only reproduces "facts") – is that the *mimetic* pretext of (Hitchcock's) cinema is an illusion dependent on the manipulated reproduction of shots, facts subject to repetition, which creates from "facts" *sinthomes* or figures. The text even opens with segmented neon letters spelling M-U-S (Music Hall), which also invokes the mother of the muses Mnemosyne.

openly theorizes from *The Lodger* on – that is, presents fully developed as a logic of the material mark, machine, signature and bar, in each case pre-informing not only the pretext of serial (i.e. representational) "murder" but the prosthesis of the visible or seeing (*theorein*), a material precession or supersession of what will come to be called "theory" as such.

In refusing to function as symbols, even imploded ones which foreclose "interpretation," *sinthoms* dislocate the function Žižek assigns them in Lacan's name, since in actuality such emblems – and one would have to include feet, hands, birds, syllabic repetitions, visual and aural puns, letters (M, P, F, R . . .), numbers (three, thirteen, four), numerous objects and gestures – totally rupture the *mimetic* surface of the film on which any logic of identification depends. This recalls what Robin Wood notes, that Hitchcock's cinema is closest of all to animation, sheer artifice, a mode of hyperbolic *writing*. It is suggestive, then, that Žižek must here escape not only into mere (inter-subjective) interpretation, the very approach he would foreclose, but into a positively regressive *mimetic* reading at that – as occurs with the first *Man Who Knew Too Much*, the "film that most directly calls for such a reading," when we are told that the real story behind the "'official' spy plot" is about "family," about "the price mother has to pay for succumbing – albeit only in jest" to the charm of a foreigner. While I will return to the role of a language that is itself beyond *and* before the wall of (symbolic) language in Hitchcock, we must first ask why *Psycho* is such an exemplary text for Žižek.

It is the final hollowness and lack of interiority of the subject that will "summarize the ultimate lesson of *Psycho*" (257) – a final emptying out of every identificatory or intersubjective approach to Hitchcock presented in the name of an American and postmodern sublime. When the "final dissolve of Norman's gaze into the mother's skull" (257) occurs, there is "not a relapse into subjectivity, but an entry into the dimension of the subject beyond subjectivity" (255). Maybe; but then, this "return to . . . the subject beyond subjectivity, [with] which . . . no identification" (253) is possible, is the quintessential "gaze of the Thing." It is this limit moment that Žižek recurrently circles and which *Psycho*, above all, is supposed to be a master text of, the site not only of the "collapse of the field of inter-subjectivity as medium of Truth in late capitalism" (262), but one free of "subjective identifications":

the secret epitomized by Norman's gaze into the camera, does not amount to a new version of the platitude on the unfathomable, ineffable depth of a person beyond the wall of language, and so on. The ultimate secret is that this Beyond is itself hollow, devoid of any positive content: there is no depth of "soul" in it (Norman's gaze is utterly "soulless", like the gaze of monsters and the living dead) – as such, this Beyond *coincides with gaze itself* . . . *Psycho* indexes the status of a subject which precedes subjectivity – a depthless void of pure Gaze which is nothing but a topological reverse of the Thing.   (257–258)

Unlike Jameson who, in a path-breaking reading of *North by Northwest* in the same volume, still sees Hitchcock as attempting a "solution" of the transition from private to public space (which, for Jameson, may inversely entail a nostalgic insistence on interiority), Žižek addresses a Hitchcock for whom interiority seems at first a defensive fiction.

Žižek's own Americanism *manqué* may lie in his ability to stage a materialist discourse that involves the same radical break with historicism which, despite today's critical trends, originally defined the American and pragmatist turn. From the above reading of Hitchcock, however, it would seem that in doing so Žižek inscribes himself in a vocabulary that he can invert and empty out, but not fully relinquish or transform. And this limit emerges at the very moment that a "beyond" is most asserted, when the emptied terms of identification, metaphor and subjectivization return like the undead.

If the *destitution subjective* is, at least with Hitchcock, less a gaze "beyond" language than the effect of the radical materiality of signification (or language), then its machinal dispossession of all interiority precedes even the human face and can be identified at various points with graphics or even letters irreducible to any inter-subjective model or the Symbolic automaton (I am thinking of the printing press scene in *The Lodger*, after which there are a series of faces morphed together as talking on the wireless, preceded by the newspaper truck with two eyes for windows: that is, the human head as filled with dead print, *The Evening Standard*). One might, accordingly, project a future for readings of Hitchcock which move beyond the metaphoric traps of the "gaze" (including those with fixed gender) and toward an understanding of how thoroughly the surface of his text is generated by networking chains of infratextual citations.

Before indicating where this leads, we should note how this materiality of language is marked and theorized in virtually every Hitchcock text. We might choose, for instance, the example of *Spellbound*, which has the advantage of caricaturing the psychoanalytic hermeneutic (indeed, exceeding the very site and apparatus Žižek's psychoanalytic robotics attempts to re-instate – a kind of neo-Lacanian Green Manors, the sanitorium in that text). In the film, we might say, the binding "spell" of the title refers not only to the totalizing hermeneutic of psychoanalysis (parodied in the opening scenes), but of what even precedes *spelling* on a linguistic level. If to be "spell-bound" (like Adorno's "bewitched" spot in his letter to Benjamin) is to be bound to a certain narrative construction of language, this is virtually or in effect dispossessed and preceded by the central motif – itself recurrent throughout Hitchcock – that is associated at the same time with Gregory Peck's amnesia and putative psychosis, that of *a series of bars*, knocking or parallel lines. It is this series which William Rothman calls Hitchcock's "signature." Rothman, however, only tries to convert this essentially pre-semiotic marker into some sort of psychological *symbol*: "I call this pattern of parallel vertical lines Hitchcock's / / / / sign. It recurs at significant junctures in every one of his films. At one level, the / / / / serves as Hitchcock's signature: it is a mark on the frame, akin to a ritual cameo appearance. At another level, it signifies the confinement of the camera's subject within the frame and within the world of the film . . . It is also associated with sexual fear and the specific threat of loss of control or break-down."[10] One could undertake an entire reading of Hitchcock in which this prefigural "signature" – sometimes called a "bar" simply (*Vertigo*'s "*bar* at the top of the *Mark*") – shifts interpretation from the identificatory, narrative, recuperative models in which even Žižek's notion of the "gaze" seems to linger, into one that interrogates his cinema as interactive surfaces of writing or marking. In fact, "it" denotes (or rather, presents, since the bar-series dissolves all *mimetic* representation) what might be called the primal or even prefigural domain of semiotic differentiation,

[10] William Rothman, *Hitchcock: The Murderous Gaze* (1981), 33.

marks preceding words or even spelling. Like the conceit of "shock" in Benjamin, the bar motif recalls a kind of *ur*-primal scene, or séancing (precisely the metaphor Hitchcock uses for his cinema opening *Family Plot*). We might also call this series of *bars* a figure of radical exteriority over against whose prefigural recurrences images coalesce, linguistic consciousness emerges. This seems demonstrated in pixyish fashion at the early supper scene in the asylum. Here Gregory Peck is viewed rubbing the tablecloth with his mock-phallic butter knife to efface the oval-shape of parallel lines traced by the fork of Ingrid Bergman, parallel outlines obscenely resembling a vaginal opening – a *too* literal trope of origin. In fact, though, the parallel lines simultaneously supplant any vaginal trope with the hypnotic or psychotic emblem of a sheer semiosis or, for that matter, sheer anteriority, narration, castration, "death," and so on. By repeatedly installing this *non*-figure, Hitchcock notes where the visual is not *mimetically* conceived as a reproduction (what he calls, dismissing other films, "pictures of people talking"). It is hardly incidental, of course, that so many names in Hitchcock with a cluster of defacing implications associated with the syllable mar(k) – Marnie, Marvin, Margaret, Martin, Margo, Markham, Marion, Marlow, indeed, Mark itself (or the word explicitly, as noted above) and so on. These include affiliations with the bar-series and record a field of marking precedent to the effect of the eye (on the most banal level, but not only, the imprint of celluloid itself), the prosthesis of the visible *tout court*, and hence get displaced as a chain in Hitchcock into other tracks, including chains leading from recording machines, wheels (or rings), memory (in *The 39 Steps*, again, Mr. Memory is called a "re*mark*able man") and the letter "r" for repetition ("old man 'R'," the originary spy-master in *Secret Agent*, say) through the black sun, feet or steps, birds, dogs, chocolate, inscription (the Spies' Post Office, a Chocolate Factory, again in *Secret Agent*) and so on. It is also not accidental that, in *Spellbound*, the salient image coming from the famous Dali dream-sequence is that of the eye cut (i.e. preceded) by scissors (the bar sequence), that of vision itself generated and cut off in advance, become other and lodged in a premimetic zone by differential signifying sequences. What distinguishes the allegorical moment, here, is the act of remarking a movement in and constituency of material signs preceding the *faux* perception of the projected image or screen.

If Žižek goes beyond neo-pragmatist retro-humanism – or is a half-measure corrective to it – he nonetheless repeats the gesture of desired transparency in his projection "beyond" language. Instead, we must revise the site of the Thing, of the specter of materiality itself, as woven into a prefigural use of material language.

This is an opportune site to return to a different conception of the "sublime" than is represented by the interiorist tradition to which Žižek adheres – an alternate conception, intervening in the very configuration of the historial, which Hitchcock openly theorizes in conjunction with memory as early as *The 39 Steps* (and, in fact, before). In that film, the "McGuffin" of the secret formula for a "silent" warplane engine – a certain sublime of flight – is tied to the memorization of banal "facts," of *number and letters* in fact, whereby the routine of Mr. Memory (less that of the "Symbolic" automaton (Žižek) than the mimetic pretense of film, of brute recording) converts representation, through the sheer repetition of signifiers, into a formal discourse, the play of reflexive and infratextual signifiers in Hitchcockian cinemallographics. In that early text, it is the *faux* muse of "Anna*bella* Smith," the veiled lady assassin with the knife in her back she is unable (reflexively) to reach, that ironically rewrites the aesthetic trajectory of the *ana*gogic dialectic in Plato (in a text where "up" and "down" appear the same – as in "Professor" Jordan's remark to Hannay of being led "up – or is it down – the garden path"). Such a textual moment is linked to the aesthetic, perceptual, basis of memory – what Benjamin might call the link between cinema (as a machinal corollary to "allegory") and the historial sensorium. Thus in *Psycho* we see an invocation of a certain material "sublime" not in a neo-Lacanian anthropomorphization of "mother" (always, in Hitchcock, a machinal, non-human, generation-cancelling, linguistic site) but in the record-player in Norman's bedroom on which Beethoven's *Eroica* is seen. What is "heroic," in a certain transposition of the romantic tradition (that is, in fact, little more than an over-accurate reading of it), is the dispossession of any trace of interiority the emblem purveys – a figure, that of the record or phonograph, long a staple of Hitchcock's theorization of filmic "consciousness," of the voice, of time, of representation (in *Blackmail*, the first *Man Who Knew Too Much*, *Secret Agent* – where the record is associated with the toilet, hence shit, sound, memory, the black sun, feet, dogs, and so on). It is in a similar vein that Paul de Man, in "Hegel on the Sublime" (for de Man will locate an entire materialistic project in the key Enlightenment texts thought, precisely, to have purveyed the opposite), that the "Longinian model of the sublime as representation" (114)[11] is voided by a certain conception of mnemonic inscription – much as the black disc that represents a record for Hitchcock cites not only repetition and circularity, but an eclipsed sun at that.[12] If for de Man this material notion of the "sublime" in Hegel is "self-destroying in a manner without precedent," that site of self-cancellation which is allied, in Hitchcock, with "mother" does not constitute an overt foreclosure: on the contrary, it becomes a proleptic principle of passage, of crossing, of translation initiated at the material site where such inscription is registered as sheer exteriority. From the framework of cinema, the "technological sublime" would not be a literal machine but the mnemotechnology that, in this fashion, recasts the very domain of the house (*hôte* or motel – in which we may anagrammatically hear *le mot*), the "psyche," the *norm*.

By pointing to graphic and pun-based networks that preinhabit Hitchcock's writing surfaces which precede the installation of any ocular-centrism – what it may not be useful to term hieroglyphic, despite Hitchcock's open nod toward Egyptian (that is, pre-alphabetic) metaphorics in *The Lodger* (the pyramid), *Blackmail* (the British Museum) and elsewhere – we indicate where the de-anthropomorphized domain of "mother" can be assimilated to the manner in which Derrida reads the Platonic *khora*. That is, to seek the *mater*iality that adheres to this (linguistically) determined site – one which, across Hitchcock, anagrammatically binds the locus of "mother" not to *origin* as such but first a *series* of M- terms (memory, mountain, music, murder, machine) and the letter M itself (Hitchcock's mother's name, too, being "Emma") – we might recall how this mock-originary site is read, by Derrida, outside of any binarized gender form:

She is a third gender/genus (48e); she does not belong to an oppositional couple . . . *Khora* marks a place apart, the spacing which keeps a disym-

---

[11] See Paul de Man, *Aesthetic Ideology*, 105–118.
[12] This is particularly obvious in the first *Man Who Knew Too Much*, what with its references to the Temple of Sun Worshippers and the scene with the "skeet" shoot where this black sun, as trace, would be (photographically) shot.

metrical relation to all that which, "in herself," beside or in addition to herself, seems to make a couple with her. In the couple outside of the couple, this strange mother who gives place without engendering can no longer be considered as an origin. She/it eludes all anthropo-theological schemes, all history, all revelation, all truth. Preoriginary, *before* and outside of all generation, she no longer even has the meaning of a past, of a present that is past. Before signifies no temporal anteriority. The relation of independence, the nonrelation, looks more like the relation of the interval or of spacing to what is lodged in it to be received in it.[13]

Such an interval, like a *lodging* bar-series, also marks a place from which "gender" appears in Hitchcock dismantled, a perpetual site of performance before that which itself precedes identity. If many feminist treatments of Hitchcock have depended on situating a mock-patriarch-auteur as backdrop and foil (Modleski's *Women Who Knew Too Much*, for instance), they stand to be reconfigured by a further marking of where the (often reversible) performances of "gender" seem incessantly dislocated by a machinal, "material"/maternal locus adverting to a pre-gendered site.[14]

Indeed, the (a)topos of the American him-, her- or rather it-"self," coincides in the second *Man Who Knew Too Much* with the return of an Egyptian and anti-solar motif (Doris Day, not incidentally "gift of the day," to begin with, as "mummy"). Here taxidermy gets (re)introduced with an aggressive delegislation of a *generational* time whose mock-restoration by the parental couple (their apparent goal) barely conceals a ferocious allographic formalism marked by the film's being Hitchcock's only explicit auto-remake (and, for that matter, the thumbed through phone-book). But it is the reflexive aesthetic of compulsory interruption which positions the mock-political narrative's (again, failed assassination, here of a foreign Prime Minister by his *own* (foreign) "embassy") more genuinely political – which is to say, epistemo-political (knowing "too much") – excess.

[13] Jacques Derrida, "Khora," in *On the Name*, 124–5.
[14] This insight into the pre-gendered markings of Hitchcock's work is developed further in the next chapter, with regard to *Sabotage*.

5

Sabotaging the ocularist state

The end is beginning, signifies the apocalyptic tone. But to what ends does the tone signify this? The apocalyptic tone naturally wants to attract, to get to come, to arrive at this, to seduce in order to lead to this, in other words, to place where the first vibration of the tone is heard, which is called, as will be one's want, subject, person, sex, desire (I think rather of a pure differential vibration, without support, insupportable).

> Derrida, "Of an Apocalyptic Tone . . ."

The cinema is war pursued by other means.

> Paul Virilio, *Pure War*

Careful at the *crossing*.

> Mrs. V to Stevie, *Sabotage*

The preceding reflections cast a different role that "Hitchcock" may serve today, if we see in the name not simply the auteurial mark of a production, but the signature of a materialist practice, marked as such, that can be tracked as a site of resistance to the ideology of cinematic modernism itself. That is, to successive networks of interpretive labor founded on mimetic, ocular-centric, and auteurist-identificatory traditions which have also been associated with film theory to date. Yet how, within the web of such labor, can one cast a specific politics within the ruptures of Hitchcock's style, or for that matter the distribution of everything not generally noted that may be implied by the gesture of the cameo? What is the virtual crossing – in representational models, in the options of the "sensorium," the human face, the graphematics of history, the politics of memory – adherent in the unobserved logics less of this cinematic "style" than the expropriation of cinema (as an epistemo-critical program and reserve) marked by the name, Hitchcock? Expropriation here is heard as submitting the constitutive logics of "cinema" itself to a radical exteriorization, translating all of its properties or underlying technicity into a semiotic and materialistic domain. This virtual blinding, as of a Cyclopean surveillance (an allusion evoked in the fire-works scene of *To Catch a Thief*), manifests itself at times in relation to the official or unofficial censor – noted by the certificate typically preceding the credits in the British series – yet entails, as well, an eviscerating deregulation of the perceptual "sensorium" itself as a program of interpretation, of stable signs, of temporal management.

Few films pretending to a "classic" model incarnate the problematic loss of pleasure and narrative which any loss of aura implies – a movement, in short, to a post-anthropomorphic fold – more than Hitchcock's *Sabotage*, which seems to investigate the formal problem of performing an aesthetico-political intervention when that involves a textual or mnemonic model. How do we define an act, say that of "sabotage," which operates from within a larger system, state, or representational milieu? How can a certain practice of defacement – a rewiring of a received hermeneutic, or the coding of the senses (say, "sight") – ever be affirmed aesthetically, if it can only be known by the traces of its failure? How, bringing these two together, can we begin to assess a program of writing that conceives both of these tasks so clearly, that it can appear caught in the specular trap of representing this performance as a performance of that representation?

The close reader of Hitchcock often encounters a strange effect unlike that of viewing other "cinema": characters seem displaced and objects, diverse signifying constellations move in and out of the frame, assuming active roles in the text. Among these signature-effects Hitchcock mobilizes – overt signs and repeated gestures, paronomasia extending across different films, visual and aural or letteral "puns" that serve as relays, nameplay – one of the more persistent if semantically elusive is the bar-series motif that Rothman first identified. This insignia, a *series* of slashes or *bars*, or alternately intervalled sounds like knocking, shows up across all of Hitchcock's films. While Rothman termed it a "signature" of sorts, it less enforces a stable sense of authorial import than interrupts and threatens all representational codes (is a face itself made up only, in the end, of graphic bars or shading?).[1] To the reader of Hitchcock this insignia recurs not only in benign patterns (shadows cast by a staircase) or sound (knocking), but as mobilized or echoed in a series of proper names designed to recall, as in some nonetheless premimetic code, the event: Barlow Creek in *Family Plot*, Judy Barton in *Vertigo*, Detective Barton in *Number 17* – or, in *Sabotage*, the name on the film canister with in which the bomb is carried, "Bartholomew the Strangler." Yet if we stop to consider the import of this, a certain radical evacuation of meaning on an almost *formal* basis has been evoked as another Hitchcock trademark (one recalls his declared pleasure in an empty horizon). We have become, following Benjamin, more aware of the potentially transformative import that a *formal* principle of linguistic difference may have as a caesura, a tool for intervening in received narratives, ideological habits, historical foreclosures (the "task" of the (cultural) translator). In Hitchcock these and other agents of writing function differently than elsewhere, since rather than organize "modernist" associations reflecting on the text's apparatus, they seem unexpectedly to circle a place beyond the mourning inherent in representation (crystallized after Handell Fane's somewhat Orphic suicide in *Murder!*). What is sometimes called "mother," accordingly, functions beyond any maternal, originary, or even gendered associations to link up with a series of "M" terms (memory, machine, murder, music . . .) which suggest, finally, a sort of topos for mnemonic imprinting, (dis)inscription, or the event.

Of commentators only Fredric Jameson seems to have found this bar motif worth pondering – as, uniquely, when he notes the pattern's return on the giant faces of Mt. Rushmore in *North by Northwest*. For Jameson, who is here concerned with the sheer exteriority of "space," the series confirms a site "which has no inside and cannot be penetrated."[2] Having just remarked "the peculiar inscriptions" of the cropduster scene's field, "a set of

---

[1] In Truffaut's book on *Hitchcock*, we read the latter noting: "We must bear in mind that, fundamentally, there's no such thing as color; in fact, there's no such thing as face, because until the light hits it, it is nonexistent. After all, one of the first things I learned in the School of Art was that there is no such thing as a line; there's only the light and the shade. On my first day in school I did a drawing; it was quite a good drawing, but because I was drawing with lines, it was totally incorrect and the error was immediately pointed out to me." (133)

[2] Fredric Jameson, "Spatial Systems," 64.

parallel lines not without some distant affinity with the 'trauma' of *Spellbound*," he observes of the monumental faces:

> Here, far more abstractly, we confront the same grid of parallel lines, systematically carved into the rock surface like a strange Mayan pattern. Again, what is confirmed by this pattern, and scored into the space of the scene, is the primacy of surface itself: the earth as a surface upon which the ant-like characters move and agitate . . . (64)

It is interesting that for Jameson this pattern emerges in association with a general reconsideration of the term allegory.[3] It is uniquely applied to Hitchcock, and with obvious, if unmarked, reference to the path Benjamin opens with his remarks on cinema (in which, briefly, the mnemonic apparatus of image succession and projected imprint simulate not only a projection of "consciousness" or a precession of sight itself but where the chain of mnemonic imprints stand to be altered, modified as a chain, invoking the figure of "shock").[4] Yet how does such a series operate as a "signature," a coda, and of what if it puts any "of" precisely and at all points in question? What is its relation not only to spacing, but temporalization, the visible itself, intervals, materiality, "death"? If it recurs not only as a pre-visual marker of difference but as sound or knocking (the window pane in *Marnie*), like the tappings beneath a séance table, what is its association with the figure of hypnosis (in the first *Man Who Knew Too Much*), or that of the mock-séance opening *Family Plot* by which Hitchcock depicts his cinema as a certain necromancy? After all, the reason that this "bar series" is remarked by no one is that it signifies nothing – retains *no* linguistic content, precedes all punning networks, stands to dissolve not only narrative but all *mimetic* projections of representation, including face itself? Why should Hitchcock keep at hand, or deploy, a motif of prefigural difference that puts the mimetic promise of film at risk, reminding of the technical origin of the image in the play of light and dark, alternations of intervals that precede – yet also cut-off – any perception? What is this motif's relation – which, perhaps, only

---

[3] See, first of all, Jameson's review of Rothman's work, "Allegorizing Hitchcock," 99–127. Interestingly, the first version of this essay, appearing in the journal *October*, was called "Reading Hitchcock," and both titles appear to retain an (effaced) trace of de Man.

[4] The text where this seems most addressed in Hitchcock is *The 39 Steps*, around the "allegorical" character of Mr. Memory.

Jameson picks up on – to allegory? What in Hitchcock's practice remains political in a unique sense informed by the precedence he gives, over any mimetic logic, to discursive networks and a sort of prefigural graphematics? What, in Hitchcock, associates the mimetologics of "official" or "classic" cinema with a blind hermeneutic law, with England, even with a Euro-fascist tradition that creates across numerous films (starting with the British "political thrillers" down through *Saboteur*, *Foreign Correspondent*, the propaganda shorts, right up to *Frenzy*) a sort of German-English-American poetic "axis"? Where does there emerge a kind of *cinemallographics*, mobilizing the transformative and mnemotechnic project inherent in Benjamin's arrested transposition of "allegory" on behalf not only of a semiotic disruption fully theorized in his texts, one that devolves to a serial slasher motif, but one that carries the signature of an "epistemo-critical" marker – the irrecuperable bar-series Rothman will note, the pandemic syllable *Mar-* itself, morphing across proper names? To sabotage an official, or ocularist ideology is to do so in the name of a prefigural rift within the topos of *light* – radically destabilizing the hegemonic metaphorics of (cognitive) blindness that classic "cinema" may have been converted institutionally to enforce, as has occurred throughout film "theory's" hermeneutic and mimetic biases.

Indeed, even to call this a "signature," as Rothman does, remains in ways naive, if we mean (as he does) that it evokes the silhouette of the god-like auteur as we imagine him – importing moral and thematic concerns into that icon that permit us to contain if not close off the agitated and transformational field of a text at all points traversed by anti-Oedipal, post-humanist, and transvaluative inscriptions. Even the famous cameos for which Hitchcock's works are renowned – where the director seems (often) to appear "himself" – dissolve: rather than stamping an auteurial presence, they collapse the very pretext of mimetic fiction that the photograph pretends (importing the mugging, portly figure), fold the out-of-frame into its own mock-interior, scattering the dismembered outline of the Hitchcockian body into so many familiar signifiers (baldness, fat, droopy lips), that indeed recur across often marginal characters (an impresario, a barroom nudge). They present a signature for the anamorphic logic of diverse insignia that undo auteurial, identificatory logic as such. The bar-series seems to incarnate a precessional excess, a structural interruption or caesura; while a trope of seriality, it also depicts a prehuman space or gap precedent to any letteration or outline – similar to the shots of the waltzing couples inserted periodically in *Shadow of a Doubt*.

If the problem of "allegory" returns for Jameson specifically in addressing Hitchcock, with this bar-series in attendance, it will lead him to propose a mode of reading that breaks with the auteurist traditions of Hitchcock criticism – and hence with identification as such, or the "aura." Jameson suggests a "better, non-subjective way of telling the story (doing away with consciousness, 'character', and the anthropomorphic)" (51). The impasse in Jameson's invocation lies in the very logic that moves him, under the auspices of allegory, to the outer rim of the "anthropomorphic" tradition of film criticism. For him modernist allegory is reflexively focused, in a sense, on the account of the work's mode of production (or consumption) – something, by the way, fully present in Hitchcock's *Sabotage*, with its making Verloc run a movie house, deal with patrons, sabotage the *light* source itself. As such, the approach remains mimetic. What prevents Jameson, here, from fully realizing a Benjaminian dimension of the term is seeing how this "reflexive" or "modernist" moment proceeds to alter, and modify (or sabotage) the historical model out of which itself is projected – a fact that will make the term "sabotage," could that be defined (and the film, *Sabotage*, opens by invoking a dictionary definition), a homonym for allegory in one sense. To proceed beyond the "anthropomorphic" tradition and toward an interrogation of the materiality of Hitchcock's writing practice would mean acceding from the image to the premimetic mark – a process Jameson stops short of, imagining any recurrence to word patterns must relapse to an intentionalist model.

Yet if "allegory" should return at this site for Jameson, one might recall where the prefigural bar-series as a "signature of the visible" suggests in an irreducible and even material sense what Benjamin calls in the "Task of the Translator" a certain rhythmic effect of *pure language*. (To relate this effect to what, in Hitchcock, is meant by "pure cinema" would entail a complicated but not unthinkable itinerary.) But in Benjamin's text, there is a ceaseless quest for that reflexive and linguistic *techne* of historial intervention that evokes different names, among them allegory, translation, "materialistic historiography," and the figure of cinema.[5]

Benjamin seems to accord to cinematic imprinting and projection a mnemotechnic similar to that of linguistic consciousness itself (a prospect explored in *Spellbound*, among other films). The old notion of allegory and the traditional one of cinema both pretend to a privileged relation to – and role as guardian of – classical *mimesis* (the allegorical signified, the photo's referent). Each term is accordingly positioned, when transposed in his text, to undo (reverse, displace, negate, transfigure proleptically) precisely that particular regime.

In asking what may be the relation of (dis)inscription to the *event* in Hitchcock's "political thrillers," and what is political there, we will address the early British thriller, *Sabotage*, which seems to perform (and theorize) the failure of its own act – a failure that pervades the film and its reputation, but which testifies nonetheless to a certain success. It may help, briefly, to recall Hitchcock's story line. The film turns about the attempt by a foreign agent, Mr. Verloc (Oscar Homolka), to commit an act of sabotage that disrupts London. The narrative moves from Verloc's opening act of sabotage – placing sand in the city's generators, thereby putting out the lights – to the escalated plot to bomb Piccadilly Circus (called "the *center* of the world"). Verloc, a free-lancer, also displays an apocalyptic side in a vision at the Zoo aquarium of buildings melting away in general devastation. Verloc's handler scoffs at his first act, having merely put out the lights, noting that the Londoners' response was primarily *laughter*. In contrast, the time-bomb is intended to stop the laughter, to kill, to intervene definitively in the socius. Meanwhile Scotland Yard has had Verloc under surveillance by agent Ted Spenser, who is also disguised, here as a *fruit seller* in the grocery adjacent to the Bijou. From the start he initiates a flirtation with Mrs. Verloc (Sylvia Sidney). In a seemingly de-sexed relation, she is bound to Verloc because of his "care" for her young brother Stevie. Spenser continues to ply *Mrs. V* (as she is repeatedly called, in letteral fashion) for information while courting her. After Spenser stumbles into a meeting with conspirators in the office *behind the film screen*, Verloc sends the time-bomb – which had been delivered by the portly bird-store owner in a bird cage – with Stevie, concealed with two film canisters. The bomb has a

---

[5] Most specifically, of course, in "The Work of Art in the Age of Mechanical Reproduction," in *Illuminations*, 217–253.

precise time that it is to go off (1:45), which in code is referred to as when the *bird* will "sing." Stevie, repeatedly interrupted on his mission by the Lord Mayor's Show Day parade, is delayed and blown up on a stalled bus. Mrs. Verloc, figuring out the cause of Stevie's disappearance, almost involuntarily stabs Verloc with a steak-knife over supper as he falls on it trying to disarm her. Spenser, wanting to save Mrs. V, tries to take her away, but *she* is determined to tell Inspector Talbot – who has just arrived with his men to surround the Bijou – of her hand in Verloc's murder. During this time the bird-man arrives at the Bijou to find Verloc dead and himself surrounded. As Mrs. V cries out about Verloc's death, the bird-man blows up the Bijou, virtually erasing all evidence of the murder. The Inspector can not remember whether Mrs. Verloc's confessional cry came before – or after – the explosion. Spenser leads her away to conceal her act of murder and, presumably, enter a marriage (that could both be a trap and a site of blackmail). The problem posed for an allographic reading – that is, one turned back on itself to open the possibility of intervening in (sabotaging) a received representational system and altering that scene – is how to read the fact of Verloc's running a movie house.

1. A broken contract

There is a sense among critics that a trauma pervades Hitchcock's *Sabotage*, yet rather than represent a defect or deficiency, the effect appears related to the way the film sets up and comments on Hitchcock's own "political" cinema. In saying political we do not mean in the routine sense – in which, even on the greatest of contemporary matters, Hitchcock did not assume simple positions nor tend to declare himself in passing historical terms (the propaganda films of the war, even, could not be used, for their implied critiques of the French and British racism along with the German much as *Lifeboat* was suspected of being teutonophilic, and *Saboteur* seemed not even to have been seen as indicting American capitalism as co-fascist with the Germans). Rather, we may point, first, to the way a representational assault on the aesthetic "state" is mounted in the British films that assaults an entire cultural metaphysics permeating determinations of gender and hermeneutics, and which positions a certain "Hitchcock," invariably, with the always failed anarchic or revolutionary projects of the – nonetheless, most frequently, aesthetically elite and necessary – "villians," (Abbott, the Professor, Verloc), a positional identification that sometimes veers toward a failed crossing of borders, borders that, while marked geographically, may be read in a para-Nietzschean fashion as the projected passage to an other representational field, system, or apprehension of time than that of the hermeneutic or aesthetic state, peopled by the violence of police and tourists ("England").[6] The initial emptying out of Verloc's own movie-house, the Bijou, when the electric is sabotaged (by himself), seems to anticipate the effect the text has encountered since: this first interruption (of narrative at its origin, as it were) seems to have haunted and passed through the work's after-life. Yet the way that Hitchcock inscribes his cinema in Verloc's mercenary missions of sabotage, perhaps, is exceeded only by the diverse ways language overruns the film itself – in issues of definition, translation, and signs at first. Indeed, the unique (for Hitchcock) use of a "high literary" model (Conrad's *The Secret Agent*), could not but evoke awareness of translation and comparison, the relation of original and copy, of cinema and writing. Yet in an oeuvre filled with transcodings and texts, *Sabotage* sports one of the strangest graphematic allusions when a reporter takes down shorthand following the bomb explosion on the bus. Noting the name of the film in the canister that the boy Stevie carried – blown to bits while bearing the package unwittingly for Verloc – the reporter's hand draws squiggles across the page, as though transcribing the explosive film contents itself into a non-mimetic type of script.

One recent critic, Mladen Dolar, speaking in a Lacanian vein, has called *Sabotage* "perhaps the only [one of Hitchcock's films] in which the traumatic wound does not heal": "Although all Hitchcockian films are centered around a traumatic event which involves a confrontation between the subject and his/her desire (in the purest form with that "What do you want?" at the end of *Rear Window*), *Sabotage* remains perhaps the only one where the

---

[6] Thus, in the first *Man Who Knew Too Much*, Abbott (Peter Lorre) plots the assassination of the ambassador Ropa, a name affiliated with the emblematics of "rope" in Hitchcock, associated not only with strangulation (or decapitation, the loss of natural consciousness with knowledge of a certain semiotic excess) but narrative time – exemplified in the unravelling of the "jumper" in the dance-assassination scene.

traumatic wound does not heal, it cannot be squeezed back into a fictional mould."[7] The question remains whether the project of "sabotage" registers a dilemma in Hitchcock's own aesthetics which he can only try to blow himself *out of*. One way this occurs is when Hitchcock scores his textual surface with various *signifying agents* (the play of aural and visual puns, signatures, numbers, letters, infratextual relays and such) that pointedly disrupt the mimetic contract of viewing and remark his film a scene of *reading*. That Hitchcock himself viewed it as such is marked in Hitchcock's earliest prolonged cameo, that of *Blackmail*, where he appears interrupted while *reading on a train* (that is, a trope of cinema) in the Underground (figure of cinema's own *after-life*). This cameo signals not just that a mode of reading interrupts the illusory continuum of mimetic film narrative – he (Hitchcock) is interrupted (in turn). Cinema here is itself a figure for *and* interruption of reading, and it is this interruption (of an interruption) that opens the possibility of political sabotage, disinscription and blacking out, which is marked at the beginning of *Sabotage* when London's lights go out. It may also not be incidental that *Blackmail*'s interruption is effected by a young boy figure – one in a sense not unlike Stevie.[8] One image that comes to mind with this analogy is that by blowing up Stevie, Hitchcock will either aim to restore a disturbed reading scene (that is, obliterate the interrupting boy), or render that scene itself permanently ruptured. (We might repeat that Hitchcock's cameos, rather than purveying an auteurial imprimatur, are the signature of a perpetual anamorphosis along the surface of Hitchcockian writing, the guarantor of this caesura-effect by a folding of the outside frame and behind-the-camera (the director) into the screen sign-system – guardian of a collapsing of frames which will pose the text itself as an event.)

The first transposition from Conrad that Hitchcock performs is to make Verloc's cover that of running a cinema, the Bijou. This displacement opens up a reflexive dimension that is immediately complicated when the movie-house itself is shut down, even emptied *at the start* – and this, by the same (reflexive) act of

[7] Mladen Dolar, "The Spectator Who Knew Too Much," in *Everything*, 132.
[8] Not coincidentally, a still from this sequence is used on the cover of *A Hitchcock Reader*, ed. M. Deutelbaum and L. Poague (Iowa City: Iowa State University Press, 1986).

sabotage or rupture that is aimed at London in general. *Preceding* its own opening with a darkness that never seems to quite leave the film, the text at once performs and thematizes a break down and disruption so thoroughly that we almost miss remarking it. Much is made of the fact that the Londoners respond not with anxiety or a sense of catastrophe, but laughter. So curious is the opening act of sabotage – lights out, a hand discovering sand in some universal generator (source of all London's "juice" and *light*), laughter in the Underground, debates about returning ticket money – that we may well want some explanation for just what is happening. If such unbenign darkness voids all referents, we might regress to the credit sequence for explanation. Yet the pre-opening credit shot of the dictionary definition of "sabotage" operates on several troubling levels – and seems to do anything but provide a working explanation or definition. Why the focus on word, letters, *definition*? Indeed, the very definition of definition becomes problematic. Not only because it invokes sheer convention and official meanings, but because, inversely, that official literalization itself becomes a means of escaping the overdetermination and metonymic errance of language in general. One thrust of the dictionary *definition* is echoed in the word itself, in which a negation (de) of *finitude* (or time) is echoed. However official the printed text looks, it draws our attention during its magnified close-up not only to the *luminous* letters on the page (like the neon ones opening *The 39 Steps*) but to a general crisis in meaning. And hence interpretation – one that puts the lights out and empties the theater before any narrative has a chance to begin. That is, the dictionary shot raises the question of *other* forms of meaning, more disruptive or sabotaging, more allegorical, more letteral. This is italicized by the fact that the shot follows the compulsory display of the state's certificate of censorship for the film, which marks that the work itself may be a double text operating within the constraints (and sabotaging) an official surveillance and aesthetic regime of the state. Yet there is a problem here. If the official definition replicates the state's aestheticopolitical power as evidenced in the certificate of censorship, the definition of the *word* "sabotage" is turned against that which frames its definition. The word is immediately broken, as if exploded, by the facticity of its own material parts and phonetic character: "Sa-botage, sa-bo-tarj":

Sa-botage, sa-bo-tarj. Wilful destruction of buildings or machinery with the object of alarming a group of persons or inspiring public uneasiness.
Sa-bre (-er), n. & v.t. Cavalry sword with a curved blade (the s., military ...

Letters and sound; official definitions, called into question by the very giving (following the state's certificate of censorship), mapped by the diacritical rupture of phonetic caesuras one scarcely notes. Indeed, the following entry, barely readable, for *"Sa-bre (-er), n. & v.t.* Cavalry sword with a curved blade," makes the connection between word and sword, cutting the sabre (with) itself – a sword with a *curved* or parabolic blade. The possibility of another form of definition, of *allegory* or allographics, is marked. It is anything but accidental, therefore, that the movie-house operator Verloc will be from the start pursued by a Scotland Yard detective with the name Ted *Spenser* – that is, by an agent bearing the name of the most "classic" of allegorical English poets. It is as if a traditional literary model of meaning, an agent of the state hermeneutic police, means to contain Hitchcock's explosive cinematic writing *and his turn toward a subversive definition of allegory (or cinema) itself*. Toward, in short, an expropriation of the mimetic premises in which cinema has been held that activates a purely graphematic model, an aesthetico-political project that will resist and exceed both mere hieroglyphic analysis (as a formal procedure) and the mimeto-identificatory, ocular-centric readings of auteur-based criticism. But perhaps something else is afoot – with even *feet* themselves at issue, as when Spenser asks if he can "tempt" the police officer who complained of cabbage on the ground that might make one slip and "break a leg" with an orange, noting they are "good for the feet": *or*anges, substituting for the edenic apples, figures of the *or*(eille) or ear, round, restituting one's footing, measure, or knowing. For *sabot*, after all, derives from the French for shoe, a citation of feet or steps as those figure, say, in *The 39 Steps* for Mr. Memory – where, too, they appear linked to the *legs* whose materiality echoes *legein*, or for that matter *logos* (as does *The Lodger*), legibility and legality, legacy and *legere* itself.

The word "sabotage" has to do above all with *action* and agency, particularly secret agency, defined as intervention in the system. It draws attention to a more ambitious question: where or how does the structure of the word, of a text, exceed the aesthetic and pleasurable (even laughable) play of meanings and shift abruptly to becoming an act or event with historial consequences – shift, in short, from merely putting out the *blinking* light-bulb ("light" as an effect of its own absence) to paralyzing the state or altering causal chains in history? Why must the act in question be conceived of as primarily destructive ("Wilful destruction of buildings or machinery")? If both the imposition and disruption of official meaning(s) is thus marked *before* the film begins, implying the violence of each, at least two things occur: the word is broken apart phonetically while the close-up focuses on (our) reading (indeed, the camera *forces* us to read), and this itself seems linked to the black-out that Verloc initiates at the outset. If in *Blackmail*'s cameo Hitchcock's reading is interrupted by a boy reminiscent of Stevie, here "reading" itself, one notch further, both effects that interruption and is (again) interrupted. *Reading*, in one sense, becomes one site of real sabotage – not in a fictional London seen on the screen, but at the origin of seeing itself (London's "generator"), the site of the reader's consciousness which the film is staging or generating. This black-out precedes the text and forestalls the narrative from occurring, even though, in order to do so, the latter will fold back on the former as its ostensible, if undefined, subject. The act of "sabotage" associated with the dictionary that opens *Sabotage* – and, in a sense, prevents it from proceeding – imparts a founding death immediately remarked when the camera wanders through London's *Underground* (a trope, again, of film's own site as afterlife, now including all of the people, the stars, the audience).

Necessarily, the Law itself enters – or seems to, or enters while seeming not to, seeming even against itself. And, as we will see, it is at least in part a law of allegory, or at least one version of it, *hunting*, seeking out, empowered to arrest its cinematic heir. Only the Law can deal with the effects of a break-down, the public chaos, or the ostensibly "legal" attribution of cause and effect or financial responsibility. The trouble is that, in the person of Ted Spenser, the Law's representative is in disguise, is a dissimulating agent, and his interests at this point – cultivating and protecting Mrs. Verloc – go against the public's. Accordingly, the Law's agent invokes the Law equivocally, making it clear that *it* itself is something other than (itself) "the Law." There ensues a street debate between "Mrs. V'" and the patrons leaving the cinema as to whether the house must return their ticket money. Ted Spenser joins in with legalese double-talk in an attempt to defend Mrs. V's right to keep the money. The exchange turns, as a customer says, on whether Verloc has "broken" his "contract" with the paying audience. The first patron says: "You broke a contract – therefore you broke a law." If one example of an act of providence is "a baby," as someone blurts out, or "your face," as Spenser quips, the loop of non-responsibility is complicated by Verloc's having himself secretly *caused* the chance occurrence or rupture. Whatever else occurs here, *Sabotage* marks the interruption and vacating of the pleasure contract of popular cinema (the cinema as the escapist site of identification, mimesis, and pleasure) as one of its premises or gambles.

If the dictionary entry focused on *reading* over viewing (or the look, or gaze), the film immediately turns to the "legal" definition of an *act*. The word "act" of course picks up on *Con*rad's title, a title that is effaced in part, of course, because it was already the name of Hitchcock's immediately preceding film, *Secret Agent*. The word "act" threads every variant pun on the problem of acting and agency. This is echoed in the text's second "definition" of a word, that in Ted's tautological double-talk concerning the legal responsibility for the black-out: "As laid down in the Act of William 4th, where an act is *defined* as an activity actuated by actual action." Here the word is repeated to the point of depriving it of real sense, while inserting the routine into the mocking-image of historical authority and precedent. The Law is invoked as something that can always be bent by or cover for its own agents (as will happen most explicitly at the film's end when Spenser conceals Mrs. V's crime). This is so particularly where the notion of a "contract" can always be arbitrarily re-*defined* by it. Reading, *legere*, which echoes both legitimation and legibility and is already invoked by the opening dictionary shot, curls up around the problem of defining an "act" before the Law itself – much as it is here deployed by its own agent, Spenser, to shield Mrs. V's interest in retaining the money. Like the bombing later, the subject of *Sabotage* at this point is possible to know largely as an absence, rift, interruption, break, or discontinuity – and the narrative both en*acts* this break and "begins" in an arrested posture as the retroactive attempt to *account* for it.[9] The text begins, differently put, as a (failed) act of virtual interpretation,

---

[9] We might add that one of the interesting things that the text here theorizes – and picks up on from the first *Man Who Knew Too Much* – is where "death" is conceived of not biologically but as a semiotic or linguistic event, one "known" or cognized (negatively) as an interruption, intervention, or break in a system of relays.

an attempt to account for a break down that is the effect of its own material structure. Accordingly, the problem of defining an *act* is complicated by the obvious charade of Ted's defense of Mrs. Verloc – a defense she rejects a moment later when Verloc tells her to give the money back, at which point the lights return anyway and the crowd goes back to the movie.

A certain wreckage is strewn over the very opening of the film – as if in the wake of an unwitnessed explosion which Stevie's bomb may seem a weak attempt to repeat or, however oddly, master. If *Sabotage* opens with a black-out that precedes light or perhaps cinematic life this rupture or *caesura* enters and arrests the narrative as well.[10] Indeed, we may seem to be in a prefigural state with regard to narrative production, like Verloc's office *behind* the film screen. This is reflected in Oscar Homolka's lethargic and impassive performance throughout, like one virtually dragging himself through a film over before it begins. Yet as Verloc's handler points out later the supposed "first" act of sabotage fails. Meant to disrupt the socius and fill it with anxiety and break down, the public instead *laughs*. That is, to translate this yet again, Hitchcock is addressing the problem that his audience remains (merely) entertained or amused by his metaphysically aggressive and defacing productions, which they cannot read anyway.

We may again note an explicit tension between the classical notion of allegory – in which a text refers to represented meanings, a view that perversely parallels a mimetic understanding of film itself – and a more active and deforming sense which Hitchcock engages. This *other* definition, more Benjaminian, involves exploding the very model that separates original and copy, reference and sign in the first tradition.

Thus Hitchcock's "broken contract" extends beyond the contract to massage the paying audience with the escapist pleasures of formulaic suspense so akin to sexual tension (Verloc, at least,

---

[10] The concept of the *caesura* – a site where a representational system can appear to turn upon itself in a temporal rupture – is elaborated by Philippe Lacoue-Labarthe in his essay on Hoelderlin's Greek *translations*, "The Caesura of the Speculative," in *Typography*, 208–235. Lacoue-Labarthe notes of this *caesura* – which bears affinity to the "bar-series" that runs throughout Hitchcock's films – that it "suspends the 'catastrophic' process of alternation" (234), and supplants melody (figuration) with rhythm (prefigural measure). To relate such an infra-linguistic event to the "bombing" in *Sabotage* has innumerable consequences for the idea of sabotaging reading or mimesis itself that I will address.

offers the money *back*). It extends beyond letting young Stevie get blown up. If the bomb, as in Conrad's novel, suggests an attempt to fix (or negate) time by gathering all into an illusional *punctum* – the pretext of still photo-graphic logic – the image can also be misread. In a sense, while Stevie's bomb draws our attention to one obvious reason Hitchcock's film *seems* to fail, it may also be a decoy or not really be the point. By making Stevie somewhat idiotic, less so than Conrad but still to some degree, Hitchcock is already toying with the mimetic machinery of identification he himself would deface. Moreover, as we have suggested, if anything the bomb sequence merely *repeats* the rupture of cinema at the opening (itself the repetition of something unrepresentable, an effect of representation itself), and it does so with an event (the explosion) that is likened by the Professor – the bird-man who purveys the bomb to Verloc and later blows up the Bijou when surrounded together with himself – to *a bird's whistle* or *song*, to sheer warbling sound. Hitchcock, stepping out of his supposed contract to entertain, cannot pretend to simply resume that anymore than Verloc takes interest in his cinema's business after this. The film *Sabotage* is already doomed to taking a different course. What is unclear is whether the very failure of the film to present subjectivities with which this audience can identify is not, inversely, a different testimony to the "success" of a still to come definition of "sabotage." For a certain "Hitchcock," clearly, cinema is theorized in advance as an anti-mimetic, hence anti-statist war-machine. It has both a nomadic and anarchic function – one whose contaminated inscription in that state order, institutionally and as a mode of production witnessed by the certificate of censorship in the British films, renders that *faux* anarchism itself a type of gamble, or *crossing*. But, where to?

2. "Instantaneous arrest"

When Stevie is waylaid on his way through the Lord Mayor's Show Day parade by the toothbrush and hair ointment salesman, the latter thrusts Stevie into the chair before the teeming crowd to advertise his product's ("Salvo-Dent") power of "instantaneous arrest" of *decay*. What, indeed, saves teeth, or is saved (from what) by them? While the trope involves an initial glance at the technology of the photographic still, it supplies an underlying gloss on the implications of the time-bomb itself (to some extent, this film) – and beyond that to the illusion of a specular system. Such a *mise en abyme* seems in fact to occur in a least likely spot, the Disney cartoon sequence run in the movie-house evoking Mae West (that is, a certain impure graphics or "animation"), during which Mrs. V – in shock over Stevie's death – will be drawn into a kind of mad laughter beyond mourning. The phrase also returns us to the allegorical problem of Hitchcock's relation to a powerful primary text or novel. We might say that the film's relation to its own textual original, Conrad's *The Secret Agent*, is effaced when Hitchcock changes the work's name to assume Hitchcock's allographic priorities. Yet a remainder lingers – and if Hitchcock pre-empts the title by using it in his previous film, the exploitation and neutralization of Conrad's work, in advance, not only erases the latter's authorial priority, but attaches the *words* themselves to a citational network in which their philosophical resonances are, quite simply, released like the errant birds, dogs, and black cats – animated animal traces – that operate as signifying agents elsewhere. Emblematically, it is this historial relationship of priority and secondariness that Hitchcock deregulates with his time-bomb – in which the cinematic *techne* reflects, first, on its materiality, or role in mnemonic inscription, or place as a relay of the historial sensorium.

William Burroughs once said that he had written little of power, and would know that he had written a good sentence when the reader died on the spot. Hitchcock, too, is questing for his killer text, but "sabotage" for him always operates within a hermeneutic economy or system – one of reading, as Deleuze suggests. Absorbing the cultural function of literary writing (or the novel), Hitchcock's cinema is inhabited in turn by the specter of the material word with which the film opens: that word is something that, however broken down (dictionary entries, letters, marks, or phonemes), precedes the eye or the gaze, and in effect generates visibility as a technological effect of reading *signs*, of repetition, or memory as a machine. On the plus side, it displaces the illusion of mimesis itself – movies conceived as "pictures of people talking," the phrase by which Hitchcock mockingly dismissed almost every other film. On the minus side, this cinema consciously inhabits an intolerable site of mechanical recurrence. To intervene in this system – to act on it, to sabotage or change it – involves, as we saw, a reflexive exertion. Coming out of the Underground, after all, the Londoners are laughing: they cannot be hurt or killed by Hitchcock's text, which only seems to accommodate them more and more. Cinema, like language, is technically no different than consciousness and assimilates the latter. One cannot quite kill what is already technically "dead," already the product of material signs or representation, emerging in its after-life. This may be one implication of another narrative interruption that occurs in the film, the scene when Mrs. V, reeling from the death of Stevie, takes a seat in the movie-house momentarily. What appears on the screen is the Disney sequence about human-birds, and the killing with an arrow of the serenading "Cock Robin" – a cartoon killing that cuts off seduction and song in mid-stride. Thus the singing, linked to the time bomb and birds, of "Who killed Cock Robin?" enfolds and memorializes its immediate precursor (Cock Robin singing), though the role of the shootist, the black bird or *shadow*, also suspends any answer to the "who." Nor can be suspended the chain the name releases – cock, Hitchcock, bird, (a)phallus, rob(b)in(g). One of Spenser's first remarks is: *"Blinkin'* shame, *robbin'* the poor people like that" – making a direct link between "blinking" (and alternation of white and black, as exploited with the drummer man in *Young and Innocent*) and "robbin(g)," a theft identified here with cinema, of money, of being. At all events, the autobiographical moment – which is also that of cinema, an alternate "Hitchcock" signature-logic – is notched in other ways, such as by Spenser's cover as a green-grocer, the occupation of Hitchcock's father. This is noted when Mrs. V speculates on why Spenser is a grocer yet has money to go to Simpson's for lunch – being the son of the owner? – though there is a covert erasure of Oedipal logics, gender markings, and "fathers" altogether (as the bird-man says of his granddaughter: "There you are – no father, no discipline"). To some degree, the opening black-out registers a dissolution of mimetic reference that is the pure, formal expression of the medium. All of Hitchcock's cinema, it has been said, is so much the product of calculated artifice that it may seem close to animation – another way of saying that, in Hitchcock, "consciousness" or "life" are co-effects of semiosis or (cinematic) writing. As a sheer and citational semiosis, this cinema would cut off the mimetic reference which film above all mediums begins by seductively invoking, or promising,[11] or would, if the mimetic referent itself were not generated by this semiosis instead. It is not accidental that, after his death, Stevie keeps returning to Mrs. Verloc as a hallucination – as cinematic ghost, his face pops up in crowds or is attached to other running children, unable to definitively leave a scene in which the categories of life and death are dovetailed, unable to initiate a cycle of mourning since he has been not so much killed as (technically) erased. Sabotaging the written word, Hitchcock exceeds and supplants "the book" yet *gets* inhabited and sabotaged by the latter's remainder, by the scriptive trace as unsublatable effect. In response, he again raises the stakes. For in blowing up not only Stevie but, in the final scene, the Bijou itself (or, in effect, in sacrificing the film *Sabotage* in a sort of meta-gesture), Hitchcock seems willing to sacrifice *the very logic and spectacle of sacrifice* that holds the representational economy of identification, narrative, and aesthetic pleasure in place to begin with.

It is at this point that there is a certain fall – what elsewhere in Hitchcock might be termed *vertiginous*. In privileging material signs over the mimetic promise of images, Hitchcock cuts off with the "juice" any natural or iconic relation such figures bear to their potential meaning. This momentary loss of *assured* reference is one implication of the opening black-out in the film that is linked to a dictionary and develops the logic of the "McGuffin." When the lights return the surviving agents of signification – now operating as aural and visual puns, infratextual relays, and graphic ciphers – have curtailed any natural logic of origination in the process. If Hitchcock's film is itself "arrested" by an aporia that one can only try to bomb one's way out of, it may be similar to that which pervades his preceding work, preemptively named *Secret Agent*. That film, after all, features John Gielgud as a character who, Hamlet-like, could not "act" in multiple senses (he cannot perform on screen, decide, or kill). There are interesting resonances to recall here in the definition: if "sabotage" is defined as the "destruction of buildings or machinery," it involves less a surface than a *structural* intervention, as witnessed in the opening act of

---

[11] Much as Mr. Memory in *The 39 Steps* is said to memorize mere "facts" (film's promised *re*production of the real) – "facts" or images which when marked and selectively repeated become virtual signifying agents, steps or feet that are sites of material events ("feats").

sabotaging the generator, while the terms of action, "alarming" and "inspiring," are associable with the *poetic* sublime. That the collapse is that of buildings or structures should be underlined, particularly given the brief shot of the street across from the Bijou, of workers in a construction site or dig. Aside from drawing attention to the sabotaging act as being one intended to assault or re-define structure as such – the underlying grid of representation – the site indicates a type of clearing work associated with the film itself (the Bijou).

If we again ask what *sabotage* means, part of the answer may lie in the target in this film and in those surrounding it that deal with espionage: *England*. But England is here understood as *home*, as interior (Inspector Talbot explains to Spenser that the sabotage is undertaken by foreign agents to distract the populace from what is going on outside: it represents an outside within the interior). England, land of ruddy-faced angels – that is, of hermeneutic *messengers* (from the Greek *angellein*) – also names a hermeneutic situation. With all sorts of discriminations, we may call this her-meneutico-political scenario which Hitchcock's cinema aims to sabotage that of mimesis, of humanism, of an aesthetic of identifi-cation or the subject. The "problem" with the film *Sabotage* is not only that Stevie (as child) is wasted so perfunctorily – indeed, children flood the text, but in a weird way, as they do in *The Birds'* school-house scene, where they appear as repetitive and machinal (like the child, Anne, in *Shadow of a Doubt*, who only *reads*) – but in the film's refusal to provide characters to identify with, refusing narrative pleasure, refusing finally to give the audience subjectivi-ties to consume, the nasty corollary of Verloc's putting sand in the generators to begin with.

One logic of the term "sabotage" is that of a radical exteriority that inhabits and dispossesses from within an interior or the pretext of *interiority* itself: a house, a self, a family unit, an aesthetics of identification, "meaning" as property. The premise of this exteriority seems manifest in the Lord Mayor's Show Day street scenes, the public parade, or the *ritual spectacle*. It is an exteriority which can only redouble or virtually implode – and blowing up the Bijou finally. The film must seem to sacrifice itself (as sacrifice), short-circuit itself not for the mock-recuper-ation that produces the couple at the end (the depressingly preprogrammed Ted and the blackmailed Mrs. V), but to take the "system" down in a mock-apocalyptic that, it knows, can only be caught in the eternal recurrence of an endlessly respun spool. As such, it represents and enacts Hitchcock's evisceration of the state apparatus of mimetic ideology and humanism. "Sabotage," we are virtually told, needs a definition – *another* definition. We will risk the following: while on the one hand it attempts to name the prospect of an *"act"* that Hitchcockian writing would effect, one parallel to a subversion of an aesthetico-political order that is mock apocalyptic, it cannot locate that event as a discrete intervention, a moment that can be isolated, but only across a general catastrophic field that the present is already an after-effect to, humans another effect of a grand *zoographics*. This makes it the more mystifying, since it takes on the form of the double-chase, proleptically pursuing the specter of an event that is nonetheless the precondition of that pursuit, and is denied by the external state or semantic system (the dictionary). The "frenzy" of trying to exceed a system that is oppositionally and specularly inscribed, in a circular logic, is implied (and Hitchcock, from the first, associates this bind with the emblem of the *ring*, a temporal figure with Nietzschean inflections). To sabotage in Hitchcock's sense, we may hypothesize, means to close out any order of interiority by which the regime of *mimetic humanism* constructs its controls – an order guarded in Hitchcock by the police and, in a later film such as *Saboteur*, glancingly identified with both (American) fascism and capitalism. It is for this reason that "politics" will never be simply taking sides, since the same order inhabits home and abroad, the concept of the foreign, fascist-imperialism and its mock others (the fact, for instance, of indicating France's colonial appropriation of Madagascar as parallel to the Reich's own plans rendered Hitchcock's attempt at war "propaganda" films useless, or "inflammatory"). The result is a site where the subjectivity of even Mrs. Verloc looks blank, her performative gender vacant. The problem is that just this *active* vacating of presumed performative or narratorial "contents" is a transformative part of the director's aesthetico-political gambit that must (not) be read. One way to approach it is through re-reading the marked *zoographism* – as regards "life" as well as animal and *animated* forms – that Hitchcock deploys. It would seem that Hitchcock's praxis projects itself as (the failure of) an "act" of sabotage, implemented and arrested in any reading, of the state's apparatus of mimetic reproduction – and this, on behalf of an intercession in definition, temporal space, the "human," the aesthetocritical polis ("London").

3. Becoming meat

I return to why an apocalyptic logic overtakes *Sabotage*, as reflected in those messianic street signs ("Repent") held up in the carnivalized scenes of the Lord Mayor's Show Day, or in Verloc's vision projected onto the fish tank of the aquarium, as onto a film screen, of the total melt-down and collapse of all *structures* – in a Piccadilly Circus called, again, "the center of the world." Yet human time is not only *interrupted*, it is also portrayed as historically collapsed and sandwiched by what can only first be called pre-mammalian and post-human time. This is done during Verloc's visit to the Zoo, as it is differently inflected by the ceaseless references to birds and to eating parts of animal (as the rehearsed menu at the restaurant *Simpson's* shows). Something in this carnival "time" is awry or, as Hamlet says, "out of joint." As in *Silence of the Lambs*, where the cannibalism of Lector renders the human itself objectivized meat in order to suggest the theme of metamorphosis (associated with moths) toward a seemingly post-humanist subject, Verloc's being stabbed with a steak-knife at the dinner table gives the human subject – shown throughout eating or consuming other animals – the status of any other roast. Verloc's apocalyptic vision at the Aquarium, then, collapses human time to a parenthesis within the non-human "time" of pre-mammalian fish and birds.

Yet Hitchcock's assault on *human* time is the effect of his understanding of material language as such. We can see this not only in the film's foreclosure of *any logic of origin* (the alternation, throughout the film, of birds with eggs ("poached eggs – the worst")), but the way this spreads to subtly undo any presentation of gender or even sexual difference that is not subject to a radical desemanticization. A notorious instance occurs in the aquarium, where a stroller notes that after laying "a million eggs" a certain fish changes sexes (his girlfriend quips, "I don't blame her"), and when Stevie asks of Verloc how he will know his song-bird's sex and is told to wait until the hen lays an egg, he says it would be remarkable this time if the "gent" did so. If gender is a semiotic effect, the logic of replication supplants the pretense of sexual generation. In another scene, the bird-man's daughter has a little girl said to be without a known father. She reverses temporal priority by striking the grand-dad ("Slap me hard – grand-dad's been very naughty"). And there is a de-racinated double-text in the misleading facade of Verloc's "fam-ily" itself: seen by Ted as a family onto which he may project his clumsy Oedipal wishes (crudely making love to an indifferent Mrs. V from the start, a pitiless exposé of hetero-inscription), the "family" is chimerical: in a de-sexed marriage (Mrs. V laughs at Verloc seeing another woman: "If you only knew him"), she is no mother, but a *sister*, and what binds her to Verloc is his supposed "care" for Stevie, while the former is obviously no "father." There is, here, no father all along or, more to the point, no "gen-eration," and what we have, for fairly obscure purposes, is some-thing like a *Potemkin family*. It may seem they are another "front," not for politics alone but a profounder vacuum. If Hitchcock's text is *anti-Oedipal* or in a certain sense at once pre- and post-Oedipal, all natural "generation" seems *cut off* at or before its origin. This extreme figure is gambled, however, *in the name of a mission*, a destructive metamorphosis of the socius itself – what depends on a formalistic re-definition of a signifying order, the sensorium, the "human," itself denarrativized as laughter (for metamorphosis to (not) occur, the text needs the momentum of the one thing it confutes or denies itself from the start, narrative time). One is reminded of the figure of translation in the advice that Mrs. V gives to Stevie: "Careful at the crossing" – where a certain crossing-over (in Nietzsche's hyperbolic sense) appears inflected.[12] We may recall why Hitchcock's shift from classical "allegory" conceived as a guardian of mimesis – which links it with a mimetic notion of *cinema*, and which Detective (Edmund) Spenser may be considered traditional and literary guardian of – to an altered and allomimetic sense suggests an (epochally) translational effect. In Hitchcock's practice as in Benjamin's the-orizations, this immediately raises the issue of a historial inter-

---

[12] "Translation," as a matter of exchange between languages, different versions of voice of which none is centered, occurs more strikingly in the first *Man Who Knew Too Much*, *Secret Agent* (the predecesssor film with which *Sabotage* is diversely interfaced), *The Lady Vanishes* and *To Catch a Thief*.

vention on the level of the linguistic "event," the mnemotechnic rupture.[13]

Yet the film is nonetheless overrun with designations of all too precise *time* – titles announce successive days (Thursday, Friday), as if to insure some forward procession, the bomb will go off ("the bird sings") at precisely 1:45. The note says, "Don't forget," yet of course one can only *forget* the precise moment given cinematic time's anamorphic cast. In fact, what we witness is the temporal dilemma engendered by a material *sign* that defers the arrival of the apocalyptic moment it announces or, in its voiding facticity, effects the simulacrum of. Just before the Bijou is blown up, Mrs. V runs to the Inspector to confess to the murder of Verloc. While she is first stalled by Spenser, who wants to conceal her guilt, she nonetheless blurts out: "He's dead," just *before* the explosion erases all trace of the murder. Immediately Talbot recollects the remark, asking: Is the girl psychic? He then attempts to clarify the timing of the remark, on which its interpretation and the film's end depend. He mutters: "That 's *queer* – Is that girl psychic? *She said it before – or was it after – I can't remember!*" Too early, the word or sign always refers back to an anteriority it can never coincide with, like the black-out, or to a proleptic arrival it always misses as the projection of a recessive "past." This logic doubles the text again, separating its catastrophic rhetoric – the vision at the aquarium – from a more banal, material, permanent dislocation as void of pathos or heroism as Verloc himself. A rift opens, we might say, in which two competing rhetorical dimensions of the film can no longer make even routine contact. We can now see why, if Hitchcock's "time" is *now*, right now in our culture, when he can perhaps be read as he has never been before, he is often, still, missed, by the incessant return of a certain forgetting, a forced closure of that rift which, in opening, he deploys as a means of sabotaging the definition of definition. If the tourist viewer routinely consumes Hitchcock's films as escapist thrillers and laughs, the latter can only intervene in the historical flux – as a commodified Trojan horse, taken inside the gates – by altering from within both the

[13] Perhaps the most elaborate text on traffic and travel as a trope of cinema itself occurs during the credits of *To Catch a Thief*, when a "Travel Service" window reflecting sheer traffic and a movie marquee is presented as a double text soliciting the tourist viewers.

facile process of consumption and the definition of *the aesthetic* itself. This "time" has no place, yet "is" everywhere.

We can better see why the word "sabotage" names an act that is explosively impossible – that can never quite be timed or made to happen, yet which also already has. Within a *mise-en-scène* in which representation is predicated on repetition and memory (like film), to act does not mean simply foreclosing a type of pleasure, suspending suspense, or for that matter altering the very system from which one's own (re)production emerges – and hence sacrificing oneself, one's text, like Stevie, like Verloc, like *Sabotage*. This "act," which does not occur at any particular point, can only take place if the text activates an "event" of reading as such – which renders the film a sort of time-bomb still (recalling Mallarmé: "there is no explosion but a book"). Hitchcock is addressing the same problem that Verloc is: how, through the agency of writing/ cinema, to commit an *act* that counts, that makes an incision which subverts the false modality of the present and alters the future chain by which the real is produced. How can an event of reading/ writing occur that alters the order of things if not by altering the system of text production and consumption, of reading and writing – as the opening dictionary shot suggests? By theorizing the bombing of the "center of the world," of a fantasy that links cinema itself (the screen, the fish tank) to the site of phenomenalization, spectralization (the Underground), *phanesthai*, Hitchcock/ Verloc would sabotage the representational, historical dominance of a certain symbolic mode on which the very definition of fantasy rests. If sabotage involves some desire for Hitchcock's text to intervene in a aesthetico-political state (call it, for now, England), we might associate the time-bomb itself with that "shock" effect that Walter Benjamin, in the *Theses on the Philosophy of History*, associates with the *agency* of allegorical writing.[14]

To some extent, "sabotage" may also mean undoing the hegemony of the written word. Hitchcock must sabotage it in turn by breaking it, showing how his cinema can precede metaphor,

[14] Hitchcock's apocalyptic "now" recalls to some extent less the figure of a *punctum* or hypostasized present-moment than Benjamin's concept of the *Jetztzeit* or messianic Now-time in the *Theses* – that is, a time that, itself the effect of material language, is projected into a putative future in order to alter the past and future, intervene by rewriting a history of the "present" (a "historio*graphy*"): it is only in this sense that Hitchcock's own text may maintain that parallel to Verloc's desire to intervene, to bring down the structures of society, to "act."

narrative, or even letters altogether (triggered by the translation-effect solicited by the present of Conrad's novel as touch-stone). At one point – in which figures and toys of transit proliferate (trucks, buses) – a model boat emerges, a hobby of the boy's, which Verloc, after the former's death, tries to shield from Mrs. V's sight: the word-thing, vehicle of transit, sail as trope and model, emerges as though tearing out the center of the word sa-bo(a)t-age itself. It is interesting that the figure of Stevie seems relevant here, since we might say that, instead of being the most likable innocent in the film, he has no real place in its world and assumes a *pharmakon* role all of his own. As a *third* or neuter term without a legitimate father, Stevie is that odd figure who at once holds together and gives the lie to the fictional triangle of Verloc's "family." (He might be compared, even, to "little Betty" in the first *Man Who Knew Too Much*, who is called "it" by her mother, Jill.) If Hitchcock's cinema were a scene of writing, and it is, Stevie would function as the trace of a trace – bearing on his cap, in the parade, a *triangular* shield sporting the letter *B*.[15] His impossible erasure or obliteration, rather than bringing the marital pair together (Verloc suggests, absurdly, that they now have a child of their own), destroys even the simulations of desire that allowed for this arrangement. As such – that is, as a neuter figure himself who both defines and has no *place* in the family, is *atopos* – Stevie suggests a prefigural term, a perfect carrier for Verloc's bomb. Indeed, since Stevie recalls *the boy who interrupts Hitchcock reading* in the cameo in *Blackmail* – an interruption that also makes reading possible – blowing him up becomes Hitchcock's attempt to effect the interruption of (an) *interruption*, a self-sacrifice of readability (narrative, pleasure, identification). Such a "sacrifice" always raises the question of being done toward some other end, though it has commonly appeared the very pointlessness of this erasure that stirred dissent (or, implicitly, undefined pleasure).[16] The only "end" available

---

[15] We might compare this suggestion to how the figure of Tracy (spelled Tracey in the original silent version) functions in *Blackmail*.

[16] The little boy Arnie in *The Trouble With Harry* represents another locus for the dislocation of temporality – a figure continuing a series that includes Stevie. In that film text, Arnie elaborates his sense of time in the exchange when he speaks of "tomorrow" being "yesterday." In Hitchcock's onamastic system, we could unpack the name as "R-nie" – indeed, the letter R figures for Hitchcock in films from *Secret Agent* ("old man R," the master-agent) to *Rebecca* (the burning R on the pillow) and *Frenzy* (Rusk's tie pin), in instances associated with *repetition* itself. This would co-sign the name "Arnie/R-nie" as a site with a negation of

would be the undoing of ends itself, the proleptic "crossing" implied at every point in the interpretive apparatus that is, nonetheless, already accomplished and effaced from the start. In a certain sense which seems reflected in Stevie's mediating role in the Verlocs' mock-family (the mother is no mother, and so on), Stevie represents the third man, the predifferentiated "little boy," what might be called an *interval* himself.

This is why the bomb associated with a bird's singing is carried by Stevie with two canisters that bear the name of a specific film. As is mentioned or joked about repeatedly, the film is *Bartholomew the Strangler*. What, however, may be deemed explosive, allegorically or otherwise, in *this* title (which refers us back to the film's own)? For one thing, it contains a *pre*figural component in the word or syllable *bar*. It is a non-word that in Hitchcock's system has the covert power to dissolve mimetic representation by preceding even scriptive language (letters) or graphics. (Indeed, we hear or see the bar-series motif in the opening word of the dictionary entry, "Wilful . . . ," in the repetition of il/ul, which Hitchcock uses elsewhere to mark this site, such as Lili in *Secret Agent*, or the names Lil and Billy in *Marnie*, or what the last text in the zombie-like children's chorus calls being "ill.") It cannot denote imprisonment since the bars it suggests, when scrutinized, have no inside or outside themselves, and fail to close off a space. Rather, it denotes and performs, presents and represents a notation of radical alternating difference and material semiosis – similar to what Derrida calls "a pure differential vibration" – that both "generates" and curtails all reading, all narrative at the same time as being the predicate of its after-life. The name *Bartholomew* in this case, echoed in variant names in other Hitchcock texts, is italicized for naming a film canister coupled with the bomb associated with the "singing" of birds. The alternation and spacing which Hitchcock connects with the materiality of film imprinting is noticeable in the clack-clack of the projector, the flickering light, the illusory succession of frames, is represented for him, routinely, in the analog (and sound) of a moving train. The "bar" as such in itself puts out the light, as at first, sabotages it in advance of any

---

repetition is attempted or marked. If we read Stevie as a "third" figure, or the neuter in an almost Blanchotian sense, we do so aware of the multiple implications that the number *three* bears for Hitchcock, which Gilles Deleuze barely opens up in addressing the figure of *thirdness* in *Cinema 1: The Movement-Image*.

articulation, rendering "light" itself an *aestheme* or phenomenal product of a movement of differential marks. As a series of bars – like the serial murders of *The Lodger* – it precedes letteration and is sometimes marked by a repeated knocking: presemantic, the series implies spacing and time, anteriority and repetition, allegory and suspension, narrative and semiotic "death." (It also denotes, and ruptures, this "and.") Without interior or exterior, it forecloses any narrative that depends on a single lost object, absent reference, or inner reserve of meaning. In the present text, encrypted in a film title and associated with Verloc's time-bomb, we are encouraged to read *it* as what materially precedes consciousness, visibility, and individual words. We might hypothesize, in a manner I cannot develop here, that this "signature" becomes Hitchcock's means not only of asserting the post-humanist materiality of his textual project, but of marking a site at once incredibly banal and before representation that, like Nietzsche's phantasm of the "eternal recurrence," becomes an *agent* of transvaluation at work throughout his text. If translation evokes for us not only a focus on writing echoed elsewhere in the film but on the notion, in Benjamin, of "pure language" – of that contentless and expressionless play of material differences premising all language(s) – then Hitchcock's bar-series might be thought to evoke just that prefigural site.

We can see why "England" must send its guardian of allegorical literature, of allegory as (mere) representation, that is, (T)ed Spenser, to try to contain Verloc/Hitchcock's writing machine. This, even when Hitchcock breaks "the contract" of his cinema (in one sense: puts out the screen, announces a rupture that precedes consciousness, blows Stevie up), or when the Bijou is only the "front" for his politico-aesthetic subversions. One of the powers of Hitchcock's cinema in relation to writing is that the word itself can always be deterritorialized as graphics or sheer sound – associated in *Sabotage* with the bomb itself. By way of the very popular shocker *Bartholomew the Strangler* – that is, Hitchcock's use of the "thriller" — the time-bomb is associated with the agency of Hitchcock's most premimetic marker, the bar-series that precedes representation. It "strangles," indeed, cuts off speech, much as Stevie's mouth will appear stuffed repeatedly with food (when we first see him) or with a toothbrush in the streets. By noting the popularity of *Bartholomew the Strangler* – Stevie attests to having watched it repeatedly – Hitchcock marks where the viewer's pleasure derives from vicarious impositions of terror, of murdering and being murdered, and insinuates that the passage from that aesthetic pleasure into the (cinematic) real of dismemberment involves an "instantaneous" crossing. Or double cross, crossing back to a site already implied before the opening of a narrative system that, like Uncle Charlie leaving his boarding room slab in *Shadow of a Doubt*, consents to forgetfully begin, as after-life, again. It also checks the problematic withdrawal of the viewer from attested pleasure when the murder/dismemberment happens to Stevie – while re-marking, on yet another level, that the viewer can't complain of what is, *supposedly*, a fiction.

It is telling that the place in the film in which allegory and sheer writing converge is the Disney cartoon, shown just after Mrs. V learns of Stevie's death and just before she sits to eat with Verloc, leading to his stabbing death. It is difficult to focus on this vignette, which we mentioned above. In it Cock Robin is shot while serenading a bird-figure of Mae West – while a chorus trails off with the refrain, "Who killed Cock Robin?" It is difficult, among other things, not because the screen raises too directly the issue of cinema as writing, or because it projects a utopian fantasy space in which human and animals are *blended* together. The theater breaks out more than ever in what Verloc/Hitchcock wanted to avoid, convulsive, even Homeric laughter. But in Mrs. V's case it is a kind of *insane* laughter – tipping her beyond the despair at Stevie's murder, "beyond" mourning. If Cock Robin – the singing man-bird – is killed in the cartoon and absorbs Stevie's death, the syllable "Cock" not only implicates Hit*chcock* but forecasts Verloc's stabbing in another temporal criss-cross of causal chains. Several things (dis)converge here. Cock Robin is shot by an arrow when singing explicitly to a *Mae West* figure. Excessively round and corpulent, "she" is also what might be called a female *female impersonator* ("Mae West" as a motif that sabotages the figure of gender is used elsewhere in Hitchcock, most specifically in *The 39 Steps* and *Frenzy*). Hitchcock layers in the cartoon a primal scene of sorts. It involves not only the death of the singer-subject in which the *agency* of that death is subtracted ("Who killed . . .?") but a death occasioned during the eerie serenading of an infragendered, inter-species figure of corporeal excess whose mock-female guise (playing to the misprision of the "male") indicts the mock-romantic or muse-like pretext of song or poetic production – a relation mirrored in that of Spenser to Mrs. *V*. It renders the alibi of western sexual romance as uncomfortably "acted" as it is in the film by the boyish Sylvia Sidney – who, sexlessly possessed by Verloc and oddly sought by Ted, seems exclusively bound to her idiot brother. The trailing cartoon chorus ("Who killed (Hitch)Cock Robin?") projects a cryptic commentary over the film's dis(en)gendered erotics – a thorough dislocation that only Ted Spenser (and perhaps the viewer) persists in ignorance of by trying to impose on it a conventional narrative map of compulsory coupling. In going *beyond mourning* – since what is "mourned" (Stevie) would be either an equivocal figure, the neuter itself, or the absence of mourning – *Sabotage* opens a less chartered zoographematic space. And fails to: since what would ultimately be twisted or warped in the wreckage of Hitchcock's cinema (as Verloc's Bijou) is the model of representation, identification, reference, interpretation, and pleasure whose subtraction gives access to that terrain. Where laughter at first undermined the sabotaging of the *generative* origin itself, it is taken up as a space of madness in Mrs. V, where the import of her letteral marking asserts itself over a more general "Who . . . ?" that is first applied to animated and personified animal-humans on screen.

The association of an active deregulation of linear time with Hitchcock's "cinema" registers his prelinguistic conception of the moving image – as a switchboard and constellation of historial and would be mimetic traces and prefigural logics. In Hitchcock the dismantling of reproduction, of copying, is transposed back into the always pre-encountered domain of recording – marked in the different record players evinced in *The Man Who Knew Too Much*, *Secret Agent*, or even *Psycho*. Sam Weber recently analyzed the relation between the image and the moment of reception in Benjamin – that up-taking, associated in Benjamin with variants of the verb *aufnahmen* – in which re-inscription becomes possible:

The recording apparatus, whether visual or auditory, "takes up" everything but never looks back, never returns the glance. It *blinks* but never *winks*. Instead, what it does is to arrest and separate and reproduce the "here-and-now" again and again in a proliferating series of images which go here and there, a mass of pictures that cannot keep still even if they are instantaneous "snapshots." The German word for such "still photos" – *Momentaufnahmen* – indicates that what is ultimately arrested,

"taken up," broken down, spliced back together again and then let loose
. . . is the *moment* itself. The "time" of reproducibility is that of this
"posthumously shocked", immobilized, dispersed, recollected and finally forgotten moment, ever on the verge, always coming to pass.[17]

If there is no real Oedipal logic in the mock-family that the Verlocs
present, and hence *no mother* in the boyish Sylvia Sydney, it is not
only because Hitchcock knows something about "gender" he is
structurally forbidden to name, something about its fictionality
and interchangability that puts sexual difference and generation
at semiotic risk. What Hitchcock elsewhere calls "mother" inhabits less a gendered and maternal site in a family romance than
a machinal order (or that Derrida elaborates under the name
khora) – much as the x-ray shot reveals ticking gears in the bomb
package (citing, of all texts, Chaplin's text of anachronization,
Modern Times). The site of "mother" in Hitchcock – associated
with a series of M-terms (memory, murder, machine, music) –
tends to cover a machinal semiosis that virtually cancels before it
(re)produces, much as the bar-series does "visibility" or reading
itself. The excuse of appropriating a work of high "literary"
repute (Conrad) allows the text to focus on the relation of cinema
to writing, of secondary to primary texts, of translation, but is also
only a front – like the Bijou. In the process, he sabotages the
reigning historical and political regime of representation – though
at the price of leaving any position intact from which that "act"
can be assessed or read. The explosion condensed into the one
bombing sequence in *Sabotage* is not only scattered or multiplied
but referred to something prefigural, to sheer sound, as it was
earlier in the film to a bird's whistle. At this point, when the world
has become sheer exteriority, Hitchcock's act of sabotage – that is,
the evisceration of a *faux* tradition of meaning and mimesis with
its attendant politics of reference and genealogical time – renders
itself *passé*. One is left, of course, with the carnage of a failure that
imprints itself, in advance, from the start in Verloc's case, by
virtue of a marked repetition. Like the laughter that first greets
Verloc's somewhat dubious effort, the laughter of the already
dead in the Underground, already in a cinematic space analogous
to semiotic "consciousness," absorbs the project of sabotaging
narrative time by the latter's necessary forgetfulness of that being

---

[17] Samuel Weber, *Mass Mediauras: Form, Technics, Media* (1996), 100.

accomplished before the fact. One cannot kill the (un)dead. Yet one can move repeatedly, so that the usual evasions and relapses become vacuous, to the site where intervention is conceived as that of the aesthetic model itself, the site of inscription, identification, the lost aura, that forecloses the anthropocentric contract.

❖❖

Tourings – or, the monadic switchboard

❖❖

6

❖❖

Echotourism: Nietzschean cyborgs, anthropophagy, and the rhetoric of science in cultural studies

❖❖

Science as a means of self-narcosis: *do you have experience of that?*

Nietzsche, *Toward a Genealogy of Morals*

As techno-science, science, in its very movement, can only consist in a transformation of the techniques of archivization, of printing, of inscription, of reproduction, of formalization, of ciphering, and of translating marks.

Derrida, *Archive Fever*

This chapter will focus on whether the trope of "science," as appropriated by cultural studies, at times indirectly preserves a long-installed humanist and *mimetic* bias at the expense of a different materiality – we will call it that of language itself, but to some extent that, too, can seem a misnomer – which remains critical to the post-human(ist): that is, whether a figure of "science" at times upholds regressive models of representation, and whether we need a more material, non-mimetic conception of the literary, perhaps even a more Nietzschean conception of "science" itself, at least, if the conjunction of literature and science is not designed to extend to us a new conceptual capital, or extend a familiar archive, but raise the specter of historical *intervention*. Thus, the term in my title, "echotourism," is double. First, it cites a certain eco-tourism – harmless enough, even desirable in ways, yet a type of *protected tourism* (I have seen it in the jungles: expensive lodges, imported cooks, prepared trails). The tourist cannot help but play into a constructed business world, a fantasy commodity predicated on the tourist's need for protection, need to be *there* and not be *there* at the same time. It is sheltered: it stays (*eco*) *in* the home, while seeming outside of it. But the word can be also broken within itself: *eco*-tourism/*echo*-terrorism. My adjustment names a *double* of this first scene, its echo, particularly if the pun questions how "science" – one materialist other of a seemingly humanist field of literature – circulates at times in cultural studies. It calls us back to the word *echo* itself, to the formal, literary, or material dimension of the signifier – and, further, to a slippage that converts tourism to the echo of terrorism, the terrorism of mere tourism, its illusory safety, and the terrorism of echoes, ghosts, rebellious signifiers for which mimetic "science" has no category but literature might. In part, this terrorism and tourism might both apply to the technoculturist who enjoys the metaphors of science as an adjusted *mimetic* problem, one supplementing rather than replacing humanist systems of reference and meaning with promising figures of alterity (the cyborg will be one over-used and overly mimetic icon of this would-be technological sublime). There is an implicit "terrorism," we might say, to the manner by which different figures of science are folded into that same system – as though, pointing at and promising an allohumanist model, it can in fact reinforce the same systems by turning to a newly historicist, mimetic, and cultural studies idiom. Yet *terrorism* adheres to the word echo itself, mostly for its de-semanticizing or nihilistic implications – as if something in the terrain of the material signifier, its supposedly apolitical formalism, harasses the humanist, mimetic and interiorist model still and holds the key to another transformation. Does a commodified figure of techno-culture, today, present a form of tourism that protects us from, rather than accesses, the allohuman? Does the question lie, rather, in altering our linguistic and mnemonic reading-systems – the hard-disk, as it were, out of which models of reference and history seem generated?

Science was long held as an institutional other of something called "literature" (as if in a subject-object binary): science as a discourse designating a materiality that ruptures the humanist models of meaning and interpretation. The "and" linking science and literature potentially frames the latter, positioning it in a space it never inhabited. Critical practice remains primarily

mimetic, today, as seen in the dominance of historicist and contex-
tualist models, instead of addressing the virtual models of
mnemotechnics texts present. (The latter, it seems, can only emerge
with a more radical conception of material language, rooted in
and *before* cognition and the phenomenalism of consciousness
dependent on the mnemonic trace.) If one invocation of "science,"
today, often evades this transformation of and within the hermeneutic model – where memory and language are reconceived
as a material field of inscription, as well as "acts" of exscription,
disinscription and reinscription which alter our very concept of
the "material," of virtual pasts and, hence, virtual futures – then
the tourism of techno-cultural tropes actually defers a more
profound transformation. This seems to happen, among elsewhere, when cybernetic tropes get wedded to *interiorist* or sal-
vationist politics, to social rhetorics of the community, to moralist
trajectories which, nonetheless, leave the problem of memory –
the locus of the material in language, and of the production of all
virtual realities – intact: it is also this site that the anti-mimetic
properties of literature have always patrolled, or have always
threatened to convert into a material, which is to say exterior,
mapping. Wherever a cultural rhetoric of technology views the
technos as something supplemental, as the added-on part of a
linear history – as occurs in invocations of the "post-modern" or a
coming age of the post-human – it leaves the humanist, interiorist
model of representation intact.

Any concept of "science" that breaks with a descriptive model
(which is always to say mimetic) must move in the direction of a
performative that is anti-mimetic or post-mimetic: it would theorize the manner in which cultural figuration – in insisting on
interiorizing metaphors – seems to evade and phenomenalize the
conflict of pre-mimetic events, inscriptions, prefigural scars of
history. It reads the aesthetic as the material, memory as an
exterior site, and voids linear historicist models with experimental chronographs that potentially intervene in, erase, and repro-
gram "memory" itself.

Such another use of *science* occurs in Nietzsche, in the "gay
science," we will recall, and it is not irrelevant that this signature
is bound, of course, to a speculation on – indeed, all considered,
including the textual figure of eternal recurrence and its use as
one site of passage, a performative engagement with – *the*

post-anthropomorphic. How does Nietzsche's thought of the *hyper-human* traverse and exceed the metaphor of the cyborg today (say, as introduced by Haraway)? Has the later image in cultural studies *passed* from promising a figure of sheer exteriority to being an icon that upholds an "old" regime of interiority – and this by reviving a romantic and mimetic tradition of the techno-logical sublime nonetheless?

I should add that we must be conscious of how Nietzsche approaches, solicits, and by-passes a certain trope of science at the end of the *Genealogy*: that is, where it becomes the last refuge of the ascetic ideal – as the proclaimed atheist becomes the last refuge of the theistic drive, the belief in the "truth" of the absence of a "Truth," and so on. Against this descriptive conception of science is posited, implicitly, the gay science, a "science," or *Wissenschaft*, that is pre-originary, hyperbolic, ruptured within the chains of historical narratives, capable of a performative (and textual) inter-vention in history – or bringing the latter to crisis, to a *caesura* in which the economies of linear time buckle, pasts and futures potentially reconfigured, what Benjamin sometimes calls "shock." It would be garishly reductive, though not inaccurate, to address this style, this project, this transvaluation out of the hu-manist-ascetic model, as dependent on a certain materiality (one we will call linguistic, but also linguistic-mnemonic: the site of that "mnemotechnics" of torture and inscription out of which, the *Genealogy* tells us, a memory was imposed, and "man" created as the animal who could promise, who could secure a certain possi-bility of "meaning"). Positing the hyper-man (or what Werner Hamacher translates as the "Out-Man," the being whose exterior-ity is linguistically determined),[1] involves transforming the agency of cognition, the model of reading and writing, shifting from a passive to an active or *proleptic mimesis*. The adjective "gay" (*fröhlich*) – read as a post-anthropomorphic agenda – recalls us to a hyperbolic stance of and within rhetoric preceding and altering the subject's emotive and experiential structure, rather than a model external to him or her: in it much is risked: it eschews the tourism of the mimetic by encountering the material as a mnemotechnics, a simultaneously textual and historial science. The allohuman emerges from the "human" not as

---

[1] See Werner Hamacher, "Disgregation of the Will," in *Premises*, especially 157–60.

temporal progression or evolutionary event (on the contrary, Nietzsche predicts the arrival of the "last man": a kind of *mise en abyme* of Modern Language Association conventions) but abruptly: it had in fact always been the case – the "human" was all along an invention, as it were, a parenthesis, a permanent detour tied to the figure of mimesis. It must invent and re-install itself violently, in and through the agency of a linguistic, indeed a *stylistically* defined "subject," by altering the very systems of reading-writing. We have reason to assume that with *this* post-human trajectory – to which Nietzsche ties, in so many words, the redemption of something called "the earth" – we engage "materiality" in an active and transvaluative way. To be brutally reductive one last time (more or less), a certain Nietzsche can be said to tie a (gay or hyper) *science* to apprehending oneself (individually, collectively) within a network of mobile inscriptions and historical *agencies*, and – through altering those inscriptions hyperbolically – to the possibility of *alternate futures* (at least, to those predicted retroactively by genealogical and causal chains). Alternate futures are tied to the possibility – as Donna Haraway notes – of creating alternative *pasts*. (It is not accidental that, in *La Double Séance* as in *Specters of Marx* and throughout his project, Derrida re-writes "science" as "séance": that is, the place of meeting of the dead and the "living," the living and the unborn and unborn dead – for here, in the opening and séancing of the mnemonic field, which the literary text offers only one privileged model for, mnemonic systems may be brought to a crisis, to a proleptic crossing or transformation in which the trace-chains of the past and the future are gambled, redecided, deferred, missed or lost as an "event," and so on.)

My point here – leaving Nietzsche for a moment, and leaving open altogether where and whether the figure of "eternal recurrence" serves merely as a chronographic marker for this crossing – is that to the degree which, in contemporary cultural studies, "science" has become the latest discursive trope to evade the materiality of (anterior) inscription, and the performative transvaluations that a post-anthropomorphic project requires (the two are not identical), it *risks* being another touristic way of distancing that materiality. This loop in cultural studies is haunted by its double: it becomes at once the promise of a certain outside, of an escape from the "literary" according to the old humanist model, and its other, the re-enforcement of interiors, of mimesis, of mere escape from the sciencing/séancing of the literary. The "literary" names one site for engaging such models, but only after the institution of difference-management called "literature" is historically closed, transformed perhaps into a mobile system of relays, inscriptions, virtual caesuras, semiotic and phenomenal conjurings, mnemotechnics.

If science is oriented toward materiality (rather than its institutional definition) – if it is solicited by the aesthetic in or under that capacity – and if materiality must be thought as it is (forgetfully) experienced in (a) history, through *mnemotechnics* and as inscription, then we must consider that the yoking of science and literature today potentially conceals and evades its double, incarnates the double of what it often sees itself as. Indeed, the "aesthetic" – where so-called consciousness or perception (*aisthanumai*, in Greek) arises from the phenomenalization of inscription – marks the site of the material from an epistemological-ideological perspective. Rather than "literature" representing an interior opposed and exceeded by an external science, this opposition, it now appears, was ideologically motivated to perpetuate *a false interiority* associated, inversely, with that very material and performative language most capable of barring that figure: which is also to say, the economy of meaning we call the "human."

If the trope of the "cyborg" in cultural studies can appear a touristic icon of the post-human while preserving humanist models, we see how that economy is dismantled in the text of popular culture – indeed, post-humanist texts such as *Blade Runner*, *Silence of the Lambs*, and *Natural Born Killers* jump to mind, as does all of Hitchcock. In *Blade Runner*, the cyborg-like replicants are precisely not bathed in the fantasy of the metallic-body-as-machine; on the contrary, it is the replicants who are "more human than human" (literally, more playful, loving, courageous, and so on), where both are increasingly defined alone by the installation or disinstallation of memory – the first for the replicant, the latter for the humans in a supposedly post-modernist signscape that has always been there. Memory is the ultimate preoriginary technology, *exterior* to itself, and it takes the form of writing, inscription, photographs. If the transformation of literary sciencing and séancing entails an active shift of the epistemological structure of reading itself, it would bar the passive reinscrip-

Echotourism

tion of a mimetic model that cultural studies, despite its political intent, tends to induce (historicism, humanist representational- ism, *identity* politics, science as controlled metaphor of material- ity: eco-tourism, eco-terrorism). Indeed, it seems that in order to effect the world (perhaps precisely in Marx's sense), what is called for is not a return to a referential construction, but accelerating types of figuration that alter the politics and antique models of referentiality to begin with. Should we pass from *Blade Runner* to *Silence of the Lambs*, it would be to observe where the post-human experiments with the accelerations and disruptions of ritual sacri- fice, post-gendering and a figurative and literal cannibalism in which "man" himself is apprehended as animal, transformed as meat, and this by an *aesthetic principle* which Lecter purveys. Like the Minotaur that Buffalo Bill becomes in his cellar-labyrinth – which represents a text to be negotiated – this material principle (Bill's skin-suit, like *Blade Runner*'s "skin-jobs," confers identity from the outside) involves fledgling experiments with what Lec- ter calls "transformation"; like Lecter – in which name one must hear a figure of reading – this principle performs and communi- cates largely in anagrams, puns and ciphers (that is, "echoes"). That is, a language evading the panopticon of the FBI, or the *herd*-like and degendered males that police the state, itself less a patriarchy than a *eunarchy* (to coin a phrase). The post-gendered "Bill" is not opposed to normal sexuality, since the latter pretense only covers a vaster degendering and frozen perversion of which Crawford, the FBI chief, is a cipher: it appears a rule of eunuch "males," defending a "human" and phallic imaginary. Lecter – by sacrificing Bill, that is, sacrificing the sacrifice, to Starling in a bizarre scene of instruction – tutors a new style of reading: *echo*- tourism, *echo*-terrorism. The materiality of inscription is not con- cealed from mimesis because it is persecuted; it is persecuted because it represents a scene of intervention, a science of the real, a rupturing of the trade-routes of ritual sacrifice – indeed, most of all, human sacrifice, sacrifice of the earth – that the mirage of the human has for long demanded. This can only return to a pre- originary site of writing – or the Egyptian capital of *Memphis* (here, Tennessee), where Lecter is re-empowered while eating, then assuming the identity of, a *tourist*. Today, perhaps, our real post-human(ist)s need such guises. Like the "psychopaths" of Hitchcock, Lecter represents not a deviation but an experimental

209

cipher, a trial post-anthropomorphic personality configuration erratically *en route* to a different economy: we must be understanding with such infancies. At all events, the post-human cannot be a passive category which the trope of system, information, hypertext, cyborg or even the material delivers us to the contemplation of: it has always been the case, we must conclude, *and* demands active transformation, of the figures of language, memory, America, chance, exteriority, anteriority, "time." There is *an ethics to the aesthetic*, then, which is to say to the material, the exterior, the mnemonic, the "earth," that is post-human: as in the word "earth," it may be heard in the ear, have to do with premimetic echoes and the economy of signifying chains, and it is, to borrow Lecter's words, transformative.

Today, perhaps, the *virtualization* of the real is not the province of a set of goggles, but describes the site to which pre-mimetic figures give us access within folds and ruptures of mock-narratives we have accepted as "reliable" history: so-called "figures" that interrogate the phenomenal structure of interpretation as inextricable from the destinations (often doomed) of cultural programming, figures like prosopopeia, anagrams or inscriptions, which void the terror of mimetic impositions.

From such a perspective, the virtual seems invoked as though before an (a)position where different avenues and representational options present themselves interchangeably. Such a nonsite is necessarily backlooped through a differential grid of linguistic agencies and mnemonic constellations – even where encountered as phenomenal projections (hermeneutic economies, cities, "experiential" codes). The conjuring of the *virtual* may not be discontinuous with the material manner in which certain "literary" effects function – or even the quite banal way that "novels" had functioned in bourgeois culture, as when presenting linguistic and historically positioned "character" nodes according to protocols by which readers crystallize or efface personae, narrative counter-positions, signifying constellations. Consciousness, to the degree it is semio-linguistic or material in Voloshinov's sense, partakes of a site from which "all" subject-effects or experiences can appear moments of a mutating combinatoire or archive of markings and codes – like Nietzsche's late performative claim to be every "name" in history. "Everyday" consciousness is no different. It throws its tents at the disjoint and perpetual cross-roads of retro-projected identifications and phantasmatic conjurings even where its axes and programs are called desire, goals, transference, "self" fashioning, reaction, fetish, and so on. Multiple language and semio-neural and para-genetic transmission networks always also traverse and option such effects, evaluations, fact-systems, formalizations. The (a)position summoned by a *preceding of face* implied by a pre-mimetic invocation of prosopopeia accedes to a movement before which "contemporary" recitations of linguistic selfhood are bracketed, together with an anthropomorphic investment in one way of legislating the human. As an immensely potent topos, the word *science* nonetheless prowls as a double-sided ideologeme. Conjuring associations of a restitutive notion of "nature," on the one hand, and the promise of absolute technicity (and otherness) on the other, it cannot be other than haunted, spoken through or for, evaded or invoked like a transporting Charon at the border between living and the dead or material.

It is not arbitrary that the figure of "science" should become the basis for a type of epistemological regress. As a signifier promising a certain excess to the merely human, it is entwined rhetorically with the idea of a referential real undisturbed by systems of notation. The cultural and social function of the term "science" is more than double. On the one hand, seemingly woven into a denotational system of correspondence as far from tropes as possible, pure description, it gives rise to a rhetoric of faith that, oddly, co-polices an anthropocentric semantics; on the other hand, it promises a sheer and even beneficent technicity in a generally allohuman sense. In its fallen way, it operates in part as theologeme, simulating the philosophic domain of referential "truth." We are reminded of Nietzsche's warning in the *Genealogy* that for some "modern" science functions not as an escape from the spell of metaphysics (the biases of an ascetic principle transmitted through Christian negations of the body and so on) but as the last avatar of this negational epoch. Rather than emerging from this cross-historial program, science can become the last form of such *nihilism*. Under the general rubric of "[s]cience as a means of self-narcosis" (147), Nietzsche notes: "That which *constrains* these men, however, this unconditional will to truth, is *faith in the ascetic ideal itself*, even if as an unconscious imperative –

don't be deceived about that – it is the faith in a *metaphysical* value, the absolute value of *truth*, sanctioned and guaranteed by this ideal alone (it stands or falls with this ideal)." (151) And again: "this 'modern science' . . . is the best ally the ascetic ideal has at present, and precisely because it is the most unconscious, involuntary, hidden, and subterranean ally!" (155) Such "nihilism," we may need reminding, partakes not only of representationalism but historicism itself. If "cultural studies" already evinces this symptom – that of converting a discourse of technicity into a retro-humanism – voices of the "official" science community policing their borders have moved to purge themselves even of this move, and in tell-tale ways.

In Steven Shapin's *A Social History of Truth* (1994), for example, we are given a privileged "genealogy" of this modern empirical science. Read as a symptom itself, it can appear to conflate protocols of historicist methodology with a curious sub-text that participates in this ideological maneuvering. Melding the promise of a leftist divagation ("a social history") with the rehearsal of a narrative of legitimation, the work both addresses and shores up the *trusted* referential core of "science," of shared if made facts, at once unveiling and concealing a contemporary theologization of this science. That Shapin is so overwhelmingly concerned with the institution of "trust," or where credit becomes credibility (or belief and deferral), helps make the complex intriguing. To do so, Shapin undertakes what might be called an inverse "new" historicist tactic, or at least feigns to, when presenting a *historical* account of one origin of modern empirical science in the homosocial bonding culture of the British gentleman: they alone could gain credit for, bank on, and guarantee truth-telling, of the promise of the speech-act, and this alone assured the discourse of facts. Instead of investigating marginalized voices, it is the "center" itself which is examined ("his characteristic setting was right at its center" (40)). Yet the course of this account is more than double, more than merely folded back on itself. It aims to provide a story of origins for how "truth" or "fact making" is instituted by the speech acts of gentlemen, who alone obtain the credit of trust issued between them, being amidst else "free" alone to speak truly – not under constraint. This "social history" becomes the cipher of present administration.

Yet Shapin simultaneously assures us that this story has no

impact on the nature of those facts, those truths, that is, "science" itself. It is not accidental that this inverse-genealogical tour deploys the techniques of historicist narratives, nor that it is concerned with the instituting of "empirical" facts or their maintenance, nor that it appeals to the enforced and policed "trust" of a privileged (or nominally "free") *brotherhood*: here the need to institute communal facts or "knowledge" (Shapin seems to recode the idea of truth, increasingly, as recorded information) presents a steady drum-beat against the historical shadow-discourse coded as "skepticism" *tout court*. It presents a "naturalist" need for stable *reference* surveillance and a "correspondence" model of language, echoed in his account by a phenomenological definition of the senses or their evidence. To guard this epistemological – and, as Shapin notes rightly, by projection, ethico-ontological – model, two forms of information gathering must be *co*-managed: that of the evidence or *testimony* of the senses from which reliable information comes and, simultaneously and even in advance, the testimony of other men, of the transmitters, of the old fathers, of the "truth telling" others in any way. Any notion of the archival, any tracking of its mutating surfaces and systems, is shaded first into "trust" between men, honorable individuals, and then back to the "faceless" discourse of institutions. Rehearsing the protocols of a left assertion of the community, of the "we" and its needs, a kind of *postal-police* is implicitly theorized and established since the investments of "trust" direct transmission, curtail doubters and reading, assure the relative sameness of (all) testimonial, paralleling the immediacy of perception. What may be in question too is how the class fictions of the "great civility" that control truth manage the transmission of this property, the legal relay and retention of legacies. For the senses to be trusted, for the archive to sleep well, transmission must be secured – send in, if necessary, a SWAT team of historicists, seal the area. A close bond – gathered under an account of the rules needed to institute "trust," itself *demanded* by what is called a social order, hence not literally *free* as "truth" – rests between the presumed immediacy of perception or communication and the speech acts of gentlemen partaking of a "great civility" that guarantees, or rather insures and credits, the fundamental structure of the promise. Shapin cites *Beyond Good and Evil* in an epigram on the relation of truth-telling to the nobility, but he might rather have consulted the *Genealogy of Morals* on two fronts: those passages where the prehistorical creation of a type of human *capable of promising* is forged with the manufacture of memory, of facts initiating a mnemotechnics of inscription enacted through spectacles of cruelty precedent to any "free" bonded homosocial guild, *and* the late texts where the role of the "modern" scientist as last derivative of metaphysical truth, last "Christian," last nihilist is discussed. Shapin wants "trust" to be – absolutely; it is *necessary*, the very premise of social order and, subsequently, "science." From its leftist pretexts Shapin's narrative morphs into a specular minefield of rightist epistemo-ontology and institutional violence, the domain of a Symbolic or law. It becomes naturally coercive, even punitive: "those who cannot be trusted to report reliably and sincerely about the world may not belong to our community of discourse. It is not just that we do not agree with them; it is that we have withdrawn the possibility of disagreeing with them." (36) Closeout. Beginning as a genealogy of "truth," a "social history" with whatever redundancies or ironic promise that entails, the performance mutates toward and exemplifies a policing apparatus – and muted contemporary theology. Opening as a divagation into the "social" foundation of fact "making," the narrative reflects back into the present of the historian, rehearsing all the latter's psychotropic battles with its discursive others, avatars of so-called skeptics. Surprisingly, what is *not* most interesting here is how "science" doubles as an ideologeme of the real or "truth" itself (as Nietzsche critiques), or that this premise is intertwined by citation or parallel with every other school or technique dependent upon the affirmed transparency of evidence – phenomenology, the "natural attitude" (30), historicist methodology, "correspondence with the true state of affairs" (40), assured models of reference, the founding of empiricism. Present already in the culturalist appropriation of "science," too, is a retro-humanism we saw at work in Ross. The trope of science has supplemented a *belief* system invested in – that is, deriving limited credit and credibility from – models of reference guaranteeing the undisturbed relay of inherited property, the politics of memory and the sign's effacement. What is guarded, in a parable which we are told does not in any way alter the structure or content of truth itself (or its supposedly nonetheless "made" facts), is a telecommunication center more culturally politicized than, in itself, "scientific." Why, again, does a feign to the left produce or cover a rightist epistemo-politics of the relay? The old boys' network has been shifted from the pretense of patriarchal guarantee to the corporate anthropomorphism of mnemonic *networks*. The single forward step Shapin takes – that of exposing not a "social history" but a faceless apparatus – is the one with most dangerous potential. "Shapin's" story issues like a probe into recent techniques of historicizing, not to retro-transform that history so much as to allow the present to be colonized by its mythography, to secure contemporary horizons. It is Shapin's contribution to delegitimize this temporal line or lineage by the process of its own narrative exposure.

If the legitimacy of the homosocial order of the British gentleman becomes a perverse mirror for Shapin's epistemo-political suppositions for the policing of "perceptual competence and sincerity" (36), two parallels arise. First, the *skepticism* that Shapin loves to vicariously revile is coded in the same manner as what are called today's "post-modernists" (or theorists?) before the referential model and community of reliable truth-tellers; and second, this brotherhood of truth tellers translates easily into the priest-like order of the specialist, the scientist, the professor, the archive-guard of today. In the end, the model that Shapin bonds with of a unitary truth and referentially guaranteed community is defending itself not against the liars, skeptics, post-modernists, theorists and so on, all of whom are veritable specters, but a certain radical otherness within *non-anthropomorphic logics of "science" itself*.

Shapin's retroprojected model of "skepticism" is classic enough, in that it is characterized always as secondary, an *after-thought* by a destructive "solitary" in the community, "parasitical" (29), marginal ("Distrust is something that takes place on the *margins* of the trusting system" (19)), morally questionable, leading to nescience ("they would ultimately succeed in knowing nothing at all" (19)), and to be expulsed: "Persistent distrust, therefore, has a moral terminus: expulsion from the community" (20). How then does Nietzsche hail precisely this crypto-position filled with "trust," rather, as *nihilistic?* What if whatever is coded as the "skeptic" never had been secondary at all – if that presumption represented the viewpoint of the defending "truth" alone, registered a suspicion (scientific?) of its notational base, its narration? Rather than be positioned as marginal, as *secondary*, might one rather address here a pre-originary perspective that *thinks* otherwise, according to a different understanding of the mne-monic and cross-historical networkings before which Shapin's community and its representational view of "truth" appear tem-porary, restrictive, re-active, *secondary*?[2] Such an other thinking is not "skeptical" except of the negational force-field Shapin's brotherhood uses to police *its* truths, assuming an affirming multi-technicity of materialistic networks in a manner, perhaps, *older* than the narrow and nihilistic conflation of unitary, referen-tial "belief" systems with a chain of value-terms that passes through *one use of science*. This possibility – that rather than some-thing negative, secondary and marginal, what is concealed under the term "skepticism" (or "post-modernism" and so on) involves a different epistemological model, at once more realistic and material – brings us to the point where Shapin's project swings into its alter-ego positions: seeming historicist, it proves ahistori-cal (shoring up an unchanging model of "truth"); seeming empir-icist, it is again idealist in structure (transparent perception); devoted to "truth," it becomes nihilistic. "Trust" depends on a protected notion of *experience* and the transmission of legacy – what demands in turn a policing of the excess, of reading itself, or how one reads. The structure of "trust" – which affirms the exclusionary authority of the priest and expert, professor and "scientist" – is itself one of deferral; the moral bonding with the "we," an *ir*responsibility. Not accidentally, Shapin throughout does not address *truth* as such but "trust" (in that X *purveys* the true), a mode of relay dependent as much on another's word already in circulation as on evidence, already anterior, just as in writing he tends to relate positions in both a ventriloquized and borrowed manner. This tells us less, perhaps, about the institution of "truth" strictly than the economics of already recitational or coded laws, and how a legislation of names, stories, and copying rights upholds a system of credit (and credibility), in an at times overtly punitive manner betraying more than a trace of resent-

[2] One, perhaps, even in keeping with what Benjamin calls, given a certain transla-tion effect, "natural history," as that is evoked, too, by the access of non-human time. It is again not accidental if Benjamin, beginning his final text in the *Theses*, invokes the "history of organic life on earth" to reduce and explode a nineteenth century anthropocentric concept of history, recalling "the paltry fifty millennia of *homo sapiens*" that "the history of civilized mankind would fill one-fifth of the last second of the last hour" (*Illuminations*, 263).

ment (Shapin is a bit harsh giving the "solitary" his pink slip: "The epistemological paradox can be repaired only by removing solitary knowers from the center of knowledge-making scenes and replacing them with a moral economy" (27)).

In accord with Nietzsche's suspicions of some "modern" uses of science, the category of "freedom" bestowed on the gentleman, a prerequisite for truth-telling since the unfree man is always constrained, is defined by self-cancellation. In the process, the ascetic or denying drive becomes again manifest. It must negate the gentleman's own "freedom" as its basis: he is "free" (can tell truths) only insofar as he foregoes his freedom – that is its basis or mark, "the paradox involved in the free foregoing of free action" (40). We will ignore whether "freedom" is not here a fiction to begin with, or alternatively whether it cannot mean in a more accelerated reading something very like the virtualization of pre mimetic tropes, an undecidable component. Rather, it is this fabled "freedom" defined by its own restraint and denial, forged by a principle of negation that turns its "freedom" into a lie, that marks the rule of a symbolic order, automated, inscribed. Such massive *deferral* to certain priests of science – we might add, deferral of responsibility too – is not limited to this credit-system of institutionalized "truth." It seems rampant today precisely in a general deferral toward a techno-elite in the "scientific" imaginary of popular culture and the polis at large. *It*, like a shamanistic doctor, will eventually solve all global impasses (exhausting energy reserves, erased bio-archives, pollution, ozone layers, future asteroid impacts, and whatever), at least *given time*. Yet this unsigned promise or deferred "trust" inversely serves a purpose, it exempts the citizen from addressing such issues – particularly where that impedes a major market sector. "Trust" becomes a policing code-term for a proclaimed "intersubjective" community's self-sacrificial construction of ritual law, that of *the imaginary homosocial fathers*. All of these, in turn, discretely service agencies of a "correspondence" model of the real, the anchor of mimetic-capitalism. All the while, this retro-humanist semio-ontological order evinces yet more massive deferral and colonization, even *cannibalistic* programming: "The great civility, therefore, is granting the conditions in which others can colonize our minds and expecting the conditions which allows us to colonize theirs" (36). Shapin's project has been colonized, cannibalized by rifts in the problem of the guaranteed speech act with whose establishment he began. He hoped to isolate that as secondary, supplemental to the "truth," without altering the autographematic basis of one contemporary ideology of "science." The entire episode rehearses some protocols concerning the conscription of techno-science on behalf of warring models of reference, "experience," and so on. This theologization of science, however, only apparently evinces a reverse logic to how "cultural studies" functions in this domain. Nowhere has this specular puzzle come out as glaringly as in the renowned "Sokal hoax."

Banal as it may be – evoking intellectual politics that seem fairly generic – this "affair" garnered enough public attention to have the status of a cipher. Even so, it is interesting mostly for one overlooked twist. As is known, this face-off between an "official" science community and culturalist forays into science studies was occasioned by Alan Sokal's planting of an intentionally parodic essay in a science issue of the cultural studies journal *Social Text* – later exposing the article as gibberish. This, to embarrass the project of "cultural studies" and their post-modernist diatribes as fatally contaminated by pretense and, one is supposed to deduce, ignorance.[3] Recalling Shapin's ethos, a certain "we" will, in the process, have "withdrawn the possibility of disagreeing with them." In subsequent published remarks, Sokal will even explain his hoax as having been executed on behalf of leftist sentiment, that is, to further expose the non-political trifling of cultural studies' pretentious and ill-understood theoretical jargon, and so on. If this redoubles or unwittingly accelerates that hierarchic pragmatism which "cultural studies" would itself have evinced toward "theory," in turn, it is not arbitrary. If the main thrust of Sokal's attack served to shore up the epistemo-political right by playing, through the popular press, on the demagogic rhetoric of American anti-intellectualism (leaving aside the whole problem of the "parody," and whether it is not always a citational component of linguistic experimentation), some other danger, or some other "other," lies behind the image that "cultural studies" pro-

---

[3] The "Sokal affair" began with the publication of Sokal's later-declared "hoax" essay, "Transgressing the Boundaries – Toward a Transformative Hermeneutic of Quantum Gravity," *Social Text* (Spring/Summer, 1996), 217–252. For an irreverent, plague-on-both-your-houses reading of this scene, see Michael Sprinker, "We Lost it at the Movies," *MLN*, 112 (Spring, 1997), 385–99.

jects of encroaching on science. At first glance, we might call *that* real or other target the epistemo-political implications which a so called "post-modernism" had come to denote. Yet on further interrogation, one can perceive that it may both be the latter's return to consult the materiality of language, specifically, which dislocates the founding epistemo-fictions of perceptual transparency, *and* certain implications of this "official" invocation of "science" itself. On the one hand, we would have to hear in the Sokal-type denunciation an attack on the public and political association "cultural studies" has in American coding with educational *multiculturalism* as such. Behind this gesture we perceive not just class interests of the "great gentility" at work, even in a rhetoric betraying nationalist and even racialist pressures. While pretending to speak for common-sense, for a public discourse protected from the non-sense or jargon of critical theory, there is an accord between this rhetorical system and political obsessions with closing borders, expelling "immigrants," redelineating "our" community from a vague *theirs*. But this confrontation is not only specular, *it is at least doubly inverted*. The agendas of "cultural studies" do not, from any competent reading of the critical scene, conform to the coded-space of "post-modernism" that is vicariously hurled at it by the right (the scientist's coded polemic here mirroring the accusation of implied ignorance toward "science"). That is, it does not wholly fit the corporate identity Shapin would call the more or less *radical skeptics*. This general entity we might bracket, for the moment, as a site of radical otherness.

"Cultural studies" had, after all, itself moved *toward* the figure of "science" not only in alliance with an untheorized technophilia of pop culture, but to re-anchor instinctively its reactive humanism and representationalism against the supposedly non-historical predations of, again, "theory," "post-modernism." CS, too, was questing for an onto-theological cipher that endorsed its predilections toward historicism and the mapping of experiential, or empiricist, or corporeal, or everyday fact *as* commodity. What is truly a spectacle of hilarious bad faith at work in the "Sokal hoax" involves the specular nature of both Sokal's and the culturalists' positions: the culturalists want to woo and colonize science studies, legitimately enough, yet in part to poach on the fabled terrain of the real (one sees this in Ross, in Haraway, in

Hayles); the "official" science ideologue wants to reject the culturalist, his double, in the name of that same "post-modernism" which CS, in abjecting, also cut itself away from, and so on. Both want, to different degrees, to restitute and affirm a referential, historicist model; both want to appear left, yet *can* drift toward or even become (in Sokal's case) propagandist for right epistemo-programming. And what, then, escapes this *center* stage? What two phantasms rest to the extreme of each, in the wings, where rather than being yet more antagonistic, they appear at certain moments to display an odd accord, gathered around the motif of the "material" or a shared post-anthropomorphic import? Natural science and "theory"?

To the side of the two fratricidal voices – that of the "official" science cop marketing a discourse of faith that upholds rightist epistemology *and* the left culturalist appealing to the same historicist model to evade "post-modernism" – the extremer positions on this ghost map converge beyond the sort of weary nihilism that the above shadow play ritualistically repeats. What is evaded involves the de-anthropomorphizing set of logics that adhere to the promise of "science" *and* to a materialistic technicity concealed by labels such as "post-modernism." At this juncture, for instance, where the categories of "life" and death are mutually traversed and interfaced, the materiality of science may be tracked through the shifting notational systems that culturally institutionalize or access its powers. In the tele-archivization of today, we may conflate the black-holes presented by certain "literary" effects (linked, for instance, to a disruption of referential and historicist models) with the technicity of a "science" caught, as a term, in the double history of the word *techne* – including associations of supplement, of art, of the aesthetic, of exteriority.[4] It is the proximity of this materiality – implied by the semio-mnemonic *séancing* of historial trace-chains – to the reflective technicity of "modern" *science* that seems, today, to be the dreaded monster, spirit or border-crossing other that these brothers jointly, and in self-cancelling manner, would guard themselves against.

[4] In this regard, see J. Hillis Miller, *Black Holes* (Stanford: Stanford University Press, 1998), which appropriates the figure of aporia for contemporary political impasses related to institutional shifts in the electronic archive itself.

❖❖

Altered states: stoned in Marseilles, or the addiction to reference

❖❖

Either under the influence of the narcotic draught, of which the songs of all primitive men and peoples speak, or with the potent coming of the spring . . . these Dionysian emotions awake, and as they grow in intensity everything subjective vanishes into complete self-forgetfulness.

Nietzsche, *Birth of Tragedy*

The most passionate investigation of telepathic phenomena, for example, will not teach us half as much about reading (which is an eminently telepathic process), as the profane illumination of reading about telepathic phenomena . . . The reader, the thinker, the loiterer, the flâneur, are types of illuminati just as much as the opium eater, the dreamer, the ecstatic. And more profane. Not to mention that terrible drug – ourselves – which we take in solitude.

Benjamin, "Surrealism"

A phrase which Baudelaire coins to describe the temporal consciousness of someone intoxicated by hashish can also be applied to the definition of revolutionary historical consciousness . . .

Benjamin, "Konvolut N"

Rather it would be a matter of a methodical provocation, of a technique for calling up the phantom: the spirit, ghost [*Geist*], inspiration, dictation. More precisely, and what makes the matter even more convoluted, we would be dealing here with a methodology of the counter-phantom.

Derrida, "The Rhetoric of Drugs"

What in critical terms is the lure of the *drug-effect*, hit, intoxication, or "high" – sought, relentlessly, in what Michael Taussig might term the corporeal-semio-political "nervous system," as a sort of power over time and events, under so many different names? Why is it historically pandemic, mutating across chemical, "literary," and religious borders? What is the connection between the drug trance – considered as semiotic engineering – and the political generally conceived? How does the trope of altered states (as if to say, of consciousness) forecast an altering in the epistemo-mimetic conceit of the state itself? Or, in the text of Benjamin, what has the induced trance or "intoxication" – often associated with Baudelaire – to do with other ruptures in his program: what goes by the non-names we have been discussing of allegory, shock, or finally, "historical *materialism*"? What is "life" if it is recurrently compelled toward this supplement and alterity?

The text we will examine is "Hashish in Marseilles," part of Benjamin's writing devoted to experiments with the drug. It remains one of few self-contained writings to emerge from Benjamin's many notes on a poetics of hashish – intended for a "book" on the subject. We know that the idea of the trace partakes of the figure of the illumination, or the "dialectical image" – a logic of intervention within a mnemonic programming and representational regime, a dark illumination preceding the Western metaphorics of "light" itself, in which the historial stands to be reconfigured. We can thus ask where the performative logic of the (writing) trance does not depict some eccentric or personal "experience" (or hallucinations), but enacts, at least as ritual, the protocols of such intervention? In the text we will address this occurs in conjunction with one of Benjamin's mock-descriptive archaeo-graphematics of *cities* (Marseilles, Naples, Moscow).

The drug-hit in Benjamin must be read through its entanglement with that writing *practice* he generally attempts to implement – that which would effect a historical and mnemonic intervention. The logics of the trance, as seems clear in his interpretation of surrealist practice, can be linked with a reconfiguring of historicizing consciousness, and thus allows for a "materialist" component. It manifests an active relation to the *virtual* in general. If what is alluded to as the historical "sensorium" is a hermeneutic programming of the senses, the disruption of a "natural" processing of perception connects the drug prosthesis – its suspension of "experience" – to a political motive, and with that a resistance to what might be termed the hypnologies of "normal" consciousness, installed reference systems, received historicist narratives. Thus what is called "hashish" seems affiliated with an active disturbance within the politically inflected protocols of perception and *reference* – where any hallucination, wild interpretive riffs, "altered" realities, and so on, would begin. If this presents one active parallel for what "materialistic historiography" may be about – that is, in whatever format, mnemonic intervention – it nonetheless *seems* to do so in a sort of protected or derealized rehearsal mode, as if in play. Such a scene of *recreation* suspends mimetic protocols of reference. In the process, it exposes the latter's *faux* "natural" order as itself a long-installed technology, like any other, in its way drug-like. Rather than the specter of natural consciousness being "originary" and the prosthesis of the drug-hit supplemental, the conventional order of reference is momentarily displayed as historically programmed, routinized, narcoleptic, politically determined. The epistemo-technics of the drug hit can appear to counter – as it does explicitly in Baudelaire – a regime of memory and time management whose archival rules may be too quickly taken for natural, empirical, "human," and so on. The hashish trance in Benjamin allows us to formally observe how the re-inscription of a monad is risked.

Under the rubric of a pharmacopoetics – which is also to say, a politics of the séance – we will further examine a trace-chain running through Benjamin's work.[1] That is, a certain accord struck within Benjamin's essay on hashish in Marseilles and sites marked by that peculiar use of "allegory" we perhaps still do not know how to translate, since we have not instituted reading models yet to accommodate it. This chain of terms begins in the *Trauerspiel*, again, with a notion of *Ursprung* – that is, an "origin" that is not itself originary but rather the site of hyperbolic emergence and emergency, determined by a convergence of pre-historical and post-historical effects. It proceeds with a transposed notion of *allegory* that is not to be conceived of as representational (as it traditionally is), nor even the so called "modernist" revision by which Benjamin is often thought, where allegory supposedly

---

[1] An entire metaphysical use of the double logic of the *pharmakon* appears, of course, in Derrida's reading of how the figure of Socrates (and, differently, "writing") appears manipulated within the constitutive "dawn" of philosophy in Plato. See "Plato's Pharmacy" in *Dissemination*.

names a work's reflexively accounting for its own conditions of production, or consumption (as Jameson suggests). Rather, allegory seems to evoke a site of mnemonic transformation in which anteriority itself stands to be recast, *reinscribed*, and alternative "futures" opened as virtual. Such a site passes through the figural logic of "shock," a certain invocation of cinema as mnemonic apparatus, and finally what will again be called "materialistic historiography" (*der materialistishcen Geschichtsschreibung*).[2] Yet en route it pauses for a moment in a Circean setting at Marseilles, by the sea, where some of the prefigural logics of this program-to-come of intervention might be discerned. This occurs, almost, as a classic katabasis of sorts, a return to the underworld to question the personified dead, "stoned" in their own way, in the interrogated patterns of things, words, place. Even before opening this scene of reading – for what else is any katabasis of this sort? – we can conjecture what such semio-intoxication attempts to *politically* counter or suspend. That is, not some pressure of the social real that the imbiber wills to escape but the management of anteriority narcoleptically programmed as what Benjamin will call (mimetic) historicism, the compulsory aggregation to the point of addiction of the installed archives of memory management "we" confuse or take for natural (or representational) models of empiricism and reference production. In short, *the addiction to reference*.

These observations will not have to do with the role of *addiction* – that is, the way in which the counter-state which we playfully call "stoned" may be pursued in compulsive or accelerated *repetitions* reminiscent of a "bad" literalization of eternal recurrence. Yet there seems little question that a certain Nietzsche may be said to lurk within Benjamin's program. This is not only marked through the early articulation of "allegory" in the *Trauerspiel* by way of a covert if over-accurate reading of *The Birth of Tragedy*'s epistemo-aesthetic logics, but wherever the topos of *intoxication* appears conjured not as escape from but semiotic assault on "history." We have used the word *stoned* with this complex in mind – a site, following associations that will turn up in the text, where the anthropomorphic and inorganic, living and dead, seem

---

[2] It would be interesting, no doubt, to read the Benjaminian *Ursprung* through what Derrida has alternately named *khora* (in a female and (a)maternistic metaphorics) and *archive* (within a patrilineal scheme). See Derrida, "Khora" and *Archive Fever*.

to interface. It recalls in the logic offered under the rubric of intoxication where language or voice adheres to or emerges from the inanimate, the stone, and alternately where what we recognize in language as "life" emerges posited as the prosopopeia of the non-organic – what may be, for memory, the site of inscription. From this position, between the effects of life or "death," the hashish state may appear both as linguistic hyperbolization and strategy of resistance to a regime of linear time and mimetic regulation too quickly assumed as "life." Not mortification, as in using drugs to kill or dull pain, but as a counter-stroke to the autonomization of "life" as machinal inscription, of the law or Symbolic.[3] The associations of intoxication with the Benjaminian figure of the caesura seem confirmed where the essay on Marseilles opens on a street that is itself described as a "knife cut (*ein Schnitt*)."[4]

We may now propose one condition for viewing the hashish hit as a moment in Benjamin's "materialistic" chain of non-terms (allegory, translation), as a séance-effect in which alternative systems of reference and time-management are solicited. That is, that where the *Theses* proposes such intervention as a moment of danger on whose decision the mere openness to diverse potential systems may depend, in the experimental drug episode this might be said to itself occur *virtually*, that is, as a virtual virtuality, as rehearsal for the "event." (No doubt, it is to some degree the consequences of that state – of the real effect of the virtual accessing of the virtual – that represents one of the "real" dangers of intoxication.) It is perhaps no accident that the drug-effect marked in the text on Marseilles in and with the play of material elements of language – such as puns, or anagrams – deregulates mimetic reading machines. In this movement the material trace is looped back through its own signifying practice (what the essay on "Translation" again calls: "to turn the symbolizing into the sym-

---

[3] Žižek, in reconfiguring Lacan's tripartite map, will come to associate the Symbolic itself (no doubt, in the end, an unacceptable generality) at once with language (as the play of metonymy), the law, and a virtual automatism of the living dead in which normative consciousness dwells. Another parallel of the drug hit is a *literary* effect. This association is well known through, among other sources in Benjamin's treatment of Baudelaire and the surrealists, Avital Ronell's *Crack Wars: Literature Addiction Mania* (1992).

[4] Walter Benjamin, "Hashish in Marseilles," in *Reflections*, 138 (*Illuminationen*, 345).

bolized").[5] Since in Benjamin this takes place within linguistic or mnemonic chains out of which diverse "presents" stand to be produced, being *stoned* – as deregulation of a verbal sensorium which is itself legislated by an installed hermeneutics – moves into the site of disinscription and reinscription, at least as *tourist*.

Within the drug trance as experiment, however, the subject-of-the-experience is free to traverse this zone under the protected guise of *tourist*. It is both *mere* tourism, an inconsequential simu-lacrum of movement allied with play, and what cannot return to any home-point or identity (including, finally, the identification of linguistic being with "human" subject). What we enter the text looking for, according to the protocols of "materialistic historiog-raphy," is a certain premimetic marking, knocking, or logic of bars or (a)rhythm from which a break (or *Schnitt*) with pro-grammed perception (or reading) is summoned. Toward the end of the text, stoned and listening to jazz, Benjamin evokes this sense: "I had forgotten on what grounds I permitted myself to mark the beat with *my foot* [*mit dem Fuss zu markieren*]" (144; 351). Whatever promise such a foot or leg entails – for instance, as the lower-bodily agent or material trace by which "the symbolizing (is turned) into the symbolized" – it appears with reference to what precedes figuration.[6]

The touristic nature of Benjamin's remarks on "Hashish in Marseilles" are testified to in another short piece reading the city of "Marseilles" itself as text – and we will note that this place, a port city (as it is called), seems topographically and typographi-cally marked. This, because the name-place *Marseilles* seems to carry within it the problematic of marking (Benjamin is obsessed, like Proust, with place-names) – that is to say, of the *mar*(r), sea or *mer(e)* it resides as a port or place of passage by. The nominal inhabitation of the sea or *mer* in the proper name resonates or at least suggests a *faux* maternal and material place – one whose reflective sea-surfaces appear to give way to a premimetic site, or

[5] See "The Task of the Translator," in *Illuminationen*, 80.

[6] The problem of the "legs of sense" is developed in the introduction to my *Anti-Mimesis*, and later in conjunction with a reading of Hitchcock's *The 39 Steps* in chapter 9. The discussion evokes the chain of figures Derrida explores in his treatment of Freud in *The Post Card*, where, for instance, the figure of a *legs de Freud* is understood to imply a chain involving legacy (or anteriority), legibility, and legitimation – the manner, in short, in which the law is folded into the management of anteriority or readability. The logic attributed by Derrida to the figure of the step, or *pas*, bears comparison.

marking, virtually precedent to the eye or *seeing*, hence, to perception or reading. *Marseilles* appears not only to name a magically
notorious and ancient Mediterranean port (evocative, no doubt, of
the Mediterranean cradle of aesthetic culture), but, by a chain
which the proper name puts into play, a mock-maternal pre-origin
of the senses themselves in an archaeology of marking (Mar/see,
-sea, -say, -(o)r(s)eille) – a nodal crossing of historical place with an
other to place. It turns out not to be fortuitous that the writing-of-
hashish, of intoxication, is Marseilles. The above verbal logic
suggests a place where the *aesthetic* or perception may be said to
emerge – echoing the Greek, *aisthanumai*, as if to situate the "sensorium" itself, one opens on to a scene of diverse inscriptions.

But the female itself, at once maternal and as if material (and
hence, precedent to gender, or amaternal), guards this site in
dubious fashion – that is, under the logics of the prostitute, at once
siren and betrayer of sheer figuration. Well before this, the tourist
Benjamin identifies "Marseilles" with the hypnotic effect of prostitutes, however, *apotropaic* figures evocative of the critic's eviscerating use of *Ursprung*. Prostitutes occupy a privileged space in
Benjamin associated with a knowledge of simulacra and the ability to double and exceed the mock-teleology of semen and *semance*
in the sexual real. "Whores," here medusoid, have in the
gynaeceum already harvested the caps (or heads) of a phallogocen-
tric commerce, whose (apo)trophies are as if turned to stone:

Has anyone yet probed deeply enough into this refuse heap of houses to
reach the innermost place in the *gynaeceum*, the chamber where the
trophies of manhood – boaters, bowlers, hunting hats, trilbies, jockey
caps – hang in rows on consoles or in layers on racks? From the interiors
of taverns the eye meets the sea. The high-breasted nymphs, the snake-
ringed Medusa's heads over their weather-beaten doorframes have only
now become unambiguously the signs of a professional guild. Unless,
that is, signboards were hung over them as the midwife Bianchamori has
hung hers, on which, leaning against a pillar, she turns a defiant face to all
the brothel keepers of the quarter, and points unruffled to a sturdy baby
in the act of emerging from an egg.   (132)

The prostitutes, already formalized into an organization
("guild"), give way to a supplemental sign ("signboards were
hung over them") which is the sign of midwifery – of a mediating
delivery of a new birth ("a sturdy baby in the act of emerging from
an egg"). The gesture is less the recuperation of the medusoid

figures, in painted mode, for a resituated maternalism, for "woman" as other than simulacrum (of woman), than the conversion of that very field of eviscerating, decapitating figures into a maieutic function for what, in the end, is not quite a human birth ("from an egg"). What is this other birth, untimely ripped or animal-hatched?

It is worth noting that Benjamin begins the essay with a clinical citation, describing the hit as a mnemonic effect that operates, again, as a cut or caesura, indeed, a (*Kaiser*)*schnitt*: "images and chains of images, long-submerged memories appear, whole scenes and situations are experienced . . . Connections become difficult to perceive, owing to the frequently sudden rupture of all memory of past events, thought is not formed in words, the situation can become so compulsively hilarious that the hashish eater for minutes on end is capable of nothing except laughter" (137). We will ignore the role of laughter here – as if in response to a specific mnemotechnic effect ("images and chains of images, long-submerged memories") – though we will have more difficulty ignoring what might be called, simply, Benjamin's attack of munchies. What is named "hashish," indeed, triggers mock-rituals of "ravenous" *in*corporation that returns us to stones themselves: "One often speaks of stones instead of bread. These stones were the bread of my imagination, which was suddenly seized by a ravenous hunger to taste what is the same in all places and countries" (143). When food is the topic, a disturbing *punning* begins, a dissociation of mimetic sense, as when he surveys a tavern's dishes: "In short, I came to a stop at a *pâté de Lyon*. Lion paste, I thought with a witty smile, when it lay clean on a plate before me . . . To my lionish hunger it would not have seemed inappropriate to satisfy itself on a lion." (141) *Lyon*, lion: hunger that would eat, also, itself, the *pâté* of a man-eater (later, a "train of thought" will lead directly "to images of animals" (143) and face, the nonhuman). In the word-play on *Lyon* we can perhaps hear the *on* of Being resonate too (the German for food is *Essen*: "*Aber das Essen war später*" (346)) bound to the *Ly*- echoing the German *liest* or "reading" (*Man liest die Tafeln auf den Pissoirs* (345)) as well as the French *lit* (bed), *lys* or lily (Benjamin speaks of the trance contracting in memory, monad-like, as flower: "it forms a kind of figure and is more easily memorable. I should like to say: it shrinks and takes on the form of a flower" (142)). Yet the name, *Lyon*, also appears topolinguistically marked in the "Marseilles" essay, and this in association with a semiotic "state" of revolutionary *expo-sure*:

Outskirts are *the state of emergency* of a city, the terrain on which incessant-ly rages the great decisive battle between town and country . . . The long rue de *Lyon* is the powder conduit that Marseilles has dug in the land-scape in order . . . to blow it up, burying it in *the shell splinters of every national and commercial language.* (135–6; my italics)

What is called a "state of emergency," a phrase too familiar to readers of the *Theses*,[7] is placed along a "rue de *Lyon*" said to operate explosively ("blow it up"). It splinters in *Babelesque* form "every national and commercial language" – a moment that tech-nically, and through the relays of Benjamin's text and beyond, evokes the logics of sheer exteriorization inflected in the trope of "pure language" of "The Task of the Translator." The "state of emergency," as a protocol, conjures the monadic transvaluator for whom all trace memory passes through – is dis-articulated before and re-articulated against – the site of *reine Sprache*, of measure and marking, of (a)rhythm.

The reported *explosiveness* of eating when heard as compul-sively self-cancelling *in*corporation and *in*teriorization – what we might call metamunchies – asserts the virtuality of sign-chains passing into a dislocation of *time-place*, that is, into "absolute duration and immeasurable space" (138). Indeed, Benjamin's compulsive ingesting testifies to and parodies this inability to fill what is a non-interior. At this site of virtual "emergency" or emergence, at once a political and a semiotic outpost, Benjamin fixates on *face*. That is, a non-place preceding the coalesced repre-sentation of the human itself:

For [hashish] made me into a physiognomist, or at least a contemplator of physiognomies, and I underwent something unique in my experience: I positively fixed my gaze on the faces that I had around me, which were,

---

[7] Such a "state of emergency," which accords with the phenomenalization of a reality-matrix from inscriptions become susceptible of alteration, like the instant of prosopopeia, is called in Thesis VIII *"unsere Aufgabe die Herbeiführung des wirklichen Ausnahmezustands vor Augen stehen"* (*Illuminationen*, 272). The "task" (*Aufgabe*), which registers as a release or giving-up as well as an up-giving, is to provoke an *Ausnahmezustand* – what, in turn, is heard as a Taking-Out-Situation or Stand-to (anticipating, in turn, the "standstill" (*zum Stillstand gekommen*) of Thesis XV). In the prepositional interface of *auf* and *aus* a distinct hyperbolism and exteriority erupts (as is the case in *Die Aufgabe des Übersetzers*).

in part, of remarkable coarseness or ugliness. Faces that I would normally have avoided for a twofold reason: I should neither have wished to attract their gaze nor endured their brutality. It was a very advanced post [*ein ziemlich weit vorgeschobener Posten*], this harbor tavern.   (139; 346–7)

We defer speculating on the import, here, of what might be implied by an "advanced [*vor*] post," a preposterous outpost, here as intoxicating tavern or *bar* recalling what the *Trauerspiel* might name a *Vor- und Nachgeschichte* effect. This post is both military and postal station. Face, as prosopopeia, leads not only to a non-human "alienation" of received history ("Later I noted as I looked down, 'From century to century things grow more es-tranged'" (142)). Here the *aesthetic* contour of Marseilles – this paradigm and hive of *life* – resists personification as well. The ensuing text simulates the *graphomorphic* powers and prowess of "materialistic historiography" in the *Theses*, soliciting a point of materiality as non-interiorizable trace.

This rupture of interiorizing processes – eating, words, psyche – is linked to active reading ("So I lie on the bed, reading and smoking" (138), "One reads the notices on the urinals"), much as the trance itself is to prose, or *rhythmic* prose: "rhythmical bliss of unwinding the thread. The certainty of unrolling an artfully wound skein – is that not the joy of all productivity, at least in prose? And under hashish we are enraptured prose-beings in the highest power" (142).[8] There is a moment in *The Birth of Tragedy* that has been systematically occluded by critics which Benjamin was perhaps the first to read accurately (only to erase, that is incarnate, in the *Trauerspiel*). It is that in which Apollo – that is, aesthetic formalization – momentarily *precedes* and is erased into the mock-originary effect called "Dionysus."[9] Such a pre-ori-ginary adversion to what we can term a material, irreducibly

[8] Prose, here, is to be heard also as the "lower" order of writing, banal, material, mnemonically repetitive, classically opposed to poetic writing. It is, thus, the discourse of the slave, feet or legs, as when Hegel notes in the *Aesthetics*, in a remark much-cited by de Man, that "prose begins with the slave."

[9] That is, in and as a *Musik* viewed not as primal eruption for which the mytheme of "Dionysus" serves as melo-centric cover but as the banal repetitive rhythm of self-dividing measure (this is noted, briefly, in section two, where we hear: "If music, as it would seem, had been known *previously* (that is, originally) as an Apollonian art, it was, strictly speaking, only as the *beat* of rhythm" (*The Birth of Tragedy*, 40; my italics)). This discussion of the role of *The Birth of Tragedy* in defining "allegory" in Benjamin's *Trauerspiel*, and thereafter, is developed in chapter 3 of this book and in my, "'Along the Watchtower' – Cultural Studies and the Ghost of Theory."

semio-technic, or "aesthetic" instant corresponds to where Benjamin's *stoned state* dissolves into a rhythmic *marking*, such as attending the playing of jazz – that is, in a *double-time* that suggests an other of linguistically formalized time itself. The movement of the foot in acoustic alliance precedes and occludes all perception ("blotted out") – positioning marking itself before the site of the ear or *oreille*, a sort of *mar*(s)(or)*eille*(s): "I had forgotten on what grounds I permitted myself to mark the beat with my *foot*. . . There were times when the intensity of acoustic impressions *blotted out* all others" (144, my italics).[10] This tapping, without content, pre-mimetic and material – what we might again visualize as a series of bars – seems affiliated with a name bearing the syllable *bar*: "'*Bar*nabe,' read the sign on a streetcar that stopped briefly at the square where I was sitting. And the sad confused story of *Bar*-nabas seemed to me no bad destination for a streetcar going into the *outskirts* of Marseilles" (143, my emphasis). This "bar" can be heard, too, as a syncopated series not unlike the tapping above. It returns us to that exteriorizing and exposing effect ("*outskirts*") linked to "state(s) of emergency." Bars, a signature of material semiosis precedent to all figuration or metaphor, provide the "advanced *posts*" where most observation occurs ("*Erst die kleine Bar am Hafen*" (346), "*Vor allem in der kleinen Bar ging plötzlich alles*" (351).)[11] The hashish experiment evokes a virtual, preperceptual zone of (dis)inscription allied with a disruption of "experience" we are familiar with in Benjamin from the Baudelaire or "Work of Art" essays.

We may now give this logic an extra turn, by noting that the port of Marseilles also appears as a site we might call a*por*etic. The idea of the port – door or porter, carrier and courier of posts – suggests both a site of commerce and transit as well as translation, a "materialistic" shift within the mnemonic network. Elsewhere, Benjamin attributes this prospect to the always virtual engineering of a so-called monad – a node of transit in which trace-chains

[10] For a discussion of how the trope of the foot or leg doubles as a material site within language, see my "Legs of Sense," in *Anti-Mimesis*, 1–10.
[11] If we understand rhythm in *The Birth of Tragedy* as the site for locating a certain Apollonian *formalism* – we might even call it, given more space, *reine Sprache* – then this effect, which accords with the bar-series signature, has the import of re-writing "Dionysus," who no longer seems prior to or more originary than Apollo in that mock-dialectic. Indeed, while "Dionysus" absorbs Apollo there-after in Nietzsche's text, the materiality of this Apollonian signature continues to define all the "Dionysian" motifs.

converge, the rewiring of which stands to alter the economy of "experience," history, the mnemonic itself. Given the status of Marseilles as place (sea-port) *and* name (a marring – or sea*ing* – generative of sight or the ear), it appears also a place of "crossing," of *über-gehen*. What the drug-hit provides is a cover for this mock-séancing and mock-katabasis. All of this, provided we hear *aporia* not as mere impasse but as what anticipated the translation of one signifying order into alternate systems of reference and time-management. The aporetic heralds a bar-like "crossing" which portends to reconfigure not only *archival* history – such as the epistemo-aesthetic model of "historicism" – but anteriority, materiality, virtual futures. That is, a certain *earth* – ultimate referent and (dis)inhabitation to which the exteriorizing logics of "Marseilles" advert.[12] The issue effects gravity, as well as one's own steps, or *pas*: "On the way to the Old Port [*zum vieux port*] I already had this wonderful lightness and sureness of step that *transformed* the *stony, unarticulated* earth [*unartikulierten Erdboden*] of the great square that I was crossing [*über den ich ging*]" (139; 347). This crossing or "going over [*über*]," with its hyper or Nietzschean inflection inserted in the matter of a banal step, recasts Marseilles, perhaps, as what Wallace Stevens calls "a port of air" (*Anecdote of the Jar*) – a site, proto-Mosaic, where another discursive or virtual landscape lies which the present style is barred from yet also doubles over.[13] Strange, this city. Being stoned in and traversing Marseilles, double-site of a premimetic mark, redistributes the economy of a material trace that renders "chains of images, long-submerged memories" *virtual* – -as though at an unpredetermined point. "Marseilles" here becomes another non-name for the scene of (dis)inscription evoked in the *Trauerspiel* as *Ursprung* – one, however, where the metaphorics of the maternal appears dissolved, like the brothel-fronts, into a prosthetic maieutics.

What Benjamin conjures in and as *Marseilles*, this pharmocopoetics, is allied with an effect designed to actively intervene in mnemonic or signifying orders in his writing: the figure of "allegory," then "shock," then "material historiography." This

---

[12] One would again invoke Benjamin's entire adversion toward the trope of "natural history" in the *Trauerspiel*, which is neither natural nor historical, but opens the prospect for a non-human conceit of the historial itself.

[13] To link this being "high," say, to what Nietzsche will hyperbolically proffer as an *über*-human represents a trajectory we defer.

both projects and marks a *reflexive* shift from a mimetic regime
legislating binaries of model and copy, before and after, to what
we may call a pro-active mimesis without model or copy. There is,
in this pharmacopoetic program, a nomad politics aggressing on a
hermeneutic order out of which sense "experience" would have
been legislated or phenomenalized. Famously, Benjamin identifies this "enemy" with the ideology of historicism and, in the
Theses, with "fascism" as such. Benjamin locates the politics of the
material (which is always to say mnemonic inscription), of the
"earth" (*Erdboden*), in a mode of reading allied to this *high* which
transmutes "nature" itself – that is, from a conventional trope and
cover for an installed regime of representation, an ideology for the
management of reference and anteriority. Such a translated sense
of "earth" corresponds in ways to a pre-natural and pre-originary
technicity of the trace – to, that is, an aesthetic materiality and
formalization from which an allohuman itinerary, and ethics, is
projected. This hypothetical *crossing*, in terms of a movement from
the bounds of one signifying order (and definition of "epoch")
toward an other, can be heard as crossing-over and crossing-out.
This was what the logics of allegory had also implied, evoking
and technically altering the pre- and post-historical sign chains at
the *Ursprung*.[14]

The technicity of hashish provokes a figure of cancellation that
is referred back to a depersonified "nature" itself: "hashish per-
suades nature to permit us [*die Natur zu überreden*] . . . that
squandering of our own existence . . . . [which] runs through
nature's fingers like golden coins that she cannot hold . . . she now
throws us, without hoping or expecting anything" (144–5; 352). In
order to occur as event, such a persuasion or hyperbologics (*überreden*) must be relieved of all credit or narrative calculation
("without hoping or expecting anything") – a determined null-
point or gift, now *Gift*ed in the double sense of poison or, again,
drug. Hashish as another extension of "allegory's" unrepresentable logic positions the latter's reflexive intervention in the
mnemonic order – a katabasis mimed during and by the touristic
visit to Marseilles, heard now as a kind of homonym for *khora* or
mother-board, *mer* and *mar*. (We are reminded, again, that the
contemporary understanding of "allegory" cuts off this decisive

[14] As when we hear, again in the *Trauerspiel*, that: "[Allegory] means precisely the
non-existence of what it (re)presents" (233).

shift within what must be heard as a dissimulating concept in order to keep it *representational* – which is precisely the space it dissolves: no longer the traditional "allegory" that is an icon of mimeticisim (a textual mode purveying a segregable meaning), Benjamin's eviscerating catachresis is also not that merely *reflexive* figure conceived as "modernist" today – in which reflexivity itself is stamped as a (merely) aesthetic effect. Rather, precisely the reflexive moment of this allegory is the predicate for an act of mnemonic engineering and history alteration – a shift to the mode of hypothetical event – within the epistemo-political order by disrupting, transmuting, then effacing the grounds or "nature" out of which the term proffered itself.)

This pharmacopoetics and pharmacopolitics prepares for a transmutation of memory: "in the night the trance cuts itself off from everyday reality with fine, prismatic edges; it forms a kind of figure and is more easily memorable" (142). It posits that active séance which certain texts in the *Theses* gamble the permutations of history itself on. Invariably, any séancing of ghosts of the past and *the future* preparatory to taking a decision may be accompanied by a knocking beneath the table – a metronomic or premimetic effect allied to tapping, Apollonian (a)rhythm, the deregulation of mimesis and linearity. Echoed in the name "Barnabe," or the many bars, and echoing the law offices of Melville's Bartleby whose "conveyance" of legacies will appear abrupted, what is evoked is the specter of mnemotechnic relay whose actual points of intervention Benjamin calls *monads*. The monad, whose proliferating networks will appear in their turn as "constellations," is viewed as a mnemonic-textual node on a cross-historial switchboard. It alters the very production of "reference," the structure of events, the *sensorium*.

To return to where we began, the drugged trance yields a submerged program of resistance. Here appears a different state of *emergency* or conflagration on the outskirts of the *polis*. As is registered by the auto-prosopopeia implied by being *stoned*, where the "I" remarks its fictional "life" as linguistically posited, an allohuman moment solicited under the name "hashish" appears echoed by the anagrammatic play of the animal-city Lyon-lion (*Lyon-Löwe*). If compulsion toward this site or "high" is a recurrent human trait, one cannot dismiss it moralistically as that of escape from the pressures of the real, or even the tourism of provoked fantasy.[15] It implies, as in the case of cinema (only less deferentially, since the *techne* is ingested here), the quest for an alternative to the narrativization and naturalization of mnemonic imprinting, signs, the "human." The non-human presents itself not as the evacuation of a normally full interior or psyche of "man," not the glassy stare of one stoned or emptied out, but the kenosis of a *faux* interiority that had been linked, despotically, to a socio-linguistic and aesthetico-political regime of "consciousness" itself – to the ravenous and blind consumption of mimeticism (parodied and exceeded by Benjamin's munchies), and to the latter's presentation as natural of what had all along been a politically installed and licensed *addiction to reference*. It is undoubtedly against a certain narcosis inherent to the normative assumptions of such a program – which implies the foreclosure of decision – that Benjamin recurs to the supplementary and pre-originary violence of hashish, the suspension of a legislated suspension, the counter-poison toward a "natural" trance. One can certainly place under the category of trance a legislated consciousness-effect that, in traversing the everyday, *thinks of perception as immediate, experience as private, language as communicational and transparent, property as natural, meaning as inherent, interiority as reserve*... Hashish, in this schema, inversely forecasts the greatest responsibility, only as play; mimes the rupture of *faux* interiorization, only as munchies. The allohuman, summoned in this mock séance, congeals in anagrams over which no mimetic or metaphoric code rules or suffices. It seems triggered not by an enchantment of the senses but by suspension, disruption, an *epoche* of material imprinting that the "hashish" effects and contrives to precede in that interface of "life" and "death" that the stoned state mimes. It suspends, in short, the addiction to reference – the "human" craving to blindly generate and consume spectral referents out of the anamorphic surfaces of prephenomenal linguistic orders. It is a counter-poison, an anti-dote to an invisible drug that a recognizable use of "the mimetic faculty" decrees (as Benjamin elsewhere terms it), out of which the routine effects of consump-

---

[15] Jacques Derrida, in "The Rhetoric of Drugs," speaks of the interdiction against drugs co-deriving from the perceived withdrawal of the user from a contract with the communal real; this is "the rhetoric of fantasy that is at the root of the interdiction: drugs, it is said, make one lose any sense of true reality" (*Points*, 235–6).

tion or what we call "capital" co-derive.[16] The addiction to refer-ence, we may say, corresponds to Benjamin's fascinated and wary depiction of the organized whores of Marseilles (like "a profes-sional guild") – that is, of a mimetic and historicist enchainment of the prefigural mark. In their midst, nonetheless, the midwife Bianchamori is capable of making a cesarean, or caesura. The site of this politics is what Benjamin calls the epistemo-critical, and it has no safe port to retreat to – which no one has ever suggested Marseilles was.

In this pharmacopolitics the "drug" is also the counter-poison to an undeclared stupor or stupefaction and political mortification of the senses, the "mimetic faculty" run aground. Today, this remains the domain of certain materialist practices of reading. The chiasmus associated with the word *hashish* – within which syllabic stutter the very principle of deformative repetition appears in-scribed – could be reduced to the following: whereas linguistic consciousness is apprehended, in its stupefied norm, as a machine of consumption and natural evisceration predicated on an instal-led epistemo-political regime and reflected in the invisibly au-tomaton-like consumption of and addiction to reference, the sol-icitation of the allohuman in "hashish" invokes a reading model whose materiality abruptly dissolves mimetic and historicist ac-cretions. For Benjamin, it posits a formal transvaluation – tem-poral and mnemonic – of the effect, no longer anthropomor-phized, called "earth."

This text presents a curious cipher for a program whose *techne* of historial intervention ("materialistic historiography") hinges on the impossibility of its being catalogued once for all in the itinerary of proper names. Avital Ronell has suggested that this lure, like the whiteness of crack, of a crack and a caesura inter-woven with woman, can be conjured as (or contained and erased through the misapprehension of) a literature-effect – or what might have been touristically called that in what increasingly seems to us the names of a previous "epoch." The addiction to reference relies, in this sense, on its own insatiability and the promised pacification of an imaginary debt installed in advance of one's inscription in a communal archive or discursive trough it

---

[16] Walter Benjamin, "On the Mimetic Faculty," in *Reflections*, 333–336.

pretends to service – after which contracts of debt, and deferral, appear to operate as if on their own. Seeking a politics of the virtual, and a greater responsibility, Benjamin first practices the mode of a disconnect under the guise of witness and tourist.

8

❖❖

Contretemps: notes on
contemporary "travel"

❖❖

In this realm, transfer tickets are of no avail.

> Paul de Man, "Anthropomorphism and Trope in the Lyric"

What, in the vein of memoir that has formed an elusive genre threading cultural studies, is the lure of travel writing, the writing of travel "itself" today? Is it possible to evade that pretense in which the "autobiographical" passes itself off as though nothing has happened to the status of the speaking being, lived experience, the institutional coding of the narratee? More: as though doing so involved could break with the protocols of "academic" writing, so that a trace of self-congratulation attends the supposed return to the personal, the belle-lettristic? That is, can the entire pretext of the memoir – say, "my" return to religious ritual, the recollected visit to the "other's" culture, the "experience" of the gendered, ethnic, or locale imprinting when "growing up," the conceit of experience altogether – evade folding back into a bizarrely programmatic pretense? Is each attempt, more or less unwittingly passed through something like the logic of the "Travel Service" window one encounters during the credit sequence of *To Catch a Thief* – that is, where the miniature models that will dictate recognizable genres of "experience" (for "France," say, the Eiffel Tower, champagne) are assembled anticipating the film's later reference to a "travel *folder* heaven" in which "lived experience" is made to mnemonically wander? Or can one write – or, for that matter, not write – rememoration, like Benjamin in Marseilles, out of the suspension of the model experience itself?

What does it mean to *tour*, today, the outer reaches of the empire – which is an unnamed empire ("America" will not do, nor the West, and so on – as if some programming encompasses, now, this series of terms *and* its one-time others) legislating time and fashion as well as economy? When we go, say, as pleasuring witnesses to whatever still bears the trace of a supposed other-ness: a cultural imprint (Andean natives), the laws of a climate (tundra), a history so marked by recent disfiguration that we, today, seem to find comfort in the commodity of a readable catastrophe. Unlike several decades if not years ago (but what, now, is a "year"?), it is so easy to travel, to transfer oneself for brief episodes to distant points – which, in turn, appear woven, then, more firmly, as the mock-aura of a frontier of any sort recedes. What does it mean to write travel, today – and is not every genre of such invoked, every narrative twitch (anecdote, observation, description, rumination) mobilized, as obstacle, at the first rustling of intent?

Let us suppose that what the traveler seeks is not another place, another co-ordinate on the same mapped surface, but an other to place itself. Since we must keep in play the interface between the burned-out remnants of a romantic tradition of travel – actively emptied – and a more technical, more semiotic problem which attends a rewiring of memory "today," a theoretical point of reference may be of use. Walter Benjamin makes reference to a concept of history that breaks with the familiar notions of the term. As we know, he was given to taking familiar terms (allegory, cinema, dialectics, translation) and submitting them to a process of disinvestment. He called this "translation": a site where the word passes through its own formal properties, emptied of "meaning" or interiority, and is then returned (unmarked) to usage in a sabotaging form void of subjectivity. Allegory becomes the other of the literary historical term; "materialistic historiography" dispels any *echt* Marxian hue; dialectics is unprogressive and anti-narrative, and so on. Typically, "history" survives this procedure – which aims to empty out all interiorist traces – only to re-emerge within a different referential order. Rather than implying historicist echoes, Benjamin invokes a non-human "history" that will be gestured to under the misleading rubric of "natural history" – a history, we may add again, with different, proactive folds of time. It is misleading, because it has no overt connection to nature as physis, or nature as the antinomy of language. What lies behind the hypothesis that the culture-traveler seeks not anthropological difference but an escape from anthropomorphism altogether?

It is difficult not to address sympathetically that doomed product of the industrial world's middle class, the culture-traveler. Unlike the colonialists of the late nineteenth century or the tourists of the post-war (WW II) economic booms, screened by serviceable ideologies, what becomes possible in recent decades of budget plane travel is unexampled – and parallels the transformation of the perceptual, topographical and political mapping of the world into a *faux* "global" field of interstices itself detached, in turn, from the latter's performative role as earth. *This traveler – who we will artificially bracket from the tourist, with all sorts of ironic conditions – pursues a certain self-canceling quest that parallels and partakes of the transformation of all points on the map into system outposts.* He (though "his" gender is systematically neutered in this) turns into a communicative and contributing viral agent of the very modus he or she more or less passively hopes to avoid. It is part of the system: create a need, a hoped for drug, in the remnant of a certain imaginary of the commodified "other" or exotic, that will generate the phantom of its (already remembered) consumption, then proceed beyond the detritus of this excess. The anti-promise of travel, if only by inference, partakes of a double logic: the pretense of a quest for the non-originary, for something disappeared or disappearing, masks the lure of a rape or intervention by which one's present itself would (be) buckle(d).

There are, perhaps, two types of travelers – those who want to know the language of their destination, to maintain the illusion of communication (mostly commercial), and those who are not determined by the latter need, but who, in the process, locate themselves in a certain nexus of "translation" in which their own words, sounds, and gestures operate on the same plane as alien ones, in the open, without special contents or interior. It is only at the latter point that certain questions can be posed – once the pretense of retrieved meaning, or "experience," is suspended.

The idea of a "natural history" with its perverse invocation and dismissal of science is, here, part of a shift from a representational and imperial logic into a materialist and virtual politics of the temporal. Seeking a non-human Archimedian point irreducible to the programming of an inhabited cultural semiosis, the cultural-traveler like the Benjaminian flaneur brushes against this logic of an alternate zone or real – where the disposition of concretized history threatens to return to a moment of its own virtuality, and projects, beyond this, the possibility of alternatives. This fantasm, which opens as a ghostliness of the present that faces any traveler whose eye lights on the zones of evisceration and transformation that mark the "global" today (the accelerated obliterations of rain forests, bio-diversity, indigenous economies . . .), is more than just the aesthetic by-product of a deceived quest for the drug of "otherness," even where that is already derived from the purportedly nascent culture (the media generated norms, say, of American urban images, sounds, advertisements, sanctioned interpretations). The trick of the system that produces and erases in advance the motif of the culture-traveler, with the latter's echo of *declassé* tourism always yapping at its heels, adheres to the programmatic quest that travel or transport announces – what makes multiculturalism, removed from the spur of justice, a design to efface rather than celebrate difference. (We will forego, for the moment, asking what *transport* itself may entail or fail to today: whether the figure of such movement, itself metaphorical, does not more often than not greet the idea of acceleration with the shrinkage and consumption of putative frontiers, markers of passage, movement itself.) The trick is: if what the culture-traveler seeks is a certain late notion of what had once gone by romantic indices of "experience," what remains is not an otherness to be documented, coded, stored for an anthropological imaginary no longer functional as other than a centralized mnemonic archive or informatrix; no longer the surprise of species and cultural forms one may witness at the crest of their *disappearance* (for fifty years either way means nothing), or at a momentarily different historial imaginary than our own that adheres to indigenous peoples. *Such a traveler, concealed beneath the businesses and relays that have sprung up to accommodate and anticipate him or her, only exists from time to time in excess of his or her inscription in the system that promotes this parody of "escape" for its own viral purposes.* One can well note the non-times – in a market, say, or indexing protocols of recognition with an new companion – where one is nothing but their puppet. It remains to be seen if this traveler is not a kind of walking inversion of the museum, inside-outed, to whom instantly commodified specks of otherness adhere, mortified for collection, rather than whose semiotic imprinting is revived, reprogrammed, or recalibrated by a too calculated "return." This would-be crosser of boundaries and states soon learns, for instance, that every new site visited has, at first, the dank taste of a return. (But, in truth, "crosser" presumes a certain arrival: one might rather be termed a carrier – as with drug smugglers – accepting the double role; and one could, at the same time, do away with the pretext of arrival, or the surprise that attends it: survey any iconic airport or station in this regard (Lima will do, but the smallest frontier town replicates this), and the competing hordes of agents, cab-workers, travel-hawkers and connectors have all and very precisely been expecting "you," in replica and continually, as though announced.) If the conceit of "travel" errs in presupposing the experience of movement – which, if anything, is given the lie in "cinema" itself – this conforms to a foreclosure of "experience" that precedes it. The con-temporary, con-temporal carrier, if and where he exists, seems distinguished by accepting this foreclosure in advance. If the term travel suggests, first of all, the transport of *figurative* language or displacement (as do trains in Hitchcock, say), the perversity of the term's survival, in this instance, may be that what its desert-mode quests would relieve us of, perhaps, is its own motive: the prefigural.

1. Sorata – May, 1996; or *bad timing*

What the traveler craves, in the space afforded by alien settings whose historial trajectories are differently situated (or "presented") than our own – in technology, in linguistic ritual, in temporalities – is not "surprise," otherness, the different. This last a French backpacker asserted on the ferry crossing Titicaca, noting a commodifiable preference for "Asia" to "South America" for the European on this basis (a South America in which the Euro-eye still encounters the grotesque flowering of its belated seed, siphoned through, and very much against, the "indigenous" soil, history, backdrops). The so-called traveler is the tourist who exceeds his role as "late capitalist" agent of transformation or use, and is marked by this excess. He romanticizes it not by being eco-friendly or knowing how to "contact" the other – but by seeking out in predatory fashion the jugular vein of differential temporal strata, faults in historial models and occurrences, displaced or foreclosed turns in seemingly decided trajectories, junctures that conjure still virtual turns in the system from which he perpetually seems on the point of arrival. This sort of traveler, then, is at once vampire and mock-hunter willing to parody his role as consumer to excess – like the science fiction agent sent back from a future to acquire a once extant element or knowledge to counter or forestall the coming plague or catastrophe. Only since these two time lines also are never co-incident, and since the system one derives from is also, inevitably, going to be that which transforms and ruptures whatever economies, othernesses, and "realities" one has oneself come to siphon off, one is aware of a parallel complicity and chronographic loop.

In the Residencial Sorata they show videos at night. Copied from cable TV in La Paz, the titles are not announced until late afternoon to give the manager, Luis, time to assess his mood or constituency. *Dave, The Fugitive, Blade Runner* – which last drew out the wine bottles and a fire in the immense "colonial" reading room where the VCR is locked. An old mansion at the edge of the square in this town set beneath glacial ridges and Andean villages and at the top of a valley stretching scores of miles down to the Amazon basin – passed on in the German family from early days when Sorata sat on the gold transit route, until those when the proto-Nazi patriarch, well-entrenched with the Bolivian elite, died (too soon) in forty two – it has immense rooms deteriorating around the once finely detailed edges, haphazardly plied with beddings of different sorts, each utterly individual, the half-restored rooms of past intrigue or power housing the disreputable comfort of backpackers.

The time of the valley simulates "natural" time – a factor that haunts one, peaking on occasion, as when trekking down the valley road during the requisite visit to "the cave," a stooped destination in which a rancid underground pond and squealing alarmed bats greet one in anti-climax. But the point of the walk and its parodic telos is other: to be marked, and situated within, the shifting co-ordinates of innumerable cliff faces, vistas, protrusions, lines, and absent gazes. Bolivia, like an effaced metacommentary on the Peruvian earth-inscriptions (great etchings in the hillsides or deserts meant for hypothetical non-eyes), is too hectic in the challenge of its surfaces to read up close. The Inca, who could putatively exist in some unreproduced relation to stone and topography, letting in the powers of the non-human by not-writing – by becoming a form of inscription themselves – suggest perhaps as do few others of alternate virtual trajectories, alternative mnemonic systems cut off or paths not taken in "subsequent" human time.

The Sorata valley briefly mimes an Alpine setting – which must have influenced the German patriarch. Earlier, the Aymara Indians in furious rebellion were said to have stopped up the glacial rivers above, to flood out the Spanish. Mist effaces the white peaks often, making it seem like the stone mounts across the valley dominate the stony outcroppings and rises until the clouds disperse – whereby the peaks again assert utter power and domination. This ritual of surprise is repeated daily. Across the ridge, more gold mining – down in adjacent jungles, and across the mountain. Some mines wash out the gold from Inca burial sites. Considering "Bolivia's" place in the continental and metaphysical map, one is aware that this scene will be transfigured again from without: the Japanese financed road from La Paz beyond Coroico – replacing a legendary terror-road along sheer cliffs (and of which we just heard the latest report: an Israeli got out of his bus to pee and went right over the edge at night). This lane begins two processes: one, to divest the *selva* of its timber, and two, to enhance Bolivia's use as a transit country between Brazil and the Pacific. A straw placed into the continent's heart to be sucked on by global industrial and commercial needs.

The gold mining – distant echo of the early lure of conquistadors – is an old example of the parasitism of future space witnessed elsewhere, by the clash of different times. It is the "Indians'" role to keep the standard of difference for this: the one connected to the earth, to village and subsistence economies, to the pre-Christian and pre-Columbian, trace-figures of anonymous catastrophe, black holes of illegible re-assurance, ghost commodities. Thus one encounters "gold mines" on the *altiplano* that are set over Inca tombs and graves, whereby the gold that floats up comes exclusively from trinkets. (I have noted a relief I experience in the presence of mountain people, with whom one can have little overt "communication," and whose environmental molding already postulates abysses of difference in lungs, ability, memory – one can imagine different settings for all of this had another

European patron "discovered" the then "new" world rather than the Spanish and its attendant Catholicism; it is nonetheless a pretext of communication: as if imparting gestures to people across such temporal gulfs promises more contact than using the paranoid rituals of coded English among professionals or "colleagues" at a university.)

There is an urge, at once duty and a banal romanticism, that clings like a fragile coat to travel of this sort: to witness. Not to consume or vampirize alone – which is a form of eating, or negating, what one seeks to alter. That is, the mountain heights, teeth horizons, and which formed one core of worship for the older cultures – in contrast to which the grotesque imposition of the crucified Jesus appears as a historical theft (the decaying god, corpse exposed, killed by men) – recall us to a non-human rift divesting one (including the consumers, vampires) of all kinds of *faux* mourning: as if less for some undesignable past where a catastrophe had already been decided that has yet to reach full disclosure, than for an "earth" itself. "Crackle of extinct things." It recalls our inability to remap or chart the surfaces of this today, or to predict more than the end of a certain phase of anthropomorphism with the nullification of bio-diversity and bio-systems. So "witnessing" can be confused or have a double logic: one cannot simply witness a passing or disappearance, if one is the tomb and trace of that (without knowing what it was that passed in the act of disappearance); at the same time, the gesture of witnessing returns us to a formalized stance that mimics already a non-human site or position. One seeks in part, "today," a vantage point, a bit to the side of the human (which language, ultimately, provides while bracketing). One recalls *Blade Runner*, where the photo-memories retain connections to pasts that cannot be affirmed, identities that may be defense-fostered, or where "animals" themselves are prized as token, simulated generally as rarities. The face of ecotourism itself seeks sightings of "animals" in proximity to virtual extinction (river otters); peasant livelihoods that are pre-industrial, aping indistinct structural memories, at once pre- and post-individual; medieval orders bracing with their theatrical displays of humans caught in transparent yet permanent machines (Potosi's mines, with their slave-like workers, which my French friend, Christophe, told me he refused to visit, though passing through on a train, suggesting it would be like a zoo) . . . *For what "one" encounters is, to some degree, the dissolution of witnessing: not the pretense of partaking of a feasting (or vampiric) gaze, but the loss of the pretext – not the post-human one desires to glimpse and which is all around one (in the image of the Inca, the "prehistorical" post-historical), but a kind of pan-zoographics, what displaces the effect of life-death.* (Christophe, it should be noted, I later met: he and two partners wanted to do a quick three-day trek to glacier lakes – having to catch a plane – and relied on the services of a shady "mountaineer club" proprietor: connections were not made further up, the guide delayed and route altered, the tent inadequate to the freezing nights: "and they brought only tea, no coffee. Can you imagine, for a Frenchman, 'tea'!")

The Andes, for all the mysticism of its peoples, is starkly "material" in this sense. Not as producing the commodified otherness of cultural humanism (as if this rested on visiting alternate "cultures") but by recalling the ant-swarm of human creatures over primeval land-masses. From the "point of view" of undoing the life-death dyad – and perhaps it is the latter's maintenance today, Western bio-centrist, that imperils the whole show – one peers beyond the parallel human investment in a ruinous ideology of meaning, the management of reserves. "Bio-centrism" – that is, the mimetic reflex on behalf of the linguistic endowed organism to misinterpret, by analogy to semantics or property, the effect called "life" as what must be stored up against armies of others it is only a variant logic of, inserted in the opposite sheath of logic: evisceration, accelerated cancellation. Let us call this *bio-centrism* which itself mimics a kind of paranoid semantic the ultimate "political incorrectness" – a techno-ideology dependent on what is neither living nor dead (language) to fabricate and protect a mock-interior, an unwittingly deadly home or host territory. This "beyond" is not apocalyptic, though it inherits the logics of everything that had converged about the organizing models of apocalyptics from millenarians to visions of atomic waste. Mt. Illumani – like sacred Salkantay on the walking route to Machu Picchu – purveys a certain caesura when the mists fall: not the anthropomorphized deity of a dead culture as "we" imagine it ("the Inca"), but the de-anthropomorphized site that stages such events as non-humanist clearings. They do not "look" at the present juncture from the point of view of a memorialized past – the Inca vision or sacrifice romanticized – but with the same trace-chains

of genetico-semiotic effects that preceded dinosaurs or pre-mammalian epochs. The trace, of course, is neither alive nor dead (nor
necessarily *terrestrial*), but threads this folding of space-time –
informing the effect, and affirmation, of "life" as nervous variant
of the inorganic, the receding glaciers of Illumani. (No: I recall
someone speaking of "the hush of extinct things," I don't know
where – perhaps over a pizza in Sorata – which extends forward to
extinctions of uninvented forms.) The narrativized after-human,
even as the waste of current bio-systems, will be another system-
atics indifferent to Illumani – because "nature" never existed
(quite) to be avenged, betrayed, extincted. "Nature" was never
other than the active and proto-mimetic chemical war of traces
poised in relations of camouflage, strategic and entirely sign-
oriented networks of predation and evasion, reading technologies. (Today, it is interesting to hear theories of the earth's reception of a "life" germ from Mars or elsewhere – a culture dish of
bacterial logics.) For the human epoch it would seem a certain
view of language, a certain historical error in this regard, represented a catastrophic turn within "natural history" that masked
or deferred the conceit of catastrophe by projecting the specter of a
narrative axis. In his own misleading way, Heidegger locates this
in "Plato" (but Plato, in fact, may have tried to dissipate or erase
this pressure, much as Heidegger re-implants it as an icon to stage
himself against – hence re-installing it). Mimesis, representation –
the compulsive disorder, installed like an itch, programmed supposedly at a perpetually unfindable before and after of the Greek
fold, that wishes for and practices the "as if" of a cancellation of
signs *en route* to referents, that desires to store and consume
reference as mnemonic ground, that conceals in the ideology of
referentials and its legitimizing ghost, nature, the sleight-of-hand
involved with the covert control (*still* medieval) of the past, of
difference, of that anteriority through which all signifying passes
and which bracketing spawns, it seems, the illusory maw of
interiority. What the Inca, clearly, lacked any naïve relation to
(what accounts, strangely, for the deformations of stone resisting
abstract symmetry) – for whom only prefigural inscription, nu-
meration, and the sheer aesthetic formalism of stone *mattered*.
Aesthetic formalism being, for them, the direct and violent access to
divine ecology, a theogonic theater. Mimesis – which confutes and
confuses "nature" with reference, reference with reserves, re-

serves with capital, capital with deferred yet controlled wealth. (Before "capital" – mimesis.) So, one travels – who one, not to be "one"? – to dislocate, elude, systems of mimetic imprinting (places, that is, where this apparatus has been installed faultily on which one's relation to language and mock-self culturally depend)? To elicit cracks and caesuras, errors or lapses in the historical calculus, that can be strategically pursued? That can, still, open or imply uncalculated or virtual "futures," alternative temporalities, or keep such as Archimedian points for still virtual systems of reference, terra-culture, varieties of active rather than passive mimesis (without model or copy)? The virtuality of these alternate logics should not be under-estimated: their non-existence or non-presence would not have any less power than the grotesquely doomed existents one is familiar with or surrounded by at "home." As if such home – like language – were from before the start already alien, compelling a disinhabitation of signs, advertisements, air, water, personae. What does one commune with, if the humans are not even human anymore (never were) – but the post-humans of the "past"? Of "Bolivia"? What we learn in and of the non-system we are now emissaries of (and can only be marked as by the looks and remarks we draw, by the value of our business), is that what comes, by accident, force, historical shifts, to occupy the "place" of the real may (or must) itself be non-existent. Like the array of non-ideas or non-truths, non-icons and non-thoughts that traverse the tele-screen of American English. "Poverty," here, is an *ascesis* imposed aesthetically as the allegory of the Andean. It is a mutant commodity.

At the Residencial Sorata the *Blade Runner* tape (director's cut, no voice over, wide screen) was jammed or interrupted twice. Once when Deckard sat before his piano, covered with photographs that preceded his own life-span – aggressive "implants" that did not take – the artificed human, for whom the mimetic testimony of a past, the mnemotechnics of identity, ran to the excess of innumerable shots back to the earliest days of the camera itself. Shots, substitute-ghosts of others' memories, what in the (other) replicants persist as implants but here run to excess (recalling, in fact, the tourist's hopeless addiction to the redundant and impotent violence of the camera). These replicants, more human than human (we hear), would be erased in the end. A second jam – *bad* timing – when Roy was winding down:

where only the "copy" can experience "death." When the tape stops, Bolivian television intervened with a Spanish version of *Dirty Harry*. Caesura within a caesura . . . the trace of Illumani through the elaborated circuitry.

2. Selva – or, recollecting genre

More anecdotes? It was several years before that I visited the Huorani in Ecuador – months after the death of my mother by lung-cancer, a prolonged death-rite that presented the opportunity of escort right to the portals, the retrieval of one's hands still marked by the spaces into which they had to be extended, like an inverse theft. So it was marked by this non-aura that I wanted to go to a frontier, cross the bridge in Coca where one gives up one's passport, and do so alone. Marked, only, by the comedy and scheming incompetence that mediate such abstract desires – what are calculated by some, but bridge other terrains. Having arrived in Coca sleepless from the over-night bus from Quito over the Andes and with the fever of a flu, I negotiated transport ineptly. I wanted, surveying the map, to go down (East) the Rio Shiripuno, to be taken to a remote park system. The purveyors, a local family business controlling access to some Huorani villages – the renowned Aucas ("wild ones"), one of which branches had only two years before speared a high prelate who had come to mediate their problems with Shell Oil – would deposit me at a camp they supported. The daughter who made the arrangements did not like my payment in Ecuadorian currency and punished me by depositing me with this camp, who would only take me in the wrong direction, where the rivers dried up soon and where gasoline would not have to be wasted. When I called this to their attention when in the boat, they claimed the other direction had "hostiles" in it (*Bravos*), making it dangerous and impassable – which was probably untrue. I spent a week around and beyond the camp, getting to know the Huorani who were in this middle-space: already blighted by the Christian identity-codes, they existed away from the traditional villages (about five miles walk into the jungle, forbidden unless you bore the appropriate gifts), yet not yet in the town system. They were at a peculiar, in ways stereotyped scenario, more interesting for me than the river trip I had planned. Living still off the forest, from which they would

daily bring in birds and pigs, they were constructing a wooden
building in the clearing, in which there would be a canteen –
furnished by the family business who had brought me in. (When
the Huorani found a baby "tiger," the latter took it back to Coca to
sell to the zoo "for them," and so on.) Not far away, group tourism
had burgeoned where the oil-camps with their disease and drugs
had allowed. I was deposited into a parenthesis, which is what I
could handle or absorb, a cross circuitry of virtual pasts and
impaled futures, a camp in mid construction in the jungle over-
looking an exceptionally low, mid-October Rio Shiripuno.

The players of my theater involved several principals – the son
of the family, about seventeen, who boasted of his fortunes with
girl tourists; Eugenio, the chosen future point-man with the
"tribe" who was trying to learn some English words; Canno, an
irrepressible Huorani with the long ear extensions that traditional
males bore, yet who wandered from jungle town to jungle town in
sexual exploits but without commercial purpose – a pioneer
Huorani. At the end, there was added Majo, a smaller but older,
entirely mad figure, who everyone called *loco*, yet whose laughing
face was struck with the madness of a transition that could never
be explained or absorbed. He would laugh incessantly, and one-
time, when a coral snake was pointed out, he pursued it laughing
until the terrified snake found its hole and disappeared.

But the labyrinth of mock primality (let me allude to this as a
trope), of a certain non- or counter-origin, that is the romanticist
side of the lure for a kind of contact is suffused with specular
options: open this door, and one re-enters the programmed formalism which the jungle, with its other languages, knows too;
open that, and one returns to a site of recurrence exemplified by
the self-replicating groves in which the outsider can, stepping the
wrong way, get lost without moving twenty feet away. What the
"jungle" as a trope contains as a secret, as the mystery that is
projected on it, is quite material and proactive: the chains of
predatory mimic wars between plants and animals, animals and
animals, involving camouflage and anticipatory mimesis breaks
with the Western logos not by retreating to some "primal" mias-
mus preceding the imposition of law, but the reverse, by partaking of a rigorous network or system without boundaries, utterly
aesthetic, from which the "logos" itself appears a double parenthesis. If representation creates the appearance of a past by relying

on a linguistic trope, mimesis, that posits a referential order of the word (which effaces the pastness involved), the active "mimesis" of what cannot be troped any longer as "nature" in some Enlightenment sense, involves linguistic systems of extraordinary transformative prowess that are pro-active rather than re-active. The chameleon, say, who drinks up color transformations from its environment to shield and enhance his predations, possesses, alone, a technology beyond what any human account can mark – and it does so as a retro-anticipation, a bio-transformation that reshapes the "biotic" itself as prosthesis. What the Huorani gave me without giving was a "trip" that began, as the word suggests, as a stumbling repetition anyway.

Narrative pretexts (again) for the extinction of narrative. These took place over two treks in from the river system. The first occurred after I found our canoes mired in low waters, having gone up instead of down stream. Here we camped, happily, but I required an "aim" and talked them into going to the village which was a seven hour walk inland across small ravines harboring many *culebra*. This plan was hastened by the arrival at the river bend of a hunter with his family, an Indian woman and mysteriously blond baby (the hunter, at least, was of the neighboring Shuar, once-headhunters and still alienated from the Auca), setting off depth-charges to fish. I had been given rubber boots two sizes too small, however, which became apparent about three hours into the hike – when my feet were left bleeding, and swollen. I fell repeatedly into muddy gulches crawling with furtive things, laughing outloud each time from the wet brush when seeing my companions looked down with curiosity. I had not mastered walking across the fallen wet logs, and each fall was about six to eight feet. I was intimidated by the idea of four hours more and a return walk the next day and decided to turn back. This cut off my second attempt to rescue my mere presence in the forest with this group of people by applying an aim to it. The boatman was happy to see us: having come upon a "tiger" just begun dining on rodent, he preserved the latter, headless, for dinner, and didn't have to hunt. (Behind him, the hunting family in a canoe coming up river – arresting blond child, still – let me try a very long blow gun on a dead chick (perfect), compelling a drink of chicha: then again began to set off charges in the river's bend from which fish (mostly piranha) floated up.)

On the trip in which Majo chased the coral snake, I had insisted on going to a black laguna in the forest – a hike supposed to take five hours, that no-one wanted to do. So they made it a hunting trip. *En route*, a boar was spotted and shot at – wounded, to a squeal, and the three hunters scampered into the brush looking for it. I was left alone, only to hear the creature, shot in the shoulder, huffing in the shrubs behind me. We made it to a first laguna, where a little caiman floated with his head alone on the surface, and which supposedly had electric eels. I stood amidst a bunch of giant ants and, after a minute catching my breath, was casually told to move. Congas, whose bite makes you feverish – you must break them and squeeze their body juice onto the bite to ease it. I touched a leaf, and tracks on my hand swelled up – which my guide dismissed, as indeed it went down ten minutes later. It was very hot and airless. "Tiger" tracks were near the water. The next laguna would only replicate this. We turned back and stopped only once, when Majo turned to a tree. His mother died there. It was the "sign" for me to go. The forest was sheer technology. Zoographics. It would seem one travels to "discover" – that is, learn to reread – *technicity*. The voice of the one I had, when "living," called mother had already dismissed the anthropomorphic in advance and presented me with this non-riddle. Catamnesis. *Khora*.

Writing "travel" – outside of (the) genre? Redoubling it? Not yet. Even where this program, and from the first, had included all variant logics and already been (as such) over; heard, today, as the precording of some other's present.

Select bibliography

Althusser, Louis, *Lenin and Philosophy and Other Essays*, trans. B. Brewster. New York: Monthly Review, 1971.

Bakhtin, M. M., *The Dialogic Imagination*, ed. M. Holquist, trans. C. Emerson and M. Holquist. Austin: University of Texas Press, 1981.

Problems in Dostoyevsky's Poetics, trans. C. Emerson. Minneapolis: University of Minnesota Press, 1984.

Benjamin, Walter, *Illuminationen*. Frankfurt: Suhrkamp, 1961.

Ursprung des deutschen Trauerspiels. Frankfurt: Suhrkamp, 1963.

Illuminations, trans. H. Zohn. New York: Schocken, 1969.

The Origin of German Tragic Drama, trans. J. Osborne. London: NLB, 1977.

Reflections, Trans. E. Jephcott. New York: Harcourt Brace Jovanovich, 1978.

Bloch, Ernst, et al., *Aesthetics and Politics*, trans. H. Zohn. London: Verso, 1980.

Bellamy, Elizabeth J., "Discourses of Impossibility: Can Psychoanalysis Be Political?" *Diacritics*, 23, 1 (Spring, 1993), 24–39.

Butler, Judith, *Bodies That Matter: On the Discursive Limits of "Sex'*. New York: Routledge, 1993.

Gender Trouble. New York: Routledge, 1990.

Carroll, David, "The Alterity of Discourse: Form, History and the Question of the Political in M. M. Bakhtin." *Diacritics*, 13, 2 (Summer, 1983), 65–83.

Chow, Rey, "Ethics after Idealism." *Diacritics*, 23, 1 (Spring, 1993), 3–23.

Clark, Katerina and Michael Holquist, *Mikhail Bakhtin*. Cambridge: Harvard University Press, 1984.

Cohen, Tom, "Reading a Blind Parataxis: Dostoyevsky (Nietzsche) Bakhtin." *boundary* 2 (Winter, 1989), 45–71.

"Well! Voloshinov's Double Talk." *Sub-Stance*, 21, 2 (Fall, 1992), 91–102.

Anti-Mimesis from Plato to Hitchcock. Cambridge: Cambridge University Press, 1994.

"'Along the Watchtower' – Cultural Studies and the Ghost of Theory." *MLN*, 112 (1997), 400–30.

Bibliography

Copjec, Joan, "The Orthopsychic Subject: Film Theory and the Reception of Lacan." *October* 49 (1989), 53–72.

Curtis, James M., "Michael Bakhtin, Nietzsche, and Russian Pre-Revolutionary Thought," in *Nietzsche in Russia*, ed. B. Rosenthal (Princeton, NJ: Princeton University Press, 1986), 331–355.

De Man, Paul, *Rhetoric of Romanticism*. New York: Columbia University Press, 1984.

    Resistance to Theory. Minneapolis: University of Minnesota Press, 1986.

    Aesthetic Ideology. Minneapolis: University of Minnesota Press, 1996.

Deleuze, Gilles, *Cinema 1: The Movement-Image*, trans. H. Tomlinson and R. Galeta. London: The Athlone Press, 1986.

Derrida, Jacques, *The Post Card*, trans. Alan Bass. Chicago: University of Chicago Press, 1981.

    Dissemination, trans. B. Johnson. Chicago: University of Chicago Press, 1981.

    On the Name, ed. Thomas Dutoit. Stanford: Stanford University Press, 1995.

    Specters of Marx, trans. Peggy Kamuf. New York: Routledge, 1994.

    Points. . ., ed. Elizabeth Weber. Stanford: Stanford University Press, 1995.

    Archive Fever: A Freudian Impression, trans. E. Prenowitz. Chicago: University of Chicago Press, 1996.

Gardiner, Michael, *The Dialogics of Critique: M. M. Bakhtin and the Theory of Ideology*. New York: Routledge, 1992.

Godzich, Wlad, "Correcting Kant: Bakhtin and Intercultural Interactions." *boundary 2*, 18, 1 (Spring, 1991), 5–17.

Haddad, Lahcen, "Bakthin's Imaginary Utopia." *Cultural Critique* 22 (Fall, 1992), 143–64.

Hamacher, Werner, *Premises: Essays on Philosophy and Literature from Kant to Celan*, trans. P. Fenves. Cambridge: Harvard University Press, 1996.

Hanssen, Beatrice, "Philosophy at Its Origin: Walter Benjamin's Prologue to the *Ursprung des deutschen Trauerspiels*." *MLN*, 110 (Spring, 1995), 809–833.

Haraway, Donna, "Ecce Homo, Ain't (Ar'n't) I a Woman, and Inappropriate/d Others: the Human in a Post-Humanist Landscape," in *Feminists Theorize the Political*, ed. J. Butler and J. Scott. New York: Routledge, 1992, 86–105.

Hirschkop, Ken and David Shepherd, eds. *Bakhtin and Cultural Theory*. London: Manchester University Press, 1989.

Holquist, Michael, *Dialogism: Bakhtin and his World*. New York: Routledge, 1990.

    "The Surd Heard: Bakhtin and Derrida," in *Russian Formalism: Theoretical Problems and Russian Case Studies*, ed. G. S. Morson. Stanford, CA: Stanford University Press, 1986, 137–57.

Bibliography

Holquist, Michael and Katernina Clark. *Mikhail Bakhtin*. Cambridge, MA: Harvard University Press, 1984.

Jameson, Fredric, "Allegorizing Hitchcock," in *Signatures of the Visible*. New York: Routledge, 1992.

"Spatial Systems in *North by Northwest*," in Žižek, ed., *Everything You Always Wanted To Know About Lacan . . . But Were Afraid to Ask Hitchcock*.

Kittler, Friedrich A., *Discourse Networks 1800/1900*, trans. M. Metteer, with C. Cullens. Stanford, CA: Stanford University Press, 1990.

Laclau, Ernesto, "The Death and Resurrection of the Theory of Ideology." *MLN*, 112 (Spring, 1997), 297–321.

Lacoue-Labarthe, Phillipe, *Typography: Mimesis, Philosophy, Politics*, ed. C. Fynsk. Cambridge, MA: Harvard University Press, 1989

Librett, Jeffrey S., ed. *Of the Sublime: Presence in Question*. Albany: SUNY Press, 1993.

MacCannell, Juliet Flower, "The Temporality of Textuality: Bakhtin and Derrida." *MLN*, 100 (Fall, 1985), 968–988.

Morson, Gary Saul, ed., *Literature and History: Theoretical Problems and Russian Case Studies*. Stanford, CA: Stanford University Press, 1986.

Morson, Gary Saul and Caryl Emerson, *Mikhail Bakhtin: Creation of a Prosaics*. Stanford, CA: Stanford University Press, 1990.

Morson, Gary Saul and Caryl Emerson, eds. *Rethinking Bakhtin*. Evanston: Northwestern University Press, 1989.

Mulvey, Laura, *Visual and Other Pleasures*. Bloomington: Indiana University Press, 1989.

Nägele, Rainer, "The Poetic Ground Laid Bare (Benjamin reading Baudelaire)." *Diacritics*, 22, 3–4 (Fall-Winter, 1992), 146–160.

Nealon, Jeffrey T., "The Discipline of Deconstruction." *PMLA*, 107 (October, 1992), 1266–1280.

Nietzsche, Friedrich, *The Birth of Tragedy*, trans. W. Kaufmann. New York: Random House, 1967.

Die Geburt der Tragoedie aus dem Geiste der Musik. Munich: Wilhelm Goldman, 1980.

Penley, Constance and Andrew Ross, eds. *Technoculture*. Minneapolis: University of Minnesota Press, 1991.

Plato, *The Collected Dialogues*, ed. E. Hamilton and H. Cairns. Princeton, NJ: Bollingen, 1961.

Ronell, Avital, *Crack Wars: Literature Addiction Mania*. Lincoln: University of Nebraska Press, 1992.

Ross, Andrew, *The Chicago Gangster Theory of Life – Nature's Debt to Society*. New York: Verso, 1994.

Rorty, Richard, *Contingency, Irony, and Solidarity*. Cambridge, MA: Cambridge University Press, 1989.

Rothman, William, *Hitchcock: The Murderous Gaze*. Cambridge, MA: Harvard University Press, 1982.

Bibliography

Saper Craig, "A Nervous Theory: The Troubling Gaze of Psychoanalysis in Media Studies." *Diacritics*, 21, 4 (1991), 33–52.

Serres, Michel, *The Natural Contract*, trans. E. MacArthur and W. Paulson. Ann Arbor: University of Michigan Press, 1995.

Shapin, Steven, *A Social History of Truth: Civility and Science in Seventeenth-Century England*. Chicago: University of Chicago Press, 1994.

Smith, Gary, ed. *Benjamin: Philosophy, Aesthetics, History*. Chicago: University of Chicago Press, 1989.

Steinberg, Michael P., ed. *Walter Benjamin and the Demands of History*. Ithaca: Cornel University Press, 1996.

Taylor, Mark C., *Hiding*. Chicago: University of Chicago Press, 1997.

Truffaut, Francois, *Hitchcock*. New York: Simon and Schuster, 1966.

Voloshinov, V. N., *Marxism and the Philosophy of Language*, trans. I. R. Titunik and L. Matejka. New York: Seminar Press, 1973.

"Discourse in Life and Discourse in Art," in *Freudianism*, trans. I. R. Titunik. Bloomington: Indiana University Press, 1987, pp. 93–117.

Wall, Anthony and Clive Thomson, "Cleaning Up Bakhtin's Carnival Act." *Diacritics*, 23, 2 (1993), 47–70.

Warminski, Andrzej, *Readings in Interpretation*. Minneapolis: University of Minnesota Press, 1987.

Weber, Samuel, "The Intersection: Marxism and the Philosophy of Language." *Diacritics*, 15, 4 (1985), 94–112.

"Genealogy of Modernity: History, Myth and Allegory in Benjamin's Origin of the German Mourning Play." *MLN*, 106 (Spring, 1991), 465–500.

Mass Mediauras: Form, Technics, Media. Stanford, CA: Stanford University Press, 1996.

West, Cornel, *The American Evasion of Philosophy: A Genealogy of Pragmatism*. Madison: University of Wisconsin Press, 1989.

Zavarzadeh, Mas'ud, "Pun(k)deconstruction and the Postmodern Political Imaginary." *Cultural Critique* 22 (1992), 5–47.

Žižek, Slavoj, *The Sublime Object of Ideology*. New York: Verso, 1989.

For They Know Not What They Do – Enjoyment as a Political Factor. New York: Verso, 1991.

Looking Awry: An Introduction to Jacques Lacan Through Popular Culture. Cambridge, MA: MIT Press, 1991.

Enjoy Your Symptom! Jacques Lacan in Hollywood and Out. New York: Routledge, 1992.

Žižek, Slavoj, ed. *Everything You Always Wanted To Know About Lacan . . . But Were Afraid to Ask Hitchcock*. New York: Verso, 1992.

Index

Adorno, Theodor, 2–4, 8–9
aesthetic, the, 11, 87, 96, 113–15,
    208–10, 227, 231
aesthetic ideology, 42, 88, 96, 167
allegory, 7, 11, 87, 105–6, 113–15,
    117, 122 n. 24, 124, 174, 196,
    233
allography, 2, 7–8, 12, 124, 136,
    180
Althusser, Louis, 39, 45, 50 fn 13
American anti-intellectualism,
    218
anthropomorphism, 20, 24, 51,
    109, 136, 200, 215, 220
aporia, 24, 41, 44, 50

Bakhtin, Mikhail, 5, 56–97, 206 33,
    164, 170–73, 195–6, 231–2
Benjamin, Walter, 3–15, 23, 40,
    104–8, 110–12, 122, 125, 216,
    221–3, 239
bio-centrism, 134, 208, 246

caesura, 118 n. 21, 171, 183 n. 10,
    208, 225
cannibalization, 209 10, 217
cinemallographics, 166, 173
cultural studies, 4, 7, 51, 98–108,
    135, 204, 219

de Man, Paul, 14–15, 17, 22, 31,
    41–55, 61–97, 117, 166–7
Derrida, Jacques, 17, 21, 35, 81 n.

11, 152, 167–8, 207, 223, 235 n.
    15
dialogism, 62, 71–7
drugs, 53, 221–37

earth, 21, 53, 119, 124, 134, 209–10,
    233, 240
ethics of the aesthetic, the, 113, 210
exteriority, 10, 13, 38–3'9, 49, 208,
    220

gaze, the, 148, 154–6, 163
graphematics, 113, 169, 177, 180

Hamacher, Werner, 84, n. 12, 109
    n. 12, 206
hermeneutics, 44, 119, 173, 188,
    205
historicism, 41, 48, 53–4, 107–8,
    119, 136, 224
Hitchcock, Alfred, 24, 144–7,
    156–200
homosocial, the, 214–17
humanism, 36, 52–3, 59, 188, 246
Huorani tribe, the, 249–52

identification, 24–5, 109, 188, 200
identity politics, 7, 54, 209
ideological anamorphosis, 119
ideology, 16–20, 37, 45, 55, 69,
    80–1, 87–8, 96, 109
image, the, 130–1
inscription, 16–21, 43, 49, 53, 86–7,

257